KĀLIDĀSA
IN
MODERN SANSKRIT LITERATURE

KĀLIDĀSA STUDIES - I

KĀLIDĀSA
IN
MODERN SANSKRIT LITERATURE

Dr. SATYA VRAT SHASTRI
Pandit Manmohan Nath Dar Professor of Sanskrit,
University of Delhi.

Ex-Vice-Chancellor,
Shri Jagannath Sanskrit University,
Puri (Orissa).

EASTERN BOOK LINKERS

DELHI : : (INDIA)

Publishers :
EASTERN BOOK LINKERS

HEAD-OFFICE: 5825/7, New Chandrawal,
Jawahar Nagar, Delhi-110007
Phone No.: 9811232913.

SHOW-ROOM: 4806/24, Bharat Ram Road,
Darya-Ganj, New Delhi-110002
Phone No.: 011-45797575, 9718887575
e-mail: eblindology@gmail.com

Edition: 2024

Rs.: ₹ 1500.00 (2 Volumes Set.)

ISBN: 978-81-851334-4-7
978-93-89386-41-7 (Set.)

KALIDASA: IN MODERN SANSKRIT LITERATURE
By **Dr. SATYA VRAT SHASTRI**

Type Setting : **Creative Graphics**
Printed at : **R.K. Print Service, Delhi**

PREFACE

It was in August 1973 that I had been invited by the Kendriya Sanskrit Vidyapith, Tirupati for lectures under its Śāradīya Jñāna Mahotsava Programme. As asked, I had to write them in English. Since the audience there, as per the information conveyed to me, was not wholly to consist of traditional Sanskritists, I could not, evidently, go in for a Śāstric topic. The only alternative was to think of something of general interest. In this Kālidāsa readily came to my mind. But to say something original about him was by no means easy, so much having been written on him already. While analysing various possibilities, I hit upon the idea of making a try with the modern literature on Kālidāsa. Nothing to my knowledge had been written on the subject so far. Some three or four works had by then crossed my eyes to suggest the topic to me but they would not suffice for the lecture series. I had to have more material. I set myself to the task in right earnest. I have a fairly large collection of modern Sanskrit writings which I have procured from various sources. I also subscribe regularly to a good number of Sanskrit magazines. Of a few of them, I have even the back volumes. I dived into this vast material and came out with a number of pearls in the form of writings on Kālidāsa. To be exhaustive, I wrote to specialists on modern Sanskrit literature. None of them could add significantly to the information that I had collected through my own efforts. The existing Kālidāsa Bibliographies were also not of much help in this connection.

The material available had made it clear to me that it was more than what was needed for the limited purpose of lectures. Why then not plan a book on this fascinating topic, I argued to myself. Originally I planned a single volume on it but decided later, in view of the bulk of the matter, to split it into two. The first of these is now ready for circulation. Before long the second one too would be ready similarly.

I have deliberately confined myself to only creative writings on Kālidāsa. There are articles galore on Kālidāsa in Sanskrit magazines. But apart from their Sanskrit medium, they, at least a majority of them, have little to commend. Much has been written on Kālidāsa in English and other languages, European and Indian. The articles such as *Kālidāsakāvye prakṛticitraṇam, Upamā Kālidāsasya, Abhijñānaśākuntale nāṭyavidhānam* do not take us very far. Of the creative writings too I have been selective. I have not included tens and scores of small poems on the great poet. Obviously it was difficult to bring within the purview of the present study all types of stray verses, some of which are of doubtful merit and just eulogies of Kālidāsa. In the works studied the creative talent of the authors lends them special appeal. They have provided me with many a moment of special joy. It is to share this joy with the Sahṛdayas that I have taken them up here for a detailed critical appraisal.

They have one common factor. They are all connected with Kālidāsa. They deal, on the basis of tradition and legend of course, with him; his life, his works, his achievements, his good or bad habits, as a matter of fact, with his total personality and represent by themselves practically all forms of literature.

Kālidāsa has been a perennial source of inspiration to Indian poets and thinkers, literators and connoisseurs. He shines as the brightest star in India's literary firmament. The poet and the playwright who has left practically no details about himself is the best known of the poets and the playwrights of Sanskrit in history. Inquisitiveness being ingrained in human nature, efforts continued to be made on picturing his personality, on knowing something of his life and history. A number of anecdotes have come to be connected with him : That he was a fool at first, was married deceitfully to a learned Princess, was repudiated by her was cut to the quick at the insult she heaped on him and to be worthy of her acquired knowledge through the grace of the Goddess Kālī; that he was one of the Nine Jewels, the Navaratnas (the nine noted figures) in the Court of King Vikramāditya; that he was associated with a gardener woman to whom he would recite whatever he would compose to elicit her comments; that he was attached to a harlot and that he was the darling of King Bhoja of Dhārā with whom he had shared the authorship of *Campūrāmāyaṇa.* On the basis of the above anecdotes, the modern writers of Sanskrit have sought to draw a picture of the man that Kālidāsa was. Each one of them has utilized the anecdote/s in his own way making the picture differ from work to work. Not seldom the individual drawing the picture also peeps through it giving way to his own inclinations, his likes and dislikes, his mental make-up. The picture being his creation, this is but natural. Sometimes it is one anecdote in the main with additions and alterations of course. Sometimes it is more than one anecdote or parts of different anecdotes. Sometimes it is more details and new incidents added to the old incidents. Sometimes it is a new anecdote with just a streak of the old.

The present study aims at finding out what kind of picture the modern Sanskrit writers had drawn of their favourite poet Kālidāsa and to what effect. In this a whole class of literature on Kālidāsa's personality has been put under searching scrutiny.

A first work of its kind, it touches an hitherto untouched aspect of Kālidāsa's studies.

My father, the late Charu Deva Shastri, had fully blessed the present undertaking. He would feel somewhat exasperated at the inordinate delay at its execution. How happy he would have been to see it in print in his life-time.

The printing of the work was first entrusted to a Printing Press. Due to certain circumstances it had to be transferred to another one leading to much avoidable delay. This has also resulted in the appearance of printing errors for which I implore the indulgence of readers.

I record my deep appreciation of the authors whose works I have studied. Their creativity has gone a long way to enrich Sanskrit literature. I share one common characteristic with them. They are all Kālidāsa's fans. So am I.

It is not for me to judge the success of my efforts. If scholars find it useful, I would consider my labours amply rewarded.

Bangkok
8-1-1990

Satya Vrat Shastri

CONTENTS

INTRODUCTION

Of all the Sanskrit writers it is Kālidāsa who has attracted the maximum attention. He is the centre figure of many a legend which has come to be woven round him. These pertain to different stages of his life: his childhood, his marriage, his later life and even subsequent lives. Of these the most prominent is his having been a fool earlier, attaining knowledge through the Goddess Kālī—obviously a construction on his name—who took pity on him as he cried before her having been turned out by Vidyottamā, a Princess deceitfully married to him through the machinations of the Pandits rejected by her in a scholarly disquisition (*Śāstrārtha*) in fulfilment of her vow that she would marry only the man who would defeat her in that (the Śāstrārtha) which has been taken up by the largest number of authors for delineation. As the story goes, the fool-turned-wise through the Goddess came to the Princess who locked herself in her room on getting to know of his arrival, and not willing to suffer the mortification of meeting the same old fool for the second time, putting him the question on hearing his knock at her door : *asti kaścid vāgviśeṣaḥ*, is there any improvement in speech ? and the fool with his new-found wisdom and poetic talent composing three of his Kāvyas, the *Kumārasambhava*, the *Meghadūta* and the *Raghuvaṁśa* with each of the three words of the Princess. This legend has served as the source material for eight of the fourteen works on Kālidāsa and with each of these it has undergone modification, the writers imparting something of their own to it to appear original and innovative not only in the nomenclature of the principal characters but also in the introduction of new ones and the delineation of incidents and episodes with such additions and alterations as they deemed necessary. Of the principal characters of the legend Kālidāsa has undergone change of name in three works, the *Kālidāsaḥ*, the *Mahākavikālidāsam* and the *Asti Kaścidvāgarthiyam* where he in his state of a fool is assigned different names of Kaliyā, Kūrmanātha and Kariyā respectively. As for Vidyottamā, this name is followed by two works, the *Asti Kaścidvāgarthiyam* and the *Vidyottamākālidāsiyam*. In two other works, the *Kālidāsapāṇikaraṇam* and the *Asti Kaścidvāgviśeṣaḥ* she is just referred to as the Princess, the Rājadārikā, but can be inferred to have the name Vidyottamā from the mumbling of the words of the fool Vidyā, Vidyā when he is unable to pronounce the word Vidyottamā and convey thereby that the

Princess of that name had insulted him as the kind Goddess appears before him taking pity at his cries and enquires of him as to what he wants from her. In other works she is referred to variously as Priyaṅgumañjarī in the *Kālidāsaḥ*, Vidyāvatī in the *Mahākavikālidāsam* and Vidyāvatī Kamalā in the *Kavikulakokilam*. She is shown as the daughter of Vikramāditya, the King of Avanti in the *Kālidāsaḥ*, the daughter of the ruler of Daśapura (name not given) in the *Mahākavikālidāsam*, the daughter of Māṇikyeśvarasiṁha, the ruler of Gauḍa, in the *Kavikulakokilam*, the daughter of a King (name not given) in the *Asti Kaścidvāgviśeṣaḥ*, the daughter of Sudarśana, the King of South Kosala, in the *Asti Kaścidvāgarthīyam* and the daughter of Śāradānanda, the King of Kāśī, in the *Vidyottamākālidāsīyam*. Vidyot-Mtamā's mother figures in only two of the works, the *Kavikulakokilam* and the *Vidyottamākālidāsīyam* which do not assign any name to her referring to her only as the Queen.

Now a look at Kālidāsa's parentage. Kālidāsa is said to be the son of Pandit Sadāśiva Nyāyavāgīśa of Pauṇḍra, a village near Ujjayinī in the *Kavikulakokilam*. The *Asti Kaścidvāgarthiyam*, however, makes him the son of Sadāśiva of Devagrāma who is introduced as a great Naiyāyika while the *Vidyottamākālidāsīyam* refers to him as the son of Kālīnātha Miśra of Bhāradvāja Gotra. His mother appears in three works, the *Kavikulakokilam*, the *Asti Kaścidvāgarthīyam* and the *Vidyottamākālidāsīyam*. She is not assigned any name in the first two while in the third she is called Kālī. Each one of the works has friend/s and confidant/s of the Princess : Āmramañjarī in the *Kālidāsaḥ*, Taḍillatā in the *Mahākavikālidāsam*, Mālatīlatikā and Ālokalatikā in the *Kavikulakokilam*, Vāsantī in the *Asti Kaścidvāgviśeṣaḥ*, Ilā in the *Asti Kaścidvāgarthiyam* and Suśilā, Vimalā and Kamalā in the *Vidyottamākālidāsīyam*. Each one of these—when there is more than one, they—appear in a different situation. In the *Kālidāsaḥ* Āmramañjarī serves as the mouthpiece of the Princess to convey to Vararuci, the latter's teacher, her (the Princess's) decision to marry only that man who would defeat her in the Śāstrārtha. In the *Mahākavikālidāsam* it is Taḍillatā who notices a person dead or nearly dead when she is asked by the Chamberlain to conduct Princess Vidyāvatī proceeding towards the river Narmadā for bath through pucca road avoiding the muddy one and mistakes him for a demon or a goblin, the darkness accounting for her confusion. In the *Kavikulakokilam* Mālatīlatikā and Ālokalatikā accompany the Princess to the Svayaṁvarasabhā. In the *Asti Kaścidvāgviśeṣaḥ* Vāsantī accompanies her to the royal court and serves as her mouthpiece to convey her assent for the silent Śāstrārtha with a young man introduced as a valiant Prince from Burma. She also consoles her when she is greatly disturbed with the thoughts of her husband whom she had herself turned out upon the realization that she had been tricked. In the *Asti Kaścidvāgarthīyam* the Princess shares her most intimate moments with Ilā. Stricken with remorse for repudiating her husband, she always talks to her about him. It is through the conversation with her that it is revealed that a poet of the name of Kâlidāsa has attained great fame. When Ilā suggests to the Princess that the stage performance of one of the said poet's plays be arranged, the latter tells her that that is precisely she had also been thinking of. When the procession of Kālidāsa approaches the harem for the girls, it is Ilā who first recognizes him to be the same wood-carrier whom the Princess had married. It is she again whom the Princess asks to open the door for Kālidāsa, ordering herself its closure earlier, after she had satisfactory answer from him of her query : *asti kaścidvāgviśeṣaḥ* ? In the *Vidyottamākālidāsīyam* Suśilā advises the Princess, after she had thrown out her husband, to invite him back, there being no life for a woman without a husband, he alone belonging to her and not the property and the riches of the father to which the Princess does not agree. She is, however, exceedingly happy at Suśīlā's remark at a later stage when she appears in the work in conversation with her and some others of her friends that Kālidāsa would be able to answer her question in verse. She is equally happy at the remark of Kamalā, another of her friends, that the poet would be able to compose a poem on her under the inspiration of separation.

In all works, except two, the *Kavikulakokilam* and the *Asti Kaścidvāgarthīyam* Kālidāsa is shown as a born fool. In the *Asti Kaścidvāgarthīyam* he is shown to have developed foolishness, early enough, after a chance head injury. *Kavikulakokilam* depicts him in an altogether different light. There he is shown as completely indifferent to formal education because of his intense devotion to Mother Nature which ultimately lands him in the most unenviable position of a wood cutter to support himself and his mother after the demise of his father.

The incident of the cutting by Kālidāsa of the very branch of the tree on which he is perching—there is a slight modification in this to produce a more telling impression of foolishness in making him cut the root of the branch while sitting on its fore part as in the *Mahākavikālidāsam*—as proof of his foolishness is utilized by all works except the *Kavikulakokilam* where it is just missing. Kālidāsa is shown a fool there in the sense that he is illiterate and uneducated. He is picked up, as per the *Kālidāsapāṇikaraṇam* and the *Asti Kaścidvāgarthīyam* by scholars, in the *Mahākavikālidāsam* by three Princes, and the *Vidyottamākālidāsīyam* by a learned person of the name of Bhairavanātha who were humbled in scholarly disquisition by a learned Princess who had vowed to marry only that person who would defeat her therein. The motivation in all the above works is to avenge the insult. The same is the motivation in the *Kālidāsaḥ* but it is not of suffering ignominy in Śāstrārtha. It is the misbehaviour of the Princess with her own teacher whom she ridicules for not comprehending fully the import of her words while acting as umpire in her Śāstrārtha with other scholars. In the *Kavikulakokilam* there is no motivation at all. It is the sadistic pleasure of two men out in search of fire wood. The men make fun of the poor young man who, though son of a great Pandit, had brought himself down to the despicable state of a mere wood-cutter. After he is discovered as the real fool, Kālidāsa is comouflaged differently in different works. He is introduced as a great scholar of the name of Dhurandhara Śāstrī from Kāśī in the *Kālidāsaḥ*, a well-dressed person in the *Mahākavikālidāsam*, one of the most respected scholars of the name of Kālidāsa in the *Kavikulakokilam*, a well-versed valiant Prince from Burma in the *Asti Kaścidvāgviśeṣaḥ*, a Head of a Department in a University of the name of Darśanācārya in the *Asti Kaścidvāgarthiyam* and the guru of the defeated Pandits in the *Śrīkālidāsacaritasaṅgrahaḥ*. The mode of tutoring him for the Śāstrārtha also differs with different works. He is told to act as he is asked to in the *Kālidāsaḥ*, the *Kālidāsapāṇikaraṇam* and the *Kavikulakokilam*, to participate in discussion by gestures; raise two fingers if the Princess were to raise one, raise one finger and draw a circle with it if the Princess were to raise two; to keep mum when the Princess is with him and not to answer any of her questions in the *Asti Kaścidvāgviśeṣaḥ*. The *Asti Kaścidvāgarthīyam* refers to him as having been tutored suitably. Just as it is with tutoring, so is it with interpretation of gestures. It is Vararuci in the *Kālidāsaḥ*, scholars humbled in disquisition in the *Kālidāsapāṇikaraṇam*, Narendra, a Prince humbled likewise in the *Mahākavikālidāsam*, Vipulavikrama, a rejected suiter, in the *Kavikulakokilam*, Govardhana and Dhūmraketu humbled earlier in the *Asti Kaścidvāgarthīyam* and Śivanātha, the Ācārya of Gurukula in the *Vidyottamākālidāsīyam* who interpret them. While Govardhana's interpretation is in terms of philosophy, that of Dhūmraketu is in those of Polity. While all these different interpretations are employed in different works to explain the gestures of Kālidāsa disguised variously—the *Asti Kaścidvāgarthiyam* has two persons to do so and they are Govardhana and Dhūmraketu humbled earlier in the Śāstrārtha—in at least one work, the *Mahākavikālidāsam* some one is employed to interpret the gestures of the Princess too. He is Somaśarman, the teacher of the Princess. There is no scholarly disquisition or Śāstrārtha in the *Asti Kaścidvāgviśeṣaḥ*. Hence, no gestures and no interpreter. The Princess just takes fancy to the handsomeness of the man introduced to her as a valiant Prince from Burma and assents for marriage. That Kālidāsa was handsome figures in other works too. As a matter of fact, his handsomeness works with the Princess as said in the *Kavikulakokilam* :

Vidyāvatī (*Kālidāsaṁ dṛṣṭvā svagatam)—aho apūrvadivyakāntidharo 'yaṁ janaḥ darśanamātreṇodvellati mama manaḥ anirvacanīyabhāvāvegena.*[1]

"Vidyāvatī (looking at Kālidāsa to herself)—This man has singularly divine charm. By his very sight my mind jumps up all of a sudden with indescribable upsurge of feeling."

to agree to a silent disquisition. Just as it is with gestures, so is it with their interpretations which differ with different works. Vararuci's interpre-

1. p. 47.

tation of raising of one finger in the *Kālidāsaḥ* and that of Śivanātha in the *Vidyottamākālidāsīyam* is that God is one, of the raising of two fingers by the fool is that He is twofold, one, with form *sākāra* and the other, without it, *nirākāra*, or, as in the *Kālidāsapāṇikaraṇam* one is the Supreme Self, Paramātman and the other, the Individual Self, Jīvātman or as in the *Mahākavikālidāsam* one is of the form of Īśvara and the other is that of Prakṛti. In the *Kavikulakokilam* one finger means that the primary cause of the universe is Brahman. The two mean that it is Brahman and Māyāśakti both. In the *Asti Kaścidvāgarthīyam* it is one finger of the Princess and three fingers of the fool (disguised Ācārya). One finger means that the cause of the creation is one, the three fingers means they are three : Īśvara, Jīva and Prakṛti or according to another interpretation one finger means that for the proper running of the State and its wellbeing only one person is needed, i.e., the King. The three fingers mean that it needs three, the King, the officers and the subjects. In all cases the fool takes the one finger of the Princess to mean that she wants to punch his one eye, the two fingers of his he means that he would punch her both. The next sign is raising of five fingers by the Princess and that of a fist by the fool who seems to feel by the former that the lady wants to slap him. By his fist he means that he would hit her by that. Vararuci's interpretation of these in the *Kālidāsaḥ* is that the Princess wants to know as to whether the person opposite has his five senses under control. His fist he takes to signify that he has them so as though they were in his fist. In the *Asti Kaścidvāgarthīyam* the five fingers are interpreted to signify the question as to whether the creation is composed of five elements. The fist signifies that it is so when they are together. The five fingers may well also signify the question as to whether five type of forces would be necessary for defence. The fist signifies that it is so when they are under one unified command. In the *Vidyottamākālidāsīyam*, unlike in other works, there is no second gesture after the raising of one or two fingers. In the *Kavikulakokilam* it is the raising of two fingers by Kūrmanātha—that was his name before he became Kālidāsa—and drawing a circle with it which is interpreted to signify that the Śakti or the Māyā of the possessor of Śakti could be taken to be one only if both were to produce the same effect.

The two works, the *Asti Kaścidvāgviśeṣaḥ* and the *Vidyottamākālidāsīym* stand apart from others. The former does not have the episode of the scholarly disquisition. The latter has it twice, once between Vidyottamā and Bhairavanātha and the other time between Vidyottamā and Kālidāsa, the first one in gestures and the second one in words. In the verbal one the point at issue is as to which of the two is more important, fate, *bhāgya* or action, *karman*. Bhairavanātha opts for the first and the Princess for the second. The Princess is able to carry her point more convincingly leading to the defeat of Bhairavanātha.

Four works describe the Princess as proud and conceited. In the

Kālidāsaḥ she ridicules her own teacher. In the *Kavikulakokilam* her mother refers to her getting so proud as to feel no qualms in insulting even the best among scholars which may well—that is her worry—reduce the palace to ashes. She is so unmannerly as to insult the suitors to their very face pouring ridicule on them for carrying names that do not agree with their bearing. In the *Vidyottamākālidāsīyam* she maltreats the vanquished Pandits to the point of assigning them the duty of either keeping guard at the gate or serving breakfast or meals or looking after the stable. Not giving any details the *Śrīkālidāsacaritasaṅgrahaḥ* just refers to her as haughty and arrogant.

The *uṣṭra* episode of the original narrative is utilized in the discovery of the foolishness of the person the Princess has married in five works, the *Kālidāsapāṇikaraṇam*, the *Mahākavikālidāsam*, the *Kavikulakokilam*, the *Asti Kaścidvāgarthīyam* and the *Vidyottamākālidāsīyam*. The mispronunciation of the word (*uṣṭra*) in the very night of the marriage when the grunting of the animal reaches the ears is enough to reveal the level of his learning. In other works it is discovered differently. In the *Kālidāsaḥ* it is from the mispronunciation of the word Priyaṅgu as Piṅgu and Dhurandhara Śāstrī as Ḍhundhara Śāstrī. In the *Asti Kaścidvāgviśeṣaḥ* it is from his rustic demeanour; his sleeping on the floor, his loud snoring and his fixing his gaze on the portrait of bull-fight in preference to that of Kṛṣṇa-Gopī Rāsa dance. In the *Asti Kaścidvāgarthīyam* it is from the rustic manner of his speech. In at least two of the works, the *Mahākavikālidāsam* and the *Vidyottamākālidāsiyam* something more is added to mispronunciation of the word *uṣṭra*. It is the mispronunciation of *priye* as *piye* in the former and Vidyottamā's asking the rustic to trace *uṭra* with rules of grammar and the rustic telling her that he does not know them.

After the fool in the man is discovered, he is shunted out. The *Kavikulakokilam* makes Vidyottamā call him names and kick him. The *Asti Kaścidvāgviśeṣaḥ* makes her use choice invectives. The reaction of the dullard to her ill-treatment varies with various works. In the *Kālidāsaḥ* he is just confounded and keeps looking at Vidyottamā. In the *Mahākavikālidāsam* he feels the pinch of the insult and runs away from Vidyottamā saying that it is better for him to end his life than to suffer insult. In the *Kavikulakokilam* he offers to die feeling cut to the quick at Vidyottamā's remark that it is better to end one's life than to cling to a dullard and solicits her permission for suicide but before committing it begs her forgiveness for the wrong done to her, asking her not to cry after she had realized her mistake in kicking him and rushes out. In the *Asti Kaścidvāgviśeṣaḥ* he vows before going out not to show his face to Vidyottamā again. In the *Asti Kaścidvāgarthīyam* he persistently pleads with her not to turn him out. In the *Vidyottamākālidāsīyam* too he does likewise. He agrees to Vidyottamā's stipulation that he should acquire learning to be acceptable to her with the request that she not keep him away from her mind. From

Vidyottamā's apartment he leaves for the Gurukula from where he had come to marry her.

All works depict Vidyottamā in a state of shock when she realizes that she has been tricked into marrying a dullard and, ironically enough, in violation of her resolve to marry some one superior to her in learning! She is angry and upset. She orders the dullard out and is in no mood to listen to his entreaties.

The sentence *asti kaścid vāgviśeṣaḥ* she is said to have uttered when Kālidāsa had come back to her after acquiring learning. In the *Mahākavikālidāsam* and the *Asti Kaścidvāgarthīyam*—in the latter it is *asti kaścid vāgarthaḥ*, which she utters *before* he goes out. In the *Mahākavikālidāsam* Vidyottamā asks Kālidāsa: *asti kaścid vāgviśeṣaḥ*, is there any improvement in speech ? If not, says she, he should move away from her. This sentence Kālidāsa having got knowledge through the grace of the Goddess speaks aloud repeatedly when he notices a lady with her entourage coming to take bath in the Narmadā and whispers it into her ears when she falls into swoon on hearing them. In the *Asti Kaścidvāgarthiyam* she says while turning him out even after his persistent entreaties that she would wait for him and when he would come after completing his education would put him the question : *asti kaścid vāgarthaḥ* and on his satisfactorily answering it would accept him as her husband. In the *Vidyottamākālidāsīyam* she puts the question to Kālidāsa when he comes back to her after three years of learning and wants him to answer it in verse sending him on errands again. He has to be a poet to be acceptable to her. All works, except the two, the playlet, the *Kālidāsapāṇikaraṇam* and the Mahākāvya, the *Vidyottamākālidāsiyam* depict the Princess stricken with remorse and penitence at her maltreatment of Kālidāsa. The Aryan woman that she is, she is shown pining for him and realizing that he is a poet now, a poet of high order, falling at his feet and begging forgiveness of him. As for the *Kālidāsapāṇikaraṇam*, it is too small a work to make a mention of the above. The *Vidyottamākālidāsīyam* for all practical purposes is the only work which depicts the Princesss firm in her treatment of her husband to the point of countering the views of her father and her friend Suśīlā. She is prepared to wait till her husband acquires learning. In her very presence he had promised that he would do so.

Kālidāsa acquiring learning through the grace of Goddess Kālī—in all probability a construction on his name in the traditional episode as said earlier—does figure in a few works differing only in detail, the most important of which is in the *Śrīkālidāsacaritasaṅgrahaḥ* wherein out of the laughter of the Goddess at the rustic speech of the young man the betelnut juice from her mouth is said to have slipped into that of his turning him into a unique poet. In the *Kālidāsapāṇikaraṇam* Kālidāsa is shown going to a temple after having been turned out by the Princess and keeps on trying till the next morning, till the Goddess taking pity, appears before him and grants him Vidyā, knowledge, when he mentions this word, not able to pronounce Vidyottamā for lack of knowledge of Sanskrit, implying that Vidyottamā had misbehaved with him and the Goddess thinking that he wants Vidyā, knowledge, which is very much the traditional narrative. In the *Kālidāsagauravam* the Goddess appears before Kālidāsa as he is writing his name on her face as proof of his nocturnal visit to the Kālī temple in a jungle across a fierce river which he had accepted as a challenge. Happy at his action, the Goddess offers him a boon. She agrees to his request to make him a poet well-versed in the Śāstras. In the *Śrikālidāsacaritasaṅgrahaḥ* she is shown to laugh at Kālidāsa's rustic speech when he approaches her on being turned out by the Princess. He gains poetic genius out of the slipping of the betelnut juice into his mouth from that of the Goddess as she laughs at him. In the *Mahākavikālidāsam* he follows the path of Sādhanā, devotion, under the instructions of his Guru with his stammering gone with the Mantra given by him. Sitting on a platform in a corner of a forest near the bank of the Narmadā in the Amāvasyā night, the night of full darkness, he enters into a resolve either to win the favour of the Mother or to end his life. At the end of the Japasamādhi, the concentration with muttering, appears Goddess Kālikā and on a request from him bestows on him pure knowledge, clear speech and the name Kālidāsa indicative of its attainment through her. In the *Asti Kaścidvāgviśeṣaḥ* while moving in a forest Kālidāsa notices a figure from a distance. Approaching near it he finds it that of Goddess Kālī and prays to her to take pity on him. He starts practising penance repeating *oṁ Kālyai namaḥ*. When he is not able to win her favour even after long penance, he gets ready to chop off his head and make an offering of it to her driving the Goddess to appear before him and grant him command over speech addressing him at the same time her *dāsa*, servant, leading him to being called by that name—Kālidāsa.

Some works do not follow the narrative of Kālidāsa acquiring knowledge through the grace of Goddess Kālī. The *Kālidāsaḥ* depicts him being picked up from an Ujjayinī highway by one Nicula and brought to an Ācārya in an Āśrama who advises him to devote himself to his studies singlemindedly and tells him that he would acquire learning through the grace of Goddess Kālī and that henceforth would carry the name Kālidāsa. In the *Kavikulakokilam* he is shown after repudiation to repair to a Sarasvatīkuṇḍa, pond named after Sarasvatī, and pray to the Goddess who appears before him and offers him a boon. With the sight of the Goddess there is nothing to ask for Kālidāsa now. At the behest of the Goddess he goes into the pond three times and the third time he comes out with a lotus and a water lily, the former with thorns and the latter without them which he places at the right and the left foot of the deity respectively prompting her to bless him to be *kavikulakokila*, the cuckoo among poets and to be the best among singers of poetry in the world. She agrees to Kālidāsa's prayer to dwell in his voice, tongue and pen and promises to do whatever he wants.

It is the two works, the *Asti Kaścidvāgarthīyam* and the *Vidyottamā-kālidāsīyam* which have nothing of the episode of the grace of Goddess Kālī. In the *Asti Kaścidvāgarthīyam* Kālidāsa gains or rather regains intelligence through a chance head injury by the accidental hit on his head of the branch of the Śaka tree in the fierce storm raging in the forest (from which he had been picked up earlier) to which he had repaired after having been repudiated by Vidyottamā. It is after this that he had gone to the Gurukula of the celebrated teacher Vāmadeva and had persued his studies there for five years which had enabled him to compose poetry.

In the *Vidyottamākālidāsīyam* Kālidāsa goes to the Gurukula after repudiation but its Ācārya being unwilling to give him a place therein, he meets a Sādhu and because of intimate association with him for three years during which he visits a number of places along with him acquires good knowledge of Śāstras. When even after that he approaches the Princess and is not able to satisfy her by answering her question *asti kaścid vāgviśeṣaḥ* in verse he goes to the Gurukula and begins practising poetry coming to be known the poet Kālidāsa in course of time. Poetry comes to him not through divine favour but only through dint of continuous practice which enables him to win applause in poetic symposia.

In the traditional narrative when Kālidāsa comes back to the Princess after acquiring knowledge, she puts him the question: *asti kaścid vāgviśeṣaḥ*, is there any improvement in speech ? The poet then composes three works, each beginning with each of the words of the sentence. The modern writers have followed the incident by and large with some additions and alterations here and there. In the *Vidyottamākālidāsiyam*, Kālidāsa is made to hand over the three works to Vidyottamā with the remark that it is she who is depicted as Pārvatī in his *Kumārasambhava* and the Yakṣī in the *Meghadūta*. It is she again who peeps out of his female characters like Sudakṣinā, Indumatī and Sītā. In the *Raghuvaṁśa* he has depicted the ideal husband-wife relationship which is equal to that between word and meaning. In the *Kālidāsaḥ* too he hands over his three works to Vidyottamā reciting from each one of them the first stanza and enquiring of the Princess : *asti kaścid vāgviśeṣaḥ*, is there any improvement in speech ?, a material departure from the old narrative where the Princess is said to have uttered the words in a different context, as mentioned above. In the *Kālidāsapāṇikaraṇam* Kālidāsa approaches Vidyottamā asking her to open the door : *anāvṛtakapāṭaṁ dvāraṁ dehi*. The Princess opens the door but asks the question: *asti kaścid vāgviśeṣaḥ*. A bear hug follows this and the couple is led to union. In the *Mahākavikālidāsam asti kaścid vāgviśeṣaḥ* occurs at the very time Kālidāsa is repudiated. Realizing that she had been cheated Vidyāvatī (that is how Vidyottamā is called there) asks Kūrmanātha (Kālidāsa's earlier name) *asti kaścid vāgviśeṣaḥ*, has he anything particular to say ? If not, he should be off from there. These words occur again; this time it is Kālidāsa who utters them; when he notices a lady with the entourage. Remembering at her sight the Princess he speaks aloud her last words to him : *asti kaścid vāgviśeṣaḥ* ? When on hearing these the lady falls into swoon, he approaching her and recognizing her from her diamond ring to be no other than his wife, whispers into her ears : *asti kaścid vāgviśeṣaḥ* which make her realize that the person speaking them is no other than her husband for the fact that he alone and no one else was present when she had uttered them.

In the *Asti Kaścidvāgviśeṣaḥ* the words are uttered first after the knock at the door and the second time after the second knock when the Princess wants to be sure of improvement in the speech of her husband on being assailed by doubt at the first knock of improvement in it.

In the *Asti Kaścidvāgarthīyam* the Princess utters these before turning out her husband in response to his repeated entreaties that she would wait for him and when he would be back to her after completing his education, would put him the question : *asti kaścidvāgarthaḥ*. She would allow him in only if his answer is to her satisfaction. The question of the Princess had always been uppermost in the mind of Kālidāsa. That is why he had composed the *Meghadūta* with the word *kaścit* and had started composing two of his Mahākāvyas, the *Kumārasambhava* and the *Raghuvaṁśa* beginning each one of them with *asti* and *vāgarthaḥ* respectively.

Kālidāsa being surrounded by so many legends, what some of the writers have done is that they have brought them in too in their works almost in the manner of an extension of the Vidoyattamā episode. Tradition associates the great poet with King Vikramāditya one of whose nine jewels he is said to have been. He is also associated with a gardener woman in whose house he is said to have spent most of his time. Of the eight works with the Vidyottamā episode Vikramāditya figures in four : the *Kālidāsaḥ*, the *Mahākavikālidāsam*, the *Kavikulakokilam* and the *Vidyottamākālidāsīyam* and the gardener woman, called Mālinī, in one : *Mahākavikālidāsam*. Vikramāditya serves in the works—in one of them, the *Mahākavikālidāsam*, Mālinī too along with him—as the conduit for the union of the separated couple.

In the *Kālidāsaḥ* the Avanti King Vikramāditya figures first as the father of Princess Priyaṅgumañjarī (that is how Vidyottamā is called there). He figures again when the Ācārya of the Āśrama where Kālidāsa had persued his studies speaking in superlatives about his poetry informs him that after witnessing the performance of his *Abhijñānaśākuntala* the King Vikramāditya had made the announcement that he (Kālidāsa) would occupy the highest place among his jewels and that he would be coming to the Āśrama to bring him round for the sake of his daughter. He (Vikramāditya) begs forgiveness of the great poet on his daughter's behalf.

Vikramāditya in the *Mahākavikālidāsam* is brought in when Kālidāsa after a chance meeting with Vidyottamā on the road to Narmadā goes out for a bath. He is picked up as one of the palanquin bearers for the King. It is while carrying the palanquin that he permits himself the remark : *bhāro na bādhate rājan yathā bādhati bādhate*, the weight does not pain me as much as does the form *bādhati* on hearing that of the King : *kṣaṇaṁ viśramyatāṁ jālma skandhas te yadi bādhati*, rest for a while, O despicable one, if your shoulder aches, which prompts him (the King) to ask his name which he gives out as Kālidāsa. After this he utters an eulogy of the King which charms him into appointing him as one of the nine jewels of his Court reserving for him a garden for his stay with the lady gardener serving as the connoisseur of his poems. As the King gets ready to honour him he tells him to unite him with his wife, telling him all that had happened with him in the past. Having come to know from the Daśapura ruler that the whereabouts of his daughter are not known; she having gone out in search of Kālidāsa; he goes out to look for her. In the meantime the lady gardener assuming the form a demoness appears in Vikramāditya's Court, places a *samasyā* before all the scared courtiers telling them *inter alia* that it is Kālidāsa who alone can solve it. A spy of the name of Balāhaka sent out on the orders of the King spots him and he solves the *samasyā* instantly. A lady forest dweller on the other hand comes across a distraught lady who according to Balāhaka's information from other spies is no other than the daughter of the Daśapura ruler, Vidyottamā. The Daśapura ruler is brought in under the orders of the King (Vikramāditya) as also the lady gardener (Mālinī) who by posing the *samasyā* had imparted urgency to the search for Kālidāsa. It is they, both of them, Vikramāditya and Mālinī, who become instrumental in the union of the couple.

In the *Kavikulakokilam* the introduction of Vikramāditya has little connection with what precedes. He just enters the stage with his nine jewels every one of whom he asks to point out the superiority of his discipline. The judgement being left to Kālidāsa, he points out the superiority of poetry with convincing arguments in support of his view which thrill everybody present and prompts the King (designated Emperor in the work) to confer upon him the title of Kavisārvabhauma, the Overlord of the Poets telling him that he would be Kavikokila, the cuckoo among poets.

In the *Vidyottamākālidāsīyam* he acts as the judge to decide about the application of Kālidāsa for divorce and hears arguments for and against the same in a poetic bout between Kālidāsa and Vidyottamā with the stipulation that in case the former, Kālidāsa, were to be defeated, he would have to accept Vidyottamā. If it were otherwise, Vidyottamā would be free to go wherever she likes. Since Kālidāsa cannot score over Vidyottamā, he has to accept her as his wife. In a majority of the works the Princess is shown having no hesitation in accepting Kālidāsa when he comes back to her after acquiring learning.

Another work where King Vikramāditya figures is the *Kālidāsa-caritam* in whose final stages Kālidāsa is said to have been appointed at the head of his nine jewels. That Kālidāsa was one of Vikramāditya's nine jewels is the old legend. His having been appointed as their head is its new version. So is his renouncing the honour, shortly after its conferment, taking umbrage at the Queen's stipulation that in the next play to be written by him on the life of King Vikramāditya, he (Vikramāditya) should be described to be having one wife only. Another old legend in the work is Kālidāsa's having led an embassy to the Court of the ruler of Kuntala, Kuntaleśvaradautyam. In its new version he is said to have led embassies twice, first to the Court of the ruler of Vidarbha and the second time to the Court of the ruler of Kuntala. While the old legend has nothing of the motivation for it except perhaps the projection that Kālidāsa was as much a success in diplomacy as in poetry, in its new version it is the intrigue of a character called Paṇḍitarāja who is envious of Kālidāsa's poetic talents and the favour of the King that he enjoys thereby. The Queen siding him, he wants to see Kālidāsa out of his way. The author of the work has confined himself to the very basic elements of the old legends to introduce which he has invented a whole lot of episodes and incidents like Kālidāsa being accompanied by his brother Raghunātha in Vidarbha, his being shadowed by two spies while in Vidarbha at the instance of Paṇḍitarāja, their molesting a dancing girl of the name of Sarasvatī who had been deputed by the Vidarbha ruler to extract from Kālidāsa by mixing with him the State secrets of Mālava, her crying out for Raghunātha—that is the name for Rāma that she uses, the chance appearance of Raghunātha (Kālidāsa's brother) and his rescuing of her, her getting attracted towards him and marrying him in secret, Kālidāsa being put in prison by the Vidarbha ruler and his escape from it with the help of Sarasvatī, his appearance in his house incognito just at the time when Paṇḍitarāja arranged the theft of his works, Paṇḍitarāja accusing Kālidāsa of having betrayed Mālava interests citing his association with Sarasvatī as evidence, interrogation of Sarasvatī and her satisfying the King of her *bona fides* by revealing everything to him, the Commander-in-Chief's getting upset at the special consideration shown to Kālidāsa leading to his (Kālidāsa's) being asked to submit his resignation from the External Affairs Ministry post and his doing so gladly which is preceded by his renunciation of the position of the head of the nine jewels.

The other works, apart from those with the Vidyottamā-Kālidāsa episode in this study are *Kālidāsacaritam, Kālidāsagauravam, Kavikālidāsam, Kālidāsīyakāvyasambhavam, Kavikālidāsīyam* and *Kālidāsīyam Antimam Aitihyam*. Of these the *Kālidāsagauravam* has something of the Vidyottamā episode in the propitiation of Goddess Kālī and something of the Vikramāditya connection. Kālidāsa is shown in it as an unruly student of a Mithila High School. In a spirit of bravado he agrees to swim across a river on the Amāvasyā night and go to the Kālī temple in a dense forest. After reaching the forest through frightful surroundings in pitch darkness when it has started raining he writes his name on the face of the Goddess instead of the wall for fear of its being washed away by rain water, as proof positive of his having visited the temple which pleases the Goddess who blesses him, on his asking for it, to be versed in the Śāstras as a result of which he shows his brilliance in the disquisition on the existence of God in a school in Saurāṣṭra subsequently. He surprises everybody with his fluency in prose and verse.

King Chandragupta II called Vikramāditya praises in superlatives the *Abhijñānaśākuntala* after witnessing its performance. So does he the *Meghadūta* and other works. On Kālidāsa entering his Court he embraces him and confers on him the title of Mahākavi.

The work in question is evidently an admixture of the two parts of the old narrative.

Kavikālidāsīyam is based on Kālidāsa's association with King Bhoja of Dhārā which also is supported by legend. It is mainly based on *Bhojaprabandha* of Vallālasena some of the episodes from which it seeks to retell with additions and alterations, the most important of which are Kālidāsa's stay in the house of a harlot Vilāsavatī. There does exist a legend about Kālidāsa's association with a harlot. The author has made deft use of it. Not only has she been assigned the name Vilāsavatī, she had been made the centre piece of the narrative. The King resents Kālidāsa's association with her. A learned lady of the name of Sītā in his Court defends it and requests him not to feel bad about it. On knowing the King's displeasure Kālidāsa withdraws from the Court and begins to stay incognito with Vilāsavatī. He is traced with the help of spies when he in the guise of a Cāraṇa completes the *samasyā* placed before scholars by the King as they, unable to complete it, were fleeing the Kingdom. The King begs forgiveness of Kālidāsa and allows his stay with Vilāsavatī. The author has concocted a full story out of Kālidāsa's association, as per the legend, with a harlot, to the point of the King relenting on his objection to it.

Just as a heavy superstructure has been raised on a very seminal material in the *Kavikālidāsīyam*, so has it been raised on a similar material in the *Kavikālidāsam*. Its author has rejected all the popular stories connected with Kālidāsa. The only old material that he has drawn upon is Kālidāsa's connection with King Vikramāditya one of the nine jewels of his Court he had been. The rest of the story is all imaginary. There is no tradition of Kālidāsa's love for and marriage with the King Vikramāditya's daughter Mañjubhāṣiṇī. The various incidents like Kālidāsa's chance meeting with Vararuci and their going together to the Court of King Vikramāditya, the recitation of a *śloka* by each of the nine jewels, Mañjubhāṣiṇī's love for Kālidāsa and her refusal to appear at the Svayaṁvara,

Kālidāsa's stay incognito in the house of a lady gardener Puṣpitāgrā—are figments of the author's imagination. It is this very imagination which had made him identify the Yakṣa of the *Meghadūta* with Kālidāsa and Raghu in the *Raghuvaṁśa* with King Vikramāditya. The story of the *Meghadūta* has been so reshaped that the Yakṣa is supplanted there by Kālidāsa. It is his pangs which are described in the poem, the pangs caused by the separation from Manjubhāṣiṇī due to his exile ordered by Vikramāditya under the charge of his having enticed her. Similarly the description of the Digvijaya in the *Raghuvaṁśa* is the description of the Digvijaya of Vikramāditya. The entire work is an attempt to bring out the poet in Kālidāsa even while giving an account, purely imaginary of course with the sole exception of his association with the King Vikramāditya in the form of his being one of the nine jewels, the Navaratnas, of a part of his personal life.

The story of Kālidāsa having been the Court poet of King Bhoja is also the story in part of the *Śrīkālidāsīyam Antimam Aitihyam.* Like the *Kavikālidāsīyam* it also brings in a harlot whom it also calls Vilasāvatī introducing at the same time the episode of the hacking to pieces of Kālidāsa by the same (Vilāsavatī) for the greed of winning the reward in completing the *samasyā* put forward by the King which actually the poet had completed. In this context the legend of Kālidāsa having composed the *Campūrāmāyaṇa* volunteering it to go under the authorship of his patron Bhoja; the work is also called thereby *Bhojacampū*; is introduced. This is done by the depiction of the revival of the poet with the piecing together of his body. The incomplete character of the above work (the *Campūrāmāyaṇa*) is explained by introducing the episode of death finally overtaking the poet when he came upto the Sundarakāṇḍa.

The *Bhojaprabandha* story of Kālidāsa completing the *samasyā ka kha ga gha* with reference to a little girl who was in reality Sarasvatī (the Goddess of Learning) herself in that garb, appearing in response to Kālidāsa's prayers to bail him out of the difficulty when his intellect seemed to be failing him; finds mention in the present work too, the motivation for it being ascribed to the feeling of jealousy among Kālidāsa's contemporaries who not liking the King's infatuation for him had put forward the above intricate Samasyā to test his skill in poetry.

The *Kālidāsīyam Antimam Aitihyam* is a story of the three lives of Kālidāsa. As the story goes, Sarasvatī took a little longer to respond to the prayers of Kālidāsa driving him in a fit of temper to address her as *raṇḍe*, a loose woman, which infuriated her to curse him to be born dumb in his next life.

Kālidāsa was born dumb but not in the very next life. There he was born as the son of an old Brahmin near Vārāṇasī. It was he who as a boy had revised Śaṅkarācārya's *Śārīrakabhāṣya* subsequent to the portion it had been revised by a Bhairava. It was in the third life that Kālidāsa was born dumb. When Śaṅkarācārya reached Kāñcī the Vaiṣṇavas there not taking kindly to his Advaita philosophy made the stipulation that they would fall in line with him if he were to provide speech to a dumb fellow roaming about there. Śaṅkara seeing him recognized him to be the same person who as a boy in his previous birth had revised his *Śārīrakabhāṣya* and who still remembered it. At his behest the dumb fellow sang five hymns in praise of Goddess Kāmākṣī and spoke out seven hundred stanzas in Āryā metre, collectively called the Āryāsaptaśatī, much to the delight and surprise of everybody.

Evidently the above legend invented by some of the admirers of the poet Mūka has been joined on here by making him (Mūka) an incarnation of Kālidāsa. The work, therefore, is a queer amalgam of different legends connected with Kālidāsa; his having been a protege of Bhoja, a companion of a harlot, the real author of the *Bhojacampū* or the *Campūrāmāyaṇa* and finally reborn as Mūka in one of his incarnations.

The only work which has no tradition of any sort about Kālidāsa is the *Kālidāsakāvyasambhavam.* It is based on a reference in Mallinātha's commentary on the *Meghadūta* in explanation of the derelection of duty by the Yakṣa in not gathering the fresh flowers one morning for Kubera's worship of Śiva which made Kubera pronounce a curse on him to undergo exile for a year. It was during the exile that the Yakṣa in the Rāmagiri hills noticed a cloud in the rainy season and decided to send a message through it to his beloved in far away Alakā.

It was a novel idea to dramatize the above incident and to trace the *Meghadūta* therefrom. There is no Yakṣa in the present work, no Yakṣī, not even Kubera in the form of lord of the Yakṣas. There is nothing divine or semi-divine. Every character is a human being.

The most basic change introduced refers to the person exiled. It is not the Yakṣa who is exiled here but Kālidāsa himself. It is he who sends a message to his beloved who in the present case is Mālinī, either a gardener woman to whom, as per tradition, he used to recite his compositions to elicit her opinion or a river of that name personified. Kubera is made the maternal uncle of Kālidāsa and given the name Kubera Sharma and Megha called Megharāja, is made the latter's (Kubera's) son.

There is novely not only in the content of the theme but also in its stage presentation. Kālidāsa while reciting or writing his composition is shown on the stage with a spotlight while the memories surging in his mind are shown in paintings as backdrops.

In replacing the Yakṣa by Kālidasa the author seems to be guided by the fact that the depth and the intensity of feeling can go well with the very person describing the separation and the pangs occasioned by it. It must, therefore, be Kālidāsa himself who through the medium of the Yakṣa was describing his own condition. If that be so, why have then the medium ? Why not have the person directly undergoing the experience ?

The last of the works in this study, the *Śrīkālidāsacaritasaṅgrahaḥ* has two parts. The first one in verse which is much smaller gives in summary form the Vidyottamā episode with much the traditional incidents with the exception of the two, one, it depicts Kālidāsa grazing goats in his early years and the other, his gaining poetic talent, as said earlier in a different context, out of the slip of the betelnut juice into his mouth from that of the Goddess as she laughed at his rustic speech. The second part in the form of conversation between two or three characters examines the many points of criticism against Kālidāsa and the theories held about him either traditionally or otherwise. The points of criticism are : (i) the propriety of sending a non-sentient thing like a cloud to convey a message, (ii) not describing the birth of Kumāra while titling the work *Kūmārasambhava*, the birth of Kumāra, (iii) describing in lurid details the love sports of Śiva and Pārvatī, (iv) showing indifference towards sentiments other than Erotic, (iv), employment of Yamaka, admittedly an inferior form of poetry, in Canto IX of the *Raghuvaṁśa*. These objections the work meets successfully. The theories discussed are : (i) Kālidāsa was one of the nine jewels at the Court of King Vikramāditya, (ii) as per the *Bhojaprabandha*, Kālidāsa, Baṇā and Māgha, etc. were contemporaries, (iii) Kālidāsa had friends in the Kuntala King Pravarasena and the Simhalese King Kumāradāsa (the author of the *Janakīharaṇa*), (iv) Vikramāditya, i.e., Chandragupta II, got the *Setubandha* written from Kālidāsa in the name of his daughter's son Pravarasena II, (v) Mātṛgupta described by Kalhaṇa is no other than Kālidāsa, (vi) Kālidāsa had an association with a harlot with whom he would spend his time. All these theories the work discounts. The ones it uphold are : Diṅnāga and Nicula referred to in a *Meghadūta* verse were actual characters of the name, one a critic of Kālidāsa and the other his supporter, and that there is reference, obliquely again, to the King Vikramāditya in the title *Vikramorvaśīya* and the phrase *anutseko vikramālaṅkāraḥ*.

The work is unique in that it brings together all the points of criticism against the theories about Kālidāsa and puts a searching spotlight on them. It is an attempt to sift the tradition and to find out from it what is acceptable. From the point of view of discovering Kālidāsa as an individual the discussion on the theories is much more important than the rebuttal of the charges of impropriety against him.

From the above analysis it should be clear that in some works on Kālidāsa there is more of hold of tradition than in some others. Of all the legends and the episodes it is the Vidyottamā episode with its string of colourful incidents that exercises greater hold in the modern Sanskrit writers, eight out of a total of fourteen of them having dealt with it in their works, in some form or the other. The next in popularity in the descending order are the Vikramāditya and Bhoja episodes. All these are adequately spiced by a number of old incidents involving Kālidāsa in some way or the other. These have given ideas to modern writers to base their composition on. The basics of these ideas remaining the same, the form in presenting them differs with the result that each composition even when dealing with the old theme has a character of its own and has to be judged on its own merit.

1

KĀLIDĀSACARITAM

This five-act play by Sri S.B. Velankar, was published from Bombay in 1961. Sri Velankar has woven its theme out of his own imagination basing it, as said by him in the Preface to his work, on the impressions formed from his study of Kālidāsa's writings. In creating it, he has proceeded on certain basic assumptions. One, that Kālidāsa was a contemporary of Candragupta II of the Gupta dynasty whom he identifies with the legendary Vikramāditya reputed to have nine celebrities, collectively called the Navaratnas, the Nine Jewels, Kālidāsa included in them, in his court. Two, that he was sent as envoy by his patron (Candragupta Vikramāditya) to Vidarbha.

Theme

First Act: The play opens with the preparations for the spring festival. Queen Vasudhā is shown waiting anxiously for king Vikramāditya. Time passes by but the king does not turn up. The Queen is naturally worried at this. Then appears Paṇḍitarāja with the information that Kālidāsa had insulted him in the royal court that day. The Queen is angry at this and thinks of the means to send Kālidāsa out of the capital (Ujjayinī). In the meantime comes Vikramāditya. He is full of praise for Kālidāsa's proficiency in *samasyāpūrti* and remarks that he (Kālidāsa) is certainly more learned than Paṇḍitarāja, which the Queen does not like, for she, in her heart of hearts, wants to get rid of Kālidāsa. Just then comes Kālidāsa and joins the King, the Queen and the Paṇḍitarāja. He comes with the information of Vidarbha's plot. The King likes to discuss the whole thing with his Chief Minister and his Commander-in-Chief, before making up his mind on any course of action. In the meantime, he orders a competition between Kālidāsa and Paṇḍitarāja for extemporaneous composition of verses. He asks the Queen to be the judge and to find out for herself as to who of the two is superior to the other. The competition begins with Queen Vasudhā as the judge. Both rivals compose verses and do the *samasyāpūrtis* and the like. Now here, too, Kālidāsa's verses prove far superior in merit to those of the Paṇḍitarāja. Queen Vasudhā herself has to concede this, but she cannot reconcile herself to the popularity of Kālidāsa. The seeds of jealousy sown by Paṇḍitarāja seem to have taken deep roots in her mind.

Vikramāditya comes to know from the Chief Minister that the king of Vidarbha, in collusion with the king of Kosala, is plotting to overthrow the king of Mālava. In the light of this, it is decided to send somebody to Vidarbha to lead an embassy to its court. Queen Vasudhā finds this the right moment to get rid of Kālidāsa. She advises the King to send Kālidāsa to the court of Vidarbha as ambassador. She also, at the same time, devises such measures as may make it impossible for Kālidāsa to return to Mālava. Kālidāsa very gladly accepts the assignment and in high spirits leaves for his home. Paṇḍitarāja, on the other hand, prepares a scheme for the removal from the residence of Kālidāsa of all of his works through one of his accomplices. Vasudhā sends that very accomplice to Vidarbha to keep a close watch on Kālidāsa's movements. During his visit to Vidarbha, Kālidāsa is accompanied by his brother, Raghunātha.

Second Act : Sukīrti, the ruler of Vidarbha, is extremely worried at Kālidāsa's diplomatic mission. He tries to find out from him some important secrets of Mālava, but fails. He is highly disappointed at this. He, however, comes to know that Kālidāsa is well aware of his (Sukīrti's) collusion with the ruler of Kosala and their joint plot to launch an attack on Mālava. Sukīrti is afraid of this information passing to Vikramāditya. So to prevent Kālidāsa from going back to Ujjayinī and submitting a report to his King about his (Sukīrti's) plot, he (Sukīrti) arrests him and puts him in prison. Still undeterred at his efforts in getting hold of some secrets of Mālava, Sukīrti appoints a girl named Sarasvatī, a charming singer and dancer, to keep company with Kālidāsa. To facilitate her work, he hands her over a ring with royal insignia. At this the story takes a different turn. Sarasvatī, while on her way to Kālidāsa's apartment in prison, is molested by Govinda and Gopāla, the two spies who have been assigned by Paṇḍitarāja and Vasudhā the duty of keeping a watch on Kālidāsa's movements in Vidarbha. They express their desire to Sarasvatī to marry her. Sarasvatī's honour is at stake. In these moments of distress, she prays to Raghunātha (Rāma) to save her. Now we have a dramatic irony. The name of Kālidāsa's brother, too, is Raghunātha who happens to pass that way. He thinks that a woman in distress is calling out to him for help. He appears on the scene and rescues Sarasvatī who is naturally highly grateful to him. When she comes to Kālidāsa, she tells him that she is his friend and that she would prove helpful to him in every possible way. Just as she is saying this, Raghunātha comes. Kālidāsa introduces Sarasvatī to him, little knowing that they have met each other earlier, too, by a strange turn of events. Sarasvatī very well recalls the words of praise for her husband's younger brother that Alakā (Kālidāsa's wife), her one time friend, had uttered once. She was already feeling attracted towards Raghunātha. Now, having had an opportunity to see him, she falls in love with him. She also frees Kālidāsa from captivity by some device. Kālidāsa continues to live in Vidarbha disguised as Raghunātha. Sarasvatī and Raghunātha, too, live together and marry each other by Gandharva rites.

Third Act : King Vikramāditya does not have any news from Kālidāsa while from other sources he learns that he (Kālidāsa) has been put under arrest by Sukīrti. He feels inclined to launch an attack on Vidarbha to punish its ruler for having broken the age-old convention of diplomatic immunity but the very idea of the killing and destruction which a war entails, puts a brake on him. This is one side of the picture.

The other side is furnished by the arrangements that Paṇḍitarāja makes for the theft of Kālidāsa's works during his (Kālidāsa's) long absence from Ujjayinī. At Paṇḍitarāja's instance, one Govindabhaṭṭa goes to Kālidāsa's house to remove from there by theft all his works. Now it so happens that Kālidāsa, who has slipped out of Vidarbha prison and has come back to his house in Ujjayinī the same day quietly notices the thief in his house and catches hold of him. At this, Alakā, the wife of Kālidāsa, gets up from her bed and thinking Govindabhaṭṭa to be a fool who has entered the house through mistake, requests Kālidāsa (who is disguised as a policeman) to release him. It is only after some time that Kālidāsa discloses his identity to Alakā. This rather unexpected union of the separated husband and wife provides intense happiness to both.

Fourth Act : Back in Ujjayinī, Kālidāsa tells everything to Vikramāditya who becomes all the more favourably inclined towards him and sends him to the Kuntala country as the head of a diplomatic mission. Kālidāsa's absence from Ujjayinī once again provides Paṇḍitarāja an opportunity to hatch a plot against him. He proclaims him (Kālidāsa) a spy of Vidarbha. Paṇḍitarāja goes to Vikramāditya with this allegation. As a proof for this, he points to Sarasvatī, a girl from the Vidarbha country, who is living in Kālidāsa's house. Vikramāditya tells Paṇḍitarāja that if what he had said is proved correct, then Kālidāsa would surely be punished. But if, on the other hand, Paṇḍitarāja's allegation proves false and fabricated, he (Paṇḍitarāja) will have to suffer the punishment which Kālidāsa may fix for him. Paṇḍitarāja agrees to this. Sarasvatī is called to the royal court. She reveals there the secret of her marriage with Raghunātha, Kālidāsa's younger brother, and gives satisfactory answers to the questions put to her. Paṇḍitarāja's allegations are, thus, proved untrue and he is ordered to clear out of Ujjayinī immediately.

Fifth Act: King Vikramāditya honours Kālidāsa for all the varied services rendered by him to the State and for all his poetic works composed uptil that time, which, of course, do not include the *Raghuvaṁśa*. He (the King) puts him at the head of all the nine jewels in his learned assembly.

Vikramāditya holds the view that a poet is far superior in importance to a soldier for, he saves everybody and immortalizes the bravery of the kings by his poetry. The Army Chief, however, disagrees with him. Says he, "A soldier's contribution to the safety of his country is the same as a poet's for the prestige of the country." He (Army Chief) does not like the honour done to Kālidāsa. This hurts Kālidāsa. He is further pained at the stipulation by Queen Vasudhā conveyed through Sarasvatī that in the next plays to be written by Kālidāsa on the life of Vikramāditya, he (Vikramāditya) should be described as having one wife only. Thus does Kālidāsa give expression to his injured feelings: "Who are these people to order a poet while they themselves are incapable of restraining the King from having more than one wife?" He asks Sarasvatī to carry the letter of resignation from the post of the Chief of Poets, to which he was appointed only a little while ago. Sarasvatī agrees to do so and leaves to meet the King. Just at that very time, the Chief Minister enters Kālidāsa's house and informs him that he (Chief Minister) has been sent by the King to secure his resignation. On an enquiry from Alakā, he tells her that after Kālidāsa had been honoured, the Army Chief went to the royal palace and requested the King to relieve him of his present post on the ground that if he likes Kālidāsa, the envoy, then what has he to do with the rather redundant office of the Army Chief. The King tried to pacify him and bring him round and put in efforts to persuade him to change his decision. But he was adamant and would not listen. So finding no way out, the King orders Kālidāsa to tender his resignation from the External Affairs Ministry post. The Chief Minister carries with him the draft of the resignation letter. He gives it to Kālidāsa for his signatures. Kālidāsa feels highly relieved at this and tells his wife that he is no longer a subservient royal employee. He can now breathe freely and will henceforth devote himself entirely to writing poetry. He expresses the wish to take up for the theme of his poem the history of the whole race of Śrī Rāmacandra. And that will win him fame and honour, not honour from the King, but honour from the people, young and old, learned and unlearned, till the sun and moon last. He then prays to lord Śiva. Then enters the King, the Queen (Vasudhā) and the Army Chief. They are about to enquire from Alakā as to why Kālidāsa has resigned from the post of the Chief of the Nine Jewels also. Alakā intercepts them and says that the mortals should cause no obstruction to the production of ambrosia on this auspicious moment. Kālidāsa is free from all restrictions. He comes out with the first verse of the *Raghuvaṁśa*. Flow forth then other verses followed by a shower of flowers from the sky. After this is uttered the Bharatavākya and that brings the play to an end.

Critical Appreciation

The eminence achieved by Kālidāsa in literature has made him a centre of a number of legends that have grown round him over the years. One of them is that he was a fool initially but came to acquire learning by the grace of the goddess Kālī after having been married to a learned Princess deceitfully and rejected by her. The other is that he was one of the nine jewels, the Navaratnas, in the court of King Vikramāditya. The third is that he led an embassy to the court of a king, according to some of Kuntala, according to others of Vidarbha and according to still others of Siṁhala. The fourth is that he had a friend in a lady gardener with whom he would discuss finer points of poetry. The fifth is that he was in love with a harlot and was cut to pieces by her out of greed to win a royal reward while he was staying with her. All these are not just figments of imagination. They do have a basis, though absolutely weak; just a name, either of the poet or one of his characters or his disposition as revealing itself in his works. Thus, the first legend derives itself from the name of the poet which has in its first part the name of goddess Kālī. Unmatched excellence is unusual and can be had only through divine grace. Thus ran the popular thinking. And who could that divine being be except the Divine Mother, the all-powerful Kālī, whose name the poet carries in his. The second legend is based on the name Vikrama occurring in the play, the *Vikramorvaśīya* which is taken as a reference to his patron, the king of that name, by him. The third has its connection with the now extinct play, the *Kuntaleśvaradautya*; it being taken to refer to his own story of leading a mission to the court of a ruler. The fourth and the fifth owe their origin to the universally accepted excellence of his in the depiction of Śṛṅgāra, the sentiment of Erotics on the basis that the poet who could create such descriptions must have been himself also a great *rasika* with his own love affairs.

Our playwright has picked up for the theme of his play the second and the third of the accounts as given above. Since they are too laconic to allow a full-length play to grow out of them, he has added to them much that is his own. Except for Kālidāsa and Vikramāditya all the other characters in the play are his creations. The entire episode of Paṇḍitarāja feeling jealous of him and contriving all the while to get him out of his way by being sent to Vidarbha first and to Kuntala later which runs through most parts of his play is the playwright's innovation. His other innovations are the introduction into the play of Vasudhā— that is the name that he assigns her—, the Queen who is said to have been a Princess of Udaipur before being married to King Vikramāditya of Ujjayinī and Paṇḍitarāja, the learned poet who accompanied her after marriage; he too is said to belong to Udaipur and connected with the royal Court; the reason enough for her to favour him as against Kālidāsa whose superior poetic talent had started eclipsing him and making him lose his pre-eminent position and win the special consideration from the King, making him stoop so low as to arrange for the theft of the works of Kālidāsa. The introduction of the Vedic Pandits Gopāla and Govindabhaṭṭa who are made to serve the nefarious designs of Paṇḍitarāja and their marriage with the two palace maids Madanikā and Nipuṇikā is still another of the playwright's original creations. So is the introduction of Sarasvatī described as a childhood friend of Kālidāsa's wife Alakā—, that is the name the playwright assigns her—in this he probably was motivated by the city of that name occurring in the *Meghadūta*—who arranges for the escape of Kālidāsa after he had been put under captivity by the ruler of Vidarbha and Raghunātha introduced as the younger brother of Kālidāsa who accompanies him to Vidarbha to oversee his well-being and who through a strange turn of events comes into contact with Sarasvatī and is united with her in marriage later. The originality of the playwright is also noticeable in the renunciation of the honour of the headship of the nine jewels conferred on him by the King, thus freeing him from the onerous duties of the State to enable him to devote himself fully to his literary pursuits. To add a little spice to the theme, the playwright has invented the episode of the opposition of the Army Chief to what he feels the excessive importance shown to Kālidāsa in placing him at the head of the nine jewels and a discussion on the comparative roles of the poet and the soldier in leaving a better and more permanent impact on the sands of time in which the King comes out openly in defence of the poet. Though superior in argument, the King is not able to convince the Army Chief who, out of pique, resigns his post. To salvage the situation, the King asks for the resignation of Kālidāsa from his External Affairs Ministry post, now that he has been elevated to the position of the Head of the Nine Jewels to which the Queen also makes a reference. The playwright has introduced a dramatic irony here in that the very ground on which Kālidāsa's resignation from his External Affairs Ministry post had been asked for had become redundant in that he had himself tendered his resignation from the new position of the Head of the Nine Jewels even before he had received the royal orders for vacating the earlier position of an official in the Ministry of External Affairs.

For Kālidāsa two things take place in quick succession. One position he relinquishes himself, and the other he is made to leave, thus rendering him totally a free man, free from the responsibilities of the State, free to soar high on the wings of Poesy. It was in this frame of mind that he thinks of composing a Mahākāvya on Śrī Rāma-candra and his entire solar race. He is now not to take orders from somebody as to what type of work he should compose. His free spirit had revolted at his being ordered by the Queen that he should compose the *Vikramorvaśīya* in such a way as to depict the King in it as having only one wife. It was this revolt that had prompted him to tender his resignation from the most coveted of the positions of that of the Chief of the Nine Jewels.

Kālidāsa's life as an advancing poet, as says the playwright in the Preface, is an undercurrent of the play which begins when the *Ṛtusaṁhāra* had been composed and ends when the *Raghuvaṁśa* is to begin. The *Meghadūta* and the *Mālavikāgnimitra* are shown to have been composed when Kālidāsa was an envoy at Vidarbha. His *Kunatleśvaradautya*, supposed to have been lost, is also referred to in the play.

It has been an endeavour of the playwright to show that Kālidāsa was as successful as an ambassador as a poet. That is why his story has it that Kālidāsa succeeded in stopping the hostilities between Vidarbha and Kuntala and putting them on a firm footing of friendship and cordiality. Queen Vasudhā takes him for a diplomat only.

She cannot believe that Kālidāsa can ever be gifted with poetic qualities. That is why she asks Paṇḍitarāja not to worry :

वसुधा --- तदेतमुज्जयिनीजनुषं कालिदासं पराजित्य दासं करिष्यामः ।
न भेतव्यं भवता । परराष्ट्रकार्यालयसेवकोऽयं कथं कविर्भवति ।[1]

1. p. 5.

"Vasudhā—Don't you be afraid. We may put in captivity this Ujjayinī-born Kālidāsa. How can he be a poet working as he does in the Ministry of External Affairs ?"

The rise of Kālidāsa prompts his opponents and even queen Vasudhā to continue plottings against him from beginning to end. But all their evil designs come to naught.

Kālidāsa was a simple and straightforward person possessing at the same time the rare qualities of adroitness and courage and was highly devoted and loyal to his master. That is why he says :

कथं दोष: स्पृशेदत्र विष्णोरंशं महीपतिम् ।
न स्पृशेद् रजनीध्वान्तं नभो धाम प्रभावताम् ॥[1]

"How can a King, a part of Viṣṇu, commit a wrong ? Can the darkness of the night envelop (touch) the light of the luminaries in the sky ?"

Kālidāsa is deeply attached to his wife but places his loyalty to the country above it. Alakā is eager to accompany Kālidāsa to Vidarbha but he refuses to take her which makes her unhappy. Kālidāsa notices her sadness and tries to console her in the following words :

"न मन्तव्यं त्वद्वियोगान्मे जीवनं सुखकरमिति ।
किन्तु देशकार्यं व्यक्तिसौख्यमाहवनीयम् ॥"
दुरितवृता विभवयुता प्रियसखि निजभूमाता ॥
समयोऽयं वरतनयान् जननीसेवां नेता
प्रेमपाशनाशैरपि समरं वीरो याता
सखि सदने वासमितो न च सहते रिपुजेता ।[2]

"Don't you think that in your separation I can have an easy life. But one has to sacrifice personal comfort for the cause of the nation." He further says : "Dear friend ! Our prosperous land is surrounded all over by misfortunes. The time will lead the good sons to the service of the Mother. The brave will go to the battlefield cutting through the noose of love. The conqueror of the enemies will not tolerate living in the house of his spouse from now on."

In the above words has been described Kālidāsa's love for his wife and his country. That he loves his wife is beyond doubt but when the question of his loyalty to the country comes, he does not hesitate even for a minute to sacrifice his love for his wife.

We come to know of Kālidāsa's political sagacity, his ability in diplomatic manoeuvres and his supreme quality of fearlessness when he gives

1. p. 9.
2. p. 25.

an effective reply to king Sukīrti, the ruler of Vidarbha, who had threatened him with capital punishment on account of his having carried on spying activities in his kingdom. Kālidāsa's words uttered at this most fateful moment of his life, breathe the spirit of a free citizen and show his indomitable courage. Says he :

कालिदास:---काममेव शासनं वितरतु विदर्भाधिप: । न तेन मे भीति: कार्यनाशो वा । मालवशत्रुत्वमेव भवतैतावता तु लब्धं स्यात् । राजदूतवधेन राजमण्डले घृणा च । प्रभवति खलु भवान्मम जीवितस्येदानीम् ।

तथापि :---

यत्कर्तव्यं तद्विमृश्यैव कार्यं
नाशो नित्यो वैपरीत्येन वृत्तौ ।
नेदं श्लाघ्यं यद्धि भूपाविवेकै-
र्दु:खाधेय: सर्वलोको ह्यनागा: ।।[1]

"Kālidāsa—Whatever orders the ruler of Vidarbha may pass, I am not frightened of them. They will not be able to hinder or disrupt my work. By that you would only gain the hostility of the Mālava country. The kings would hate you for murdering an envoy. Now my life is in your hands. Still I ask you to do whatever you may like but think before doing it. It is not good that innocent people may have to undergo sufferings due to the indiscriminate and thoughtless activities of their ruler."

After his return from Kuntala, Kālidāsa is honoured by his King. Even at that time, we find him steadfast in his loyalty to his country. Says he :

लाभाशया न रचितो मम वाग्विलासो
जानाति भूपतिरिदं स्वयमेव सत्यम् ।
त्यागे तनुर्न गणिता मम राष्ट्रकार्ये
जीवन् स्थितोऽत्र खलु नैष ममापराध: ।

"Not out of any desire for (material) gain did I use those words. That this is true, the king knows very well. While working for the nation, I did not care for my body. That I am still living is no fault of mine."

Kālidāsa is eminently successful in the matter of doing one's duties. He is nevertheless fully alive to the tender side of life too. That is why, he could compose the *Meghadūta* even while living in a dark

1. p. 31. 2. p. 86.

cell when his heart was touched and pained with separation from his beloved. When he feels that living far away, as he does, he is not in a position to send a word of comfort to his wife through any other means, he sends it through a cloud. The poet in the playwright is seen at his best here. The emotional upsurge in a heart is described in words which are simply matchless. Thus cries out the unhappy poet :

एक एष मेघस्त्वरया पश्चिमां दिशमुपगच्छति । रे पयोधर, सागरमग्नं दिवंसनाथमुद्धतुं नु प्रतीचीमुपयासि । रे वारिवाह, अथवा विरहशोकार्तां प्रतीचीमाश्वासयितुं न जवेन परिक्रमसे । तर्हि शुभास्ते पन्थान: सन्तु । सर्वमनुकूलमेव ते ।

मन्दं मन्दं वहति पवन: श्रान्तपीडापनोदी
वृक्षे वृक्षे कुसुमनिचयैर्गन्धित: स्पर्शशीत: ।
एको मेघ प्रचलसि नभ:सागरे नौरिव त्वं
दु:खार्तानां विपदपनये सज्जनानां प्रयत्न: ।।

एवं सति रे अम्भोद, कथं मां विपन्नं न पश्यसि ।
सन्तप्तानां त्वमसि शरणं तत्पयोद प्रियाया:
सन्देशं में हर नरपतिस्नेहविश्लेषितस्य ।
आश्वास्या सा युवतिरलका कालिदासस्य पत्नी
श्रान्ता दीना विरहविकला जीवितेशैकचिन्ता ।।

(नेपथ्ये मेघनाद:) किं गर्जसि । कथमेतत् त्वया कार्यमिति ? भो विद्युत्पते, भवान् सर्वलोकस्य जीवनं बिभर्ति तत्कथं में सन्देशं नीत्वा न तव भ्रातृजायाजीवनं कुसुमपेलव-माशाबन्धेन दृढीकरोषि ।[1]

There is only one cloud which is proceeding towards the West :

"O ye ! the cloud ! why don't thou move towards the western quarter to rescue the sun which has sunken in the ocean, or O cloud, is it that thou art speeding to console the western quarter which is feeling the pangs of thy separation. If so, auspicious be thy path. Thou hast everything available to thee.

The breeze is blowing gently, removing the pain of the fatigued. Its touch is cool while it is being made fragrant by clusters of flowers growing on every tree. O cloud, thou art the only one moving like a ship in the ocean of the sky. It is the effort of the good to remove the hardship of the afflicted.

This being so, O cloud, why don't thou pay any attention to me while I am in trouble ? Thou art the refuge of the afflicted. Can thou carry the message of me who has been separated (from his beloved) for the love of the King ? It is for thou to console Alakā who

1. p. 39.

due to separation is miserably tired and restless. The only thought in her mind is that of his lord (Kālidāsa). (Behind the curtain is heard the thunder of the cloud). Why this thunder ? Is it thou thinkest as to how thou can do it ? O thou, the lord of lightning, thou sustainest the entire world. Then how is it that thou do not make the heart of our brother's wife, which is as tender as flowers by carrying my message for her ?"

The play has a number of popular metres, the more prominent of them being Indravajrā, Upendravajrā, Upajāti, Drutavilambita, Pṛthvī, Bhujaṅgaprayāta, Mandākrāntā, Mālinī, Rathoddhatā, Vaitālīya, Vasantatilaka, Vaṁśastha, Śālinī, Śārdūlavikrīḍita, Śikhariṇī, Svāgatā, Hariṇī and so on. Some of the rather unfamiliar metres like Vidhyaṅgamālā have also been used. Apart from this, the Prakrit metres like Diṇḍī and Sākī, too have been employed. The style of singing the songs is traditional except in certain cases where the author experiments with new styles of singing and marking time.

The contemporary political activities have been conjecturally described in the play. How the kings could find out each other's secret and went to wars; their diplomatic manoeuvres and attempts at subversion have all been dealt with in the present play. True to the age-old rules of dramaturgy, the author has not depicted any scene of actual warfare or bloody conflict on the stage.

The present work is the author's second, the first one being the *Saṅgītasaubhadram*, a Sanskrit rendering of a Marathi play of the same name. The peculiarity of both lies in the absence of Prakrits and an English introduction. The author justifies the departures from the established practice on the ground that these would introduce an element of novelty into the works which would make them more interesting and useful for the present-day audiences and readers. The modern plays should not, says he, be the copies of their old counterparts in style and technique. The English introduction, too, is justified on the same ground, the intelligentsia being more familiar with English would find it easy to know the theme and to appreciate the other important features of the play.

Since the play has Kālidāsa as the hero, it was natural for the playwright to adopt verbatim some of the verses or parts thereof from the works of the great poet as may be seen from the following examples :

(क) मत्तद्विरेफपरिचुम्बितचारुपुष्पां मन्दानिलाकुलितनम्रमृदुप्रवाला: ।
कुर्वन्ति कामिमनसां सहसोत्सुकत्वं बालातिमुक्तलतिका: समवेक्ष्यमाणा: ॥[1]

1. p. 4 (*Ṛtusaṃhāra*, 6. 17).

(ख) वापीजलानां मणिमेखलानां शशांकभासां प्रमदाजनानाम् ।
चूतद्रुमाणां कुसुमानतानां ददाति सौभाग्यमयं वसन्तः ।।[1]

(ग) मन्दं मन्दं वहति पवनः श्रान्तपीडापनोदः ।[2]

(घ) सन्तप्तानां त्वमसि शरणं तत्पयोद प्रियायाः
सन्देशं मे हर नरपतिस्नेहविश्लेषितस्य ।
आश्वास्या सा युवतिरलका कालिदासस्य पत्नी
श्रान्ता दीना विरहविकला जीवितेशैकचित्ता ।।[3]

(ङ) जातं वंशे भुवनविदिते पुष्करावर्तकानां
जानामि त्वां प्रकृतिपुरुषं कामरूपं मघोनः ।
तेनार्थित्वं त्वयि विधिवशाद् दूरबन्धुर्गतोऽहं
याच्ञा मोघा वरमधिगुणे नाधमे लब्धकामा ।।[4]

(च) नद्या इव प्रवाहो विषमशिलासङ्कटस्खलितवेगः ।
विघ्नितसमागमसुखो मनसिशयः शतगुणो भवति ।।[5]

(छ) वागर्थाविव संपृक्तौ वागर्थप्रतिपत्तये ।
जगतः पितरौ वन्दे पार्वतीपरमेश्वरौ ।।[6]

The style of the playwright is easy, fluent and idiomatic. At some places, the idioms and proverbs have an old ring about them while at other places, they look strikingly modern in thought and content. A few examples of each one of these would bear us out :

1 सुप्तो हि बोधनक्षमः । प्रबुद्धं तु को नाम बोधयिष्यति ।[7]

2 न हि चतुःशालस्थिता संमार्जनी देवगृहे स्थापनीया ।[8]

3 कंटकास्तृतमेव राजसिंहासनम् ।[9]

4 न युद्धं लोककल्याणकरम् ।[10]

5 सेवापि भाग्यनिहिता ननु साऽत्र धन्या ।[11]

6 न कदांगना सहते सपत्नीम् ।[12]

7 गौरवं पीडयान्वितम् । पीडा तु नश्यति गौरवं च चिरं तिष्ठति ।[13]

8 क्रियापदं सदा वाक्ये कर्तुरन्यं न वान्वियात् ।[14]

9 न रुचिरं किञ्चिच्चिराय विचरति ।[15]

10 क्षणिकः पराक्रमः । तत्काव्यगानं तु चिरंतनम् ।[16]

1. p. 4 (*Ṛtusaṃhāra*, 6. 3).
2. p. 39 (*Meghadūta*, 1. 10).
3. p. 39 (*Meghadūta*, 1.7).
4. p. 39 (*Meghadūta*, 1. 6).
5. p. 72 (*Vikramorvaśīya*, 3. 8).
6. p. 99 (*Raghuvaṃśa*, 1. 1).
7. p. 3.
8. p. 3.
9. p. 9.
10. p. 14.
11. p. 16.
12. p. 16.
13. p. 66.
14. p. 75.
15. p. 79.
16. p. 88.

Occasionally, we meet with, in the play, some *subhāṣitas*, too, which contain happy ideas couched in an equally happy style. As an example we quote the verse below :

रज:कणै: किं चरणावलिप्तै: साधर्म्यमाप्यं किरणै रवेर्नु ।
स्पृशन्ति सूर्यस्य करा रजांसि समत्वभावाद् न समानधर्मात् ॥[1]

The play has a good sprinkling of comic element, too. When Kālidāsa gets fame and Gopāla gets wife, Govinda says, "What have I got ?" Then there begins a very pleasant conversation between Govinda and Gopāla[2] :

गोविन्द:---रे गोपाल ! कालिदासेन लब्धा कीर्ति:, भवता चार्जिता प्रीति:, अस्माकं तु का गति: ?

Govinda—"O Gopāla ! Kālidāsa has won fame and you have got love but what have I got ?"

गोपाल:---मुक्ति: ।

Gopāla—"Salvation."

गोविन्द:---कथं जीवतो मे मुक्ति: ?

Govinda—"How salvation for me when I am still alive ?"

गोपाल:---वयं बद्धा भवांस्तु मुक्त एव ।

Gopāla—"It is we who have been bound. You are indeed free."

गोविन्द:---कथं त्वं बद्ध: ?

Govinda—"With what are you bound ?"

गोपाल:---संसारपाशै: ।

Gopāla—"With the nooses of the world."

गोविन्द:---कया ?

Govinda—"By whom ?"

गोपाल:---मदनिकया ।

Gopāla—"By Madanikā."

गोविन्द:---तर्हि बन्ध एव मे प्रिय:

Govinda—"Then I like this bondage."

गोपाल:---मैवम् । प्रियवयस्य बुद्धोऽहं प्रबुद्धोऽहं विप्रबुद्धोऽहमधुना । अपि तूदके गते सेतुबन्ध इव मेऽयं प्रबोध: । मा ते स्खलनं भवतु । मा स्त्रीपाशे बद्धो भू: ।

1. p. 96. 2. pp. 89-90.

Gopāla—No, dear friend ! I have realized, I am awakened, I have clearly perceived. But this awakening of mine is like the building of a bridge while the water has run out. Don't stumble. Don't be bound with the noose of a woman."

गोविन्द:---स्वयं स्त्रीसुखमवाप्य कथं मां वंचयसि ?

Govinda—"Why is it that having first enjoyed the feminine pleasure, you do not let myself have it ?"

गोपाल:---नहि रे अप्रबुद्ध। दूरत एव नारी प्रिया। तस्या: पाणिग्रहणेन स्वहस्तयोद्दृढलोहश्रृंखला बध्यते, न केवलं हस्तयो: पादयोश्चापि।

Gopāla—"No, O fool; A woman appears charming from a distance only. With the holding of her hand one's own hands are tied in tight chains; not only hands but feet, too."

गोविन्द:---न जाने किं वदसि ? विशदं ब्रूहि।

Govinda—"I cannot make out what you say. Be clear."

गोपाल:---पश्य माम् कमपि भेदं पश्यसि ?

Gopāla—"Look at me. Do you find any difference ?"

गोविन्द:---तुन्दिलतनुर्जातोऽसि।

Govinda—"Yes. You have become pot-bellied."

गोपाल:---ननु कथमेवं जात: ? जानास्येतत् ? भो: संसारदु:खप्रस्तरा उदरे मे निविष्टा:।

Gopāla—"How have I become so ? Do you have any idea ? The stones of the worldly unhappiness have entered into my belly."

गोविन्द:---असत्यमेतत्। न किंचित्प्रविशति दुखं तवोदरे।

Govinda—"This is not true. No unhappiness would enter into your belly.

गोपाल :---अरे पश्य भोजनादिकम्। नाहं प्रभूतमत्र भक्षयामि। जानास्येवेदम्।

Gopāla "You see my food. I do not take much food. You know it already."

गोविन्द :---केवलमेकमहिषाहारस्त्वम्। नूनं न ततोऽधिकं भक्ष्यते त्वया।

Govinda—"You take food which is sufficient for one he-buffalo. Indeed, you don't take more than that."

गोपाल :---अधुना यदाहं वदामि, 'मदनिके पर्याप्तं मे भोजनं' तदा तदा सा 'नाथ स्वादु मोदकादि, अधिकतरं भक्षणीयं, जानामि ते भोजनप्रियताम्' इत्युक्त्वा पुनरपि मोदकादि प्रयच्छति।[1]

1. pp. 89-90.

Gopāla—"Each time I say to Madanikā, 'this much food would suffice for me,' she would insist with the words, 'O lord; Modakas are delicious. Have them more. I know you like (rich) meals' and saying this, would give me more."

Similarly at other places, too, we meet with comic scenes which excite laughter and provide a good relief against the intense political and diplomatic activities described in the play.

The author's language is characterized by a fair degree of alliteration. Apart from the songs where it is a must with the author it is found elsewhere too, e.g.,

(क) कुतस्तस्य स्थानं प्रकटविकटे राज्यशकटे[1]

(ख) न कालिदासप्रतिभाविलासो व्रजेद्विकासं भुवनं विनैनाम्[2]

(ग) धन्यास्मि कन्या विदिशाजनन्या नान्यो . . .[3]

There is however one verse where it is employed with the happiest of effects. The sequence in which the similar sound recurs has imparted to it a charm which is all its own. For proper appreciation we reproduce it below :

प्रत्युत्पन्नमति: प्रजाहितकृतिर्विद्याकलानां पति-
र्विघ्नारुद्धगतिर्यशश्चिरततिर्नित्यं दयासंहृति: ।
काव्यापन्नरतिर्निराहतधृतिश्चासावुदाराकृति-
स्तत्संमानभृति:, ममात्र विनति:, स्यात्सर्वसत्संमति: ।।[4]

The language is generally free from any serious irregularity. Words like *kṛntana*[31], etc., however, do jar on the ears.

The author shows his knowledge of the fundamental principles of the different śāstras in his work. Of Vedānta in :

(क) एकं सद् ब्रह्म सहते नान्यत्तत्वं जगद्भृतम् ।
राजान्तरं न सहते स्वोद्देशे भूपति: क्वचित् ।।[5]

Of Nyāya in :

(ख) यथा शब्द: प्रमाणं स्यात् सद्विधिप्रतिषेधयो: ।
तथादेशश्च भवतो युक्तायुक्तविनिश्चये ।।[6]

Of Vyākaraṇa in :

1. p. 82.
2. p. 40.
3. p. 42.
4. p. 85.
5. p. 75.
6. p. 74.

(ग) भवतो वचनादेव निर्णयो नयमण्डले ।
क्रियापदं सदा वाक्ये कर्तुरन्यं न वान्वियात् ॥[1]

The scene of the competition between the Paṇḍitarāja and Kālidāsa is very well laid in the play. Poetic bouts like the one described here were very common in ancient India and are still popular. Besides catching the spirit of the scene and presenting it to us faithfully it helps to bring out the poet in the writer from whom we have some of his finest verses here. It is indeed gratifying to read in his work verses like,

ज्योत्स्नां या मन्दहास्यैः शरदि समुचितां दर्शयन्ती वसन्ते
सौन्दर्येन्दीवरं या विकचयति तथा भास्वरं सर्वकालम् ।
धत्ते विद्युल्लताभां जलधररहितेऽप्यत्र या देवतां तां
धन्योऽयं कालदासो व्यतिकृतसमयां वन्दते कालिदासः ॥[1]

"Fortunate is this Kālidāsa, the slave of Kāla (Mahākāla) who bows to this goddess who has caused confusion in time in so far as she by her smiles has shown the moonlight in spring though it is natural only in the autumn. She causes the shining blue lotus of her beauty bloom all the time. She gives the appearance of a streak of lightning even in this free-from-cloud season."

Or

स्मृतिनिमीलितलोचनयोषिता
न विदितं रमणागमनं ननु ।
सपदि तत्करपाशधृताऽऽवृता
कुमुदिनी शशिनैव विलोपिता ।[2]

"A woman with her eyes closed while thinking of her loved one does not know his coming but just finds herself in his arms which cover her up. The water lily was made to close by the moon itself."

The play abounds in songs which lend it a peculiar charm. They are found in the author's other work the *Saṅgītasaubhadram* too. But then there is a difference between the songs of that play and this. There they are the reproductions from the Marathi original. Anna Saheb Kirloskar had already given them in his play with all the indications of the *rāgas* and the *tālas* they are to be sung in his original Marathi version and the translator merely gave them the Sanskrit garb but in the present play (which is the original production of Velankar) they are the author's own creation. They show his deep

1. p. 74. 2. p. 75.

knowledge of the science of music as also his fascination for them. It is this fascination which has given us the present musical comedy. As in the *Saṅgītasaubhadram* so in the present play songs are prefaced with the names of the *rāgas* in which they are to be sung. The indication of the *tāla* too precedes the songs the number of which is pretty large. There are atleast 32 songs some of which are to be sung in such difficult *rāgas* as Kedāra, Śaṅkarā, Rāgeśrī, Bāgeśrī, Diṇḍī, Khamāja, Jogī, Ārabī, Pahāḍī, Karṇāṭakī, Yamana, Kāfī, Jayajayavanti, Bhūpa, Garuḍadhvani, Deśa, Bhairavī, Bihāra, Sohanī, Tilakakāmoda, Māṇḍa and in such difficult *tālas* as Dhumālī, Dādarā, Jhapatāla, Ekkā, Keravā, Dīpacandī, apart from the usual Tritāla. These songs have raciness all their own. Even the ears far less sensitive than that of the Indians can appreciate their beauty. For obvious limitations we cannot reproduce any sizable number of them here, however we may be tempted to do so. We will content ourselves with the reproduction here of only one or two which can serve just as samples :

(पहाडी, --- धुमाली)

भूगतो ननु पूषा । दिविपदां भूषा ॥
सुखकरदया निखिलजनानाम् । विहिता सुलभाऽशेषा ॥
प्रजासु कुरुते प्रीतिं स यथा । न तथा नाथे योषा ॥
श्रेष्ठगुणानां जगति विधात्रा । जनितैषा मंजूषा ॥[1]

(मांड:, ---त्रिताल:)

प्रीतिरियं न च माया । मदीया । श्रेष्ठा त्वं किल जाया ॥
वचने सखी ते ममाप्यभिमते नावसर: कटुतायाः ॥
आस्ये दयिते स्याद् हास्यं ते लास्यैर्मे प्रतिभाया: ॥[2]

Now a word about the dramatic technique of the play. Each Act of it has three Scenes to facilitate its production on the stage. The Fifth Act has a Praveśaka in addition. The Prastāvanā in it depicting the beginning of the festival of spring is of the Pravartaka type.

The nature of the theme being rather peculiar, the arrangement of the Sandhis is not clear.

"The First Act takes place in Ujjayinī in the month of Caitra (April) and the Second one in the month of Āṣāḍha (July). The Third Act takes place again in Ujjayinī in Āśvina (October) of the same year. The Fourth and the Fifth Acts take place in Ujjayinī again after an interval of two and four years respectively from the incidents of the first

---

1. pp. 12-24. 2. p. 13.

three. All the incidents of the same Act take place during the same period of twenty four hours."

Of the three types of acting, the play has instances of all as can be seen from the following :

आङ्गिक : (1) भाषणेऽक्षमो नेत्रे प्रमार्ष्टि [1] (2) नेत्रे उन्मील्य[2] (3) नेत्रे निमील्य ध्यायति[3] (4) सलज्जं ससम्भ्रममुत्थाय[4] (5) तर्जयन्[5] (6) पुरः सृत्वा[6] (7) तस्मै मुद्रामर्पयति[7] (8) तथा कृत्वान्तर्गत्वा स्त्रपितः[8] (9) कृष्णवस्त्रं प्रावृत्य द्वारमभिगच्छति[9] (10) तस्य हस्तौ गृहीत्वा[10] (11) तं समाश्लिष्यति[11] (12) दक्षिणाक्षिस्पन्दनं सूचयित्वा[12] (13) ध्यानस्थ इव स्तब्धो भवति[13]

वाचिक : (1) भीतः स्खलितवाक्[14] (2) पठति[15]

आहार्य : (1) रोषेण[16] (2) प्रसन्नमनसा[17] (3) कोपाविष्टा[18] (4) ससम्भ्रमम्[19] (5) सोल्लासम्[20] (6) सकरुणम्[21] (7) ससाध्वसम्[22] (8) सत्रपम्[23]

The very fact that the play had been put on boards successfully at the Kālidāsa Samāroha on 19th November, 1961 is a proof positive of its stageworthiness.

---

1. p. 5.
2. pp. 17, 60.
3-4. pp. 22, 60.
5. p. 32.
6. *ibid.*
7. p. 45.
8. p. 57.
9. p. 58.
10. p. 61.
11. p. 60.
12. p. 66
13. p. 99.
14. p. 32.
15. p. 72.
16. p. 3.
17. p. 4.
18. *ibid.*
19. pp. 23, 33.
20. p. 33.
21. p. 56.
22. p. 59.
23. p. 66.

2

KĀLIDĀSAḤ

An one-act play in seven small scenes by Dr. Vaneshwar Pathak of Ranchi, it deals with one of the many traditional accounts of the life of Kālidāsa, with some variations.

Theme

The play opens with the Avanti king Vikramāditya in his court together with the minister, the teacher Vararuci and other courtiers. The King asks Vararuci if the Princess Priyaṅgumañjarī has completed her education to which Vararuci replies that she has become highly learned. When the King expresses his worry about her marriage, Vararuci informs him that she has taken an unusual vow to marry only that person who would defeat her in scholarly disquisition (Śāstrārtha). She conveyed this decision of hers to him through her friend Āmramañjarī who saw her in the morning. She wanted him to convey it to the King who wants to marry her to the Sinhalese Prince Kumārasena, as she was feeling shy to tell it to the King herself. The King appreciates the decision and asks Vararuci to arrange for an assembly of scholars wherein he may act as the mediator. That would provide him with an occasion to test them and his daughter. Vararuci gladly accepts the proposal and also agrees to the King's suggestion to move swiftly in the matter. The King and the courtiers get up at this. The curtain falls signalling the end of the First Scene.

The Second Scene is laid in the Assembly hall showing all scholars with their faces downcast. Enters Vararuci. He is visibly upset over the Princess having ridiculed his decision saying that he did not realize the deeper import. All this she did him, her teacher. He is out to avenge insult. If he is Vararuci, he would have her married to a fool. He asks the scholars to go back and himself proceeds to look for the biggest fool. Exit he in quick steps. With this ends the Second Scene.

The Third Scene opens with Vararuci in a forest. He had been moving about in search of a fool but so far has not met even one leading him to remark whether all are scholars in Vikramāditya's kingdom. Just then he notices a man cutting the very branch of the tree he is sitting on. He tells him not to cut the branch lest he should fall down to which the man replies that he is up there, how could he fall down. Vararuci asks him to come down, he would get him married to Princess Priyaṅgumañjarī. The man jumps down injuring his limbs which begin to ache. As he begins to change his mind and declines to marry, Vararuci tells him that his aching limbs would be back to normal again with marriage. He agrees at this to marry and also act as he asks him to. He is happy that Piṅgu (he cannot pronounce Priyaṅgu) and he, Kaliyā (his name), will be united in wedlock. Exit both. Drops the curtain. Ends the Scene.

The Fourth Scene opens in the court with the King, the Princess and the courtiers. Enters Vararuci with a man dressed as a Pandit. He tells the King that a scholar, Dhurandhara Shastri from Kāśī has come to enter into a disquisition (*Śāstrārtha*) with the Princess. Since he has taken a vow of silence, whatever questions the Princess may want to put to him, she may do so by signs. The Princess raises one finger implying that God is one. The man thinking that she wants to poke the finger into his eye, raises two fingers implying thereby that he would poke both her eyes. The Princess then raises five fingers implying whether he had put under control his five organs of perception. The man thinking that she wants to slap him raises a fist implying thereby that he would hit her with that. This over, Vararuci proceeds to give his explanation of the signs. When the Princess raised one finger she meant that God is one. When the man raised two fingers, he meant that He is twofold, with form and without it. When the Princess raised five fingers, she meant to ask the man whether he had put under control his five senses. By raising the fist the man had answered that he had them in his fist. He then asked the Princess if she was satisfied with the answers. Out of bashfulness the Princess did not say anything and kept looking downwards. Vararuci thanks the Pandit and requests the King that as per her decision the Princess should be married to him (the Pandit). The happy King asks the minister to make necessary arrangements for that. With this ends the Scene.

The Fifth Scene is laid in the Apartment of the Princess. She and the man are shown sharing the same seat. The Princess asks, the man as to why he was not speaking. The man says that it is due to the instructions of Vararuci because according to him he is a fool and should, therefore, not speak out anything. The Princess gets up and asks the man if he is a fool. 'No, Piṅgu', says the man, he is Dhundhara Shastri. The Princess notices the word Piṅgu, Dhundhara Shastri. She angrily turns him out of the Apartment. Confounded, he just keeps on looking at her. The Scene ends with this.

The Sixth Scene opens in an Āśrama with an Ācārya and his pupils. Enters Nicula with a man. He tells the Ācārya that he had noticed a man crying on the footpath of the Ujjayinī highway because of his having been turned out of house by his wife on the ground that he was a fool, and taking pity on him, has brought him along with him. The man wants to be a scholar. When Diṅnāga ridicules him, the Ācārya intercepts him saying that it is only a person like him (the man) with his feelings hurt who goes sincerely into the pursuit of learning and becomes intelligent. He (the Ācārya) notices in the man a peculiar brilliance. He feels assured in his heart that the latter would undoubtedly be an unusually learned man. He gives him a place in his Āśrama. He asks him his name. 'It is Kaliyā', says he. The Ācārya tells him that he should devote himself to his studies singlemindedly. Every morning he should, after bath, worship goddess Kālī by whose grace he would acquire learning before long. Now onwards his name would be Kālidāsa and not Kaliyā. The Scene ends at this.

The Seventh Scene opens in the study room of the Ācārya with him and Kālidāsa engaged in conversation. The Ācārya tells Kālidāsa that he had come to know that his (Kālidāsa's) poem was greatly admired in the poetical symposium. Nicula had told him that a poem like that had not been heard in the past. Kālidāsa tells him that he was at the moment busy in composing a poem where a separated Yakṣa sends a message through a cloud to her beloved in far away Alakā. The Ācārya appreciates the theme. It is a new style in poetry—the Dūtakāvya, says he. 'But Diṅnāga does not like my poem' says Kālidāsa. 'Never mind', says the Ācārya, 'Diṅnāga is opposed to you. I have heard your poem. I tell you the truth. After Valmiki it is in your poem that the real form of poetry has come into its own. There is an eternal message in your words.' The Ācārya further tells him that he is confident that so long as the earth lasts, or the literature lasts on the earth or the connoisseurs last, would last his words. A very important news about him then comes to his mind. He tells him that after witnessing the performance of the *Abhijñānaśākuntala,* King Vikramāditya had made the announcement that he (Kālidāsa) would occupy the highest place among his jewels and that he (the King) would be coming there to bring him round for the sake of his daughter. As a matter of fact, Priyaṅgumañjarī did a great service to him. She is his driving force. It is through her only that the world of literature could get a priceless jewel like him. The King at this enters with the Princess. He begs forgiveness of the great poet on behalf of his daughter who touches his (the poet's) feet and says *asti kaścid vāgviśeṣaḥ* ? The poet hands her over his three works one by one, one beginning with *asti*, the *Kumārasambhava*, the other beginning with *kaścit*, the *Meghadūta* and the third beginning with *vāk*, the *Raghuvaṁśa*, reciting the first verse from each one of them and enquiring from the Princess : *asti kaścid vāgviśeṣaḥ* ? is there anything special that she finds in them ? Everybody joins the Princess after this in wishing great glory to the poet and with this comes to an end the Scene and also the play.

Critical Appreciation

Though a small play, there is quite a lot in it to commend itself. Though it has followed by and large the traditional account of Kālidāsa having earlier been a fool and his acquiring learning by the grace of goddess Kālī on his being turned out of the house by a Princess who had been tricked into marrying him, it also introduces many innovations into it. The first pertains to the names of the Princess and Kālidāsa. While the Princess is called Vidyottamā in the traditional account, the playwright calls her Priyaṅgumañjarī. To Kālidāsa when he was a fool he assigns the name Kaliyā. The traditional account has nothing of the sort. The other, much more important, pertains to the tricking of the Princess. In the traditional account it is the Pandits smarting under the humiliation suffered by them at the disquisition who are said to do that. In the play it is Vararuci who does it. The fact of Vararuci being the teacher of the Princess is also something new. So is his taking such an umbrage at a remark of her interpreted by him to be his open ridicule as to vow revenge. Vararuci being made the judge at the disquisition is also the playwright's original idea.

The next point of originality in the play pertains to the Āśrama scene. The traditional account has nothing of the kind. According to it, Kālidāsa acquires learning by the grace of goddess Kālī who appears before him in a temple taking pity on his cries. Up to the point of his being turned out by the Princess, the theme of the play agrees with the traditional account. After this it takes a different turn. His being found by Nicula on an Ujjayinī footpath, his desire to be a scholar, his bringing him along with him to the Āśrama by Nicula and his being accepted into it by the teacher inspite of the opposition and ridicule of Diṅnāga, are all innovations of the author himself. Kālidāsa in the present play is shown to acquire learning not only by the grace of the goddess Kālī but also through his singleminded application to studies under the guidance of a teacher. It appears that the author probably could not digest the idea that a fool could be turned overnight into a scholar just by the grace of a goddess. Well, the grace of the Supreme Force has always to be there for any kind of success ; even the teacher in the present play advises Kālidāsa to offer worship to goddess Kālī every morning after his bath by whose grace he would be a great scholar before long : *pratidinam prātaḥ snātvā śrīkālīdevyā ārādhanāṁ kuru, Kālīkṛpayā tvam acireṇa mahān vidvān bhaviṣyasi.*[1] He also advises him to devote himself singlemindedly to his studies : *ekacittībhūya adhyayane nirato bhava.*[2]

The words Nicula and Diṅnāga in the *Meghadūta*[3] which, according to some scholars, are oblique references to actual persons of those names, one friendly to Kālidāsa inferred from the epithet *sarasa* going with it and the other hostile to him inferred from the expression *diṅnāgānāṁ pathi pariharan sthūlahastāvalepān*, the insolent brush of the coarse trunks of the sky-elephants,[4] have been used very skilfully and artistically by the author in his play to weave out an episode. It is Nicula who discovers Kālidāsa and brings him over to the Ācarya who notices something peculiarly brilliant in him, the making of a great scholar and gives him a place in his Āśrama, unmindful of the opposition expressed so clearly by one of his pupils, Diṅnāga.

The announcement by King Vikramāditya of accepting Kālidāsa as the best among his jewels after witnessing the performance of the *Abhijñānaśākuntala* is also the innovation of the author. So is his (the King's) coming to the Āśrama to placate the estranged poet on behalf of his daughter. In the play the penitent Princess is shown touching his (Kālidāsa's) feet in the Āśrama to which she too repairs with his father. In the traditional account it is Kālidāsa who goes to the Princess with the words *dvāram anāvṛtakapāṭaṁ dehi* while the Princess recognizing his voice asks him *asti kaścid vāgviśeṣaḥ* 'is there any improvement in his speech'. The traditional account has it that the poet composed the three of his poems taking each time the first word of the Princess's above sentence. In the present play, the poet is shown to have

1-2. p. 44.

3. *Meghadūta*, Pūrvamegha, verse 14.

4. Translation by Franklin and Eleaner Edgerton, The University of Michigan, 1964.

already composed the three poems, even before he had met her. After touching his feet, the Princess asks him : *asti kaścid vāgviśeṣaḥ* ? and he goes on handing her over his three works, one after the other. A critic may well argue here that the introduction of the question *asti kaścid vāgviśeṣaḥ* on the part of the penitent princess falling at the feet may be incongruous. It goes very well with the traditional account where the Princess speaks from behind the door and is unaware of the great learning that he has acquired. It may be said that at least once the traditional account gets the upper hand of the playwright and as he had to introduce the words *asti kaścid vāgviśeṣaḥ* he just introduced them without any justification for them. In defence of the playwright it may well be said that he probably is taking the sentence *asti kaścid vāgviśeṣaḥ* in a different sense. It could be : 'Is there any special work (that he might have composed) ?' The poet then hands her over not one but three, reciting a verse each from each one of them. And this agrees very well with his question to her in the same words : *asti kaścid vāgviśeṣaḥ*, 'does she find anything special in them ?'

Apart from the innovations which are a great relief from the monotonous reproduction of the traditional account in certain other works, the work is embellished with quite a few crisp dialogues which are certainly one of its great attractions. The play is all in prose with no verse, except of course three verses, the first ones from each of the three works, the *Kumārasambhava*, the *Meghadūta* and the *Raghuvaṁśa* giving the author an opportunity to concentrate on it. The most interesting of the dialogues is that between Vararuci and the fool in which the character of the fool comes out very vividly :

वररुचि:—अयि भ्रात: ! तां शाखां मा छिन्धि-नीचै: पतिष्यसि ।

पुरुष:—महामूर्खोऽसि । अहम् उच्चै: स्थित: कथं नीचै: पतिष्यामि ।

वररुचि:—भवतु, न पतिष्यसि । नीचैरागच्छ एकमावश्यकं कार्यमस्ति ।

पुरुष:—ऋजूक्त्या इदमेव कथं न कथयसि यदावश्यकं कार्यमस्ति । किं पुन: कथयसि नीचै: पतिष्यसि । अहं शाखया सहैव नीचैरागमिष्यामि ।

वररुचि:—नीचैरवतर । तव विवाहं करिष्यामि ।

पुरुष:—विवाह: . . . मम विवाह: . . . (हर्षातिरेकेण नीचै: कूर्दते आहत: अङ्गानि संस्पृशन्) अहो ! महती पीडा । अहं विवाहं न करिष्यामि । पण्डितजीव ! विवाहं न करिष्यामि । महती पीडा मे सञ्जाता ! आह . . . !

वररुचि:—विवाहेन सर्वा पीडा अपगमिष्यति ।

पुरुष:— पीडा अपगमिष्यति । तदाऽवश्यं विवाहं करिष्यामि । शीघ्रं कथय कुत्र कया सह मम विवाहो भविष्यति ।

वररुचिः—अस्यामेवोज्जयिन्यां राजकुमारी प्रियङ्गुमञ्जर्या सह ।

पुरुषः—राजकुमारी पिङ्गु (हा ! हा !! हा !!!) राजकुमारी ऐं · · · (विस्मृतिमभिनीय) · · · किं कथितम् ?

वररुचिः—राजकुमारी प्रियङ्गुमञ्जरी ।

पुरुषः—राजकुमारी पिङ्गु · · · (हा ! हा !! हा !!!) राजकुमारी पिङ्गु-कलिया, कलिया राजकुमारी पिङ्गु, सुन्दरः संयोगः । पण्डितजीव शीघ्रं विवाहं कारय ।

वररुचिः—आगच्छ मया सह । यदहं कथयामि तदेव कुरु । तव विवाहो भविष्यति ।

पुरुषः—पश्य पण्डितजीव ! (भूमिं कर्णौ च स्पृष्ट्वा) यदेव कथयिष्यसि तदेव करिष्यामि ।[1]

The conversation of the fool with the Princess after the marriage is also characterized by naturalness and consequently is quite interesting :

राजकुमारी—भवान् वदति कथं न ?

पुरुषः—वररुचिपण्डितेनाहं मौनमवलम्बितुमादिष्टः ।

राजकुमारी—किं कारणम् ?

पुरुषः—स कथयति त्वं मूर्खः अतो न किञ्चिद् वक्तव्यं त्वया ।

राजकुमारी—(ससम्भ्रममुत्थाय) किं त्वं मूर्खः ?

पुरुषः—नहि राजकुमारीपिङ्गु ! अहं धुन्धरशास्त्री महापण्डितः ।

राजकुमारी—(सक्रोधम्) राजकुमारी पिङ्गु . . . धुन्धरशास्त्री . . . निर्गच्छ मम गृहात् ।

The dialogues, as can be seen from the specimens above, are characterized by quick movement. Nowhere are they hampered by longwinded oration. The only exception is in Scene Seven where the Ācārya waxes eloquent at the poetic beauty of Kālidāsa and the heights he has attained. Evidently, the admirer of the master poet in the playwright gets the better of him there.

Now a word about the expression. One of the principal characteristics of this play is the influence of Hindi diction on it. Quite a few of the words and sentences owe themselves to it. The most glaring ones of it are when the upset Vararuci first quotes the words of the Princess for him *bhavān idaṁ rahasyaṁ na jānāti* and then says

---

1. p. 42. 2. pp. 43-44.

rahasyasya vatse.[1] Now this is clearly Hindized Sanskrit *rahasya ki bacci.*

The other expressions where Hindi nfluence peeps out are:

> अहं हार्दिकधन्यवादान् करोमि महाराजं प्रति ममायमनुरोधः[3],
> त्वमस्मिन्नाश्रमे रक्षितः[4] (तुम इस आश्रम में रख लिये गये हो),
> महाराजस्त्वयि एतादृशः प्रसन्नः[5]

A short play of absorbing interest, it deserves wider recognition.

1. p. 42.
2. p. 43.
3. *ibid.*
4. p. 44.
5. p. 45.

3

KĀLIDĀSAPĀṆIKARAṆAM

A tiny play in three small scenes of Sabhanath Pathak of Arrah, it deals, apiece with many other similar attempts, with the traditional account of Kālidāsa's marriage with a learned Princess Vidyottamā.

Theme

The play begins with a prayer song addressed to God. After that what is described is all too familiar to students of Kālidāsa. Scholars, humbled in scholarly disquisition by a learned Princess, are out to avenge their defeat. They see on the way a young man cutting the very branch of the tree he is sitting on. One of the scholars asks him to come down. "Why do you ask me to come down, I am cutting firewood", says the youngman. "There is something very important for you" tells him another scholar. The young man climbs down. The elderly one among the scholars tells him about a Princess. He will be married to her. The young man expresses his doubt about it. He is a poor man, how could he be married to a Princess? Even if somehow the marriage were to come off how would she stay with him? The first scholar (who had asked him to come down) tells him not to worry about that. He should just accompany them and do as they ask him to. This closes the First Scene.

The Second Scene begins with the disquisition arranged in the Palace between the Princess and the fool, the young man. The scholars are to serve as the intermediaries. One of the scholars says that the great man (fool) would carry on the disquisition in silence. The Princess raises one finger implying that God is one. The young fool raises two. This is interpreted by the scholars that Gods are two, one Paramātman and the other Jīvātman, the supreme soul and the individual soul.

The Third Scene shows the Princess and the young man in the Palace happening to hear the lowing of a camel. The Princess asks him as to whose lowing this is. The young man answers *uṭrasya,* of the camel. He cannot pronounce *uṣṭra.* Discovering that the scholars had played a trick on her, she turns him out and feels sad. The young man goes to a temple nearby and keeps on crying till the next morning. The Goddess taking pity on him appears before him and asks him as to what he wants. Ignorant of Sanskrit, the young man thinks that the Goddess is asking him as to who has insulted him. "Vidyā (meaning Vidyottamā)," says he. Taking that the young man wants Vidyā, knowledge, the Goddess blesses him with that.

The young man acquires full learning by the grace of the Goddess. He goes to Vidyottamā and asks her to open the door *anāvṛtakapāṭaṁ dvāraṁ dehi.* Noticing the voice to be somewhat familiar, she opens it and says : *asti kaścid vagviśeṣaḥ ?* (Is there any improvement in speech ?) Both of them embrace each other and that brings the Scene and the play to an end.

Critical Appreciation

A very mediocre attempt, there is nothing noteworthy here. The account is, as said earlier, just traditional. No novelty or originality in it. Nor is the treatment in any way different.

The expression is very faulty. The words *abhinayaḥ abhinetavyaḥ*[1] simply look naive. Instead of saying *ājñapto 'smi pariṣadā*, the sūtradhāra unnecessarily uses the causal suffix : *ājñāpito 'smi*[2]. The form *ekāṅkī-rūpkātmakaḥ*[3] is deep under the influence of Hindi. So is the expression in the conversation :

प्रथमः विद्वान् किन्तु . . .
युवा — किन्तु, किन्तु किम् ?[4]

The word युवाविद्योत्तमयोः[5] is wrong. It should have been युवविद्योत्तमयोः The word *rava* for the voice of Kālidāsa[6] in place of *svara* or *śabda* jars on the ears.

There is a blunder even in the very beginning of the play, in the prayer song, *Īśaprārthanā*, itself which has *sammāna* in neuter :

महिलानामिह देशे भवतु परं सम्मानम्[7]

The play has little to commend itself.

1. p. 99.
2. ibid.
3. ibid.
4. p. 100.
5. p. 100.
6. p. 101.
7. p. 99.

4

KĀLIDĀSAGAURAVAM

Jivanath Jha Sharma of Darbhanga has created this four-scene play out of his imagination. It again deals with the life of Kālidāsa, the only elements of traditional account being that of his going to the Kālī temple, the appearance of the goddess before him and her giving him the boon on his asking to be a great poet well-versed in the Śāstras as also his being the court poet of King Vikramāditya.

Theme

The play opens with the First Scene in a Mithila High School. Kālidāsa is shown there as an unruly student. He goes up a tree and comes down it. He boasts of his strength. He challenges students for a duel. He mimicks and threatens to slap a student, should he report about this to the teacher. When one of the students condemns him for his monkey-like action, he proceeds to slap him. Another student holds him back causing laughter. One of the students asks him as to how many verses he remembers. "Innumerable", answers Kālidāsa. "Can you engage yourself in Antyākṣarī" (a kind of game where a person picks up the last syllable of a verse spoken by another person and recites a verse beginning with that), questions him a student. "Can you engage yourself in a game of cowies with me?", counter-questions him Kālidāsa. A senior student then intervenes and reprimands Kālidāsa for all his unruliness. Kālidāsa does not say anything to him and goes another way. One of the students then asks him if he can swim across the terrible river nearby. "Yes, not only during the day but also during the night", replies Kālidāsa. "If you feel so proud, then cross the river alone in the Amāvasyā night after the teacher goes to bed and then go to the temple of Kālī in the dense jungle. If you do that, we would take you to be a truly brave and fearless person," say the other students. Kālidāsa accepts the challenge. Exit all. Ends the First Scene.

Begins the Second Scene with Kālidāsa in wet loin cloth with a stick on the stage. In a soliloquy he recalls that he did not follow the advice of some of the students not to cross the frightful river, over-eager as he was to show his bravery. He is now in the thick of the forest. He sees a bear and beats the ground with the stick. Fear does take possession of him. Being midnight, it is all dark everywhere. The place being covered with creepers looks doubly dark. He somehow notices a sort of a path and starts to walk on it. For a time he does not see any temple and regrets his indiscretion in accepting the challenge thrown at him by the cunning students. He does not lose heart and moves on feeling the way with the stick. He then notices the Kālī temple. It starts raining at that time. He thinks that if he writes his name on the wall, may be it is washed away by rain. He may leave a proof of his coming to the temple by writing his name on the face of the goddess herself with a charcoal. As he is doing this, the goddess appears before him. Being pleased with him, she offers him a boon. Kālidāsa in fear asks her as to who she is. "Who, he thinks, could she be", asks the goddess. Kālidāsa looks at her carefully and recognizes her to be the Mother goddess herself. He falls at her feet. When she asks him to speak out without fear as to what he wants from her, he says that he should be a great poet well versed in all the Śāstras. 'So be it', says the goddess and disappears. With this comes to an end the Second Scene.

The Third Scene is laid in the premises of a school in a Saurashtra village. All the students and teachers are having a talk centring round Kālidāsa. The people from neighbouring places are also gathered there. Kālidāsa asks if anyone among the students can enter into a disquisition with him. One of the students prefers a discussion by him (Kālidāsa) on the subject of the existence of God first. The question of disquisition would arise later, says he. Kālidāsa discusses the subject along Śāstric lines in beautiful style much to the surprise of everybody including the teacher who clearly expresses his own inability to do it so well. He cannot make out as to how a boy who could not even reproduce the matter committed to memory by him correctly could show his fluency in flawless prose and verse. When an elderly gentleman wants to give credit for this to the teacher, the devotee of Kālī, the latter refuses to accept it. He is surprised as to how Kālidāsa could suddenly acquire such a brilliance. He asks Kālidāsa about it. At this Kālidāsa recounts all that he had experienced the previous night. One of the students confirms Kālidāsa's statement. The same morning he had come back from the Kālī temple where he had seen Kālidāsa's name on the face of the goddess in charcoal. "Everything is possible by the grace of Kālī," says the teacher. He compliments Kālidāsa in full, mentioning *inter alia* that he has justified the name 'High School' of the institution and brought glory to Mithila as also brought fulfilment to them. Kālidāsa shows his humility at this. He is his pupil. He would never be ungrateful. What he needs is his blessings. Every one present blesses him and with this ends the Third Scene.

The Fourth Scene is laid in the Court of King Candragupta II called Vikramāditya. He has seen the performance of the *Abhijñāna-śākuntala* and praises it in high-flown superlatives. So does he the *Raghuvaṁśa* and the *Meghadūta*, the other works of Kālidāsa. Dhanvantari agrees with him and compliments him for his love for learning due to which all the big scholars are happy and are engaged in composing valuable works. The King, addressing the scholars, says that these are the beautiful works of the learned only that enhance the glory and prestige of a country and not a King with a charming figure who may be just a burden on the earth indulging day and night in sensuous pleasures. Amarasiṁha gives credit to the King again for supporting so many scholars. Dhanvantari at this reminds them of the auspicious time. Just at that time enters Kālidāsa. The king embraces him and offers him a high seat. He announces the conferment of the title of Mahākavi on him. At this all those present greet him with cheers. Dhanvantari then blesses both the King and the great poet and with this comes to an end the Scene and the play.

Critical Appreciation

Though Kālidāsa is not mentioned in the play in so many words as one of the nine jewels at the court of Vikramāditya, the mention of Dhanvantari and Amarasiṁha who shared among themselves this distinction (whom he joins a little later) would make him to be so. The playwright shows his historical sense by identifying Vikramāditya with Candragupta II of the Gupta dynasty who is on record to have borne this title. Since the author himself belongs to Mithila, it is natural for him to have attachment to it. Interestingly, he carries it to the extent that he makes Kālidāsa study in one of its institutions of higher learning, Uccapīṭhapāṭhaśālā, as he calls it. So far it is understandable. But what passes understanding however, is as to why he should shift him to a school (Pāṭhaśālā) in a Saurashtra village after he has been blessed by goddess Kālī. Since there is mention of the teacher also who could not be a different one in that he refers to Kālidāsa's inertness in learning earlier and compares it with his

(Kālidāsa's) competence in it. At the moment the natural presumption should be that the place should be the same from where Kālidāsa had started the previous night. What happened just in one night to shift him from Mithila to Saurashtra ? The author seems to have gone nodding here.

The playwright keeps aside the traditional account of Kālidāsa having been originally a fool. He makes him instead a rowdy in a Mithila High School who indulges in all kinds of pranks and misbehaviour. He keeps to the account inasmuch as Kālidāsa acquires learning by the grace of goddess Kālī but completely brushes aside the Vidyottamā episode, the *raison d etre* of his going to the Kālī temple and crying before the goddess. He concocts another one of a challenge thrown at him by some students to do so to prove his fearlessness, the temple being located on the other side of a fierce river and in a thick awesome jungle. The appearance of the goddess in the play also has a different account. It is when Kālidāsa is writing his name on the face of the deity that she appears before him. The reason of her being pleased with him has not been fully brought out here. The whole thing appears rather incoherent. As the young man is writing his name on the face with the charcoal, the goddess appears before him, expresses her happiness with him and offers a boon. The writing of the name on the face is hardly the justification convincing enough for the goddess to feel so propitiated as to offer a boon. In the traditional account the goddess does so out of pity at Kālidāsa's cries, which has more of a justification for it.

After going through the play one cannot but have the feeling that it has more of dramatic element in it upto the Third Scene. The fourth Scene is its weakest link. There are long passages in it and the matter is unnecessarily dilated. The playwright seems to show off his capacity to handle high-flown Sanskrit, a tendency not uncommon among Sanskritists. Works of Kālidāsa he takes up one by one and waxes eloquent on their poetic beauty, literary excellenee and all the imaginable qualities they possess. A few of these passages are reproduced below by way of specimen :

राजा — अभिज्ञानशाकुन्तलस्याभिनयं दृष्ट्वा तत्र च लौकिकमर्यादानुगतां स्वाभाविकतां विप्रलम्भशृङ्गारस्य साशंषजनतुष्टिं पुष्टिं सहासं त्रिविधरसविन्यासं भासितसाक्षात्कारं निर्वहणसन्धिं निर्वहणचमत्कारं च पर्यालोचयता तन्मयध्यानतया मया न पारितमानन्दवाष्पाणि रोद्धुम् ।।[1]

1. p. 85.

राजा — इदमपि नासत्यं यद्रघुवंशमहाकाव्यस्य सादृश्यं कर्तुं सम्प्रति किमप्यपरं काव्यं नास्तीति । तत्र हि चमत्कारपूर्णालङ्कारसमावेशः, कोमलकान्तपदावलीविलासः, प्रतिपद्यमर्थवैशद्यम्, प्रतिसर्गं नैसर्गिको विविधध्वनिः, अपुष्टतादिदोषराहित्यम्, सर्वत्र सरसता हृदयाकर्षकता विलक्षणचमत्कारिता च स्वतः प्रमाणयति तदीयं महत्वम् ।[1]

The high-flown style is also noticeable when Dhanvantari and Amarasiṁha compliment the King for his supporting the scholars, e.g.,

अमरसिंहः- देव ! वयन्तु मन्यामहे मालाकारं विना पुष्पवाटिका, तरुं विना लता, हिमालयं विना गङ्गा, धरां विना धान्यं, गुरुं विना विद्येव च भवादृशं शरणं भूरमणं विना कुत्र स्थितिं विदधीत प्रशान्तस्वान्तोऽपि विलक्षणप्रेक्षो विचक्षणगणः ?[2]

The expression of the author is not infrequently embellished with charming alliterations as can be seen from the following and also from the above examples :

धन्वन्तरिः--विविधविद्याविद्योतमानाय कविकुलगुरुकालिदासाय विद्वज्जनजीवातवे रिपुकुलकरालवाहवे विधीयमानभारतीसेवाय देवाय च स्वस्ति स्वस्ति ।[3]

In spite of his seemingly good command over Sanskrit as evinced by his high-flown style and the chain of alliterative words, the author permits himself some grammatical aberrations and expressions under vernacular influence that do not go well with genuine Sanskrit coin. In the first category could be mentioned the words or expressions like *amamni*[1] which is impossible of formation in the Imperfect from any of the *man* roots or *vṛṣṭir api ārabhamāṇo* 'sti[5] where *ārabhamāṇaḥ* in masculine going with *vṛṣṭi* in the feminine is irregular apart from being un-Sanskrit like or *janatāḥ upasthitāḥ*[6] which should be in the singular only the suffix *tal* being added to *jana* by Pāṇ. *grāmjanabandhubhyas tal* (4.2.43) in the sense of *samūha*, a gathering or *viṣayo 'yaṁ satyam*[7] where *satya* going with *viṣaya* the masculine should be in the masculine or *prathamaṁ sthānam ādadāti*[8] where *ādadāti* should be *ādatte*, Ātmanepada being enjoined to *dā* with *āṅ* by Pāṇ. (1.3.20).

1. p. 85.
2 & 3. p. 86.
4. p. 82.
5 & 6. p. 83.
7. p. 84.
8. p. 85.

In the second category could be included such expressions as *āśīrvādaṁ vitaranti*[1] (genuine Sanskrit would be *āśiṣā vardhayanti*) सत्यमिदं नाटकरत्नम् प्रथमं स्थानम ददाति उत्कृष्टतायाः[1] is almost a literal translation of the Hindi sentence सचमुच यह नाटकरत्न उत्कृष्टता में पहले नम्बर पर है, महाकाव्यस्य सादृश्यं कर्तुम्
(Cp. Hindi महाकाव्य की समानता करने में), छायावादप्रधानं मेघदूतमेव वा कतरस्मादवरं यत्र विप्रलम्भः साकारतामुपयाति[3] ।

One or two odd expressions though not strictly fitting into any of the two categories, are certainly examples of bad Sanskrit and should better have been avoided. One of these is : *caraṇān smarāmi*[4] The plural in चरणान् reference to the feet of the teacher does not go well with genuine Sanskrit. It should be *caraṇau* only. The other is *tasmai mahākavaye mahākavipadavīpradānena ca dātum*[5] where *mahākavipadavīṁ pradātum* should have been enough. What does *pradānena dātum* mean ?

In spite of the aberrations which are happily not too many, the play stands out as a good attempt on Kālidāsa which, in greater part, is out of the rut in its theme and its treatment and should be quite satisfying to connoisseurs.

1-5. p. 8 .

5

MAHĀKAVIKĀLIDĀSAM

Written specially for the Kālidāsa Samāroha* of Ujjayinī in 1961 and staged successfully there, this play in five Acts by Sri Srijiva Nyayatirtha was first published serially in the Praṇava-Pārijāta, Calcutta in its Vol. VI, Nos. 2,3,4,6, and 8, Śaka Year 1885 or A.D. 1964, and later as one whole unit in a collection of plays, the *Rūpaka-cakram* of the playwright in Śaka Year 1893 or A.D. 1968.

The play is based on the age-old anecdote of Kālidāsa; he having been a fool originally, his marriage through a manouvre with Vidyāvatī, a learned princess, his insult at her hands, his propitiation of Goddess Kālī and his attainment of knowledge through her favour. The playwright has woven a beautiful play out of it. He has so arranged the incidents that, though well known, they do not occasion loss of interest. He has made his play thoroughly enjoyable and interesting by a fair sprinkling of wit and humour in which he is past master, quite a few of his plays being farces or satires.

Theme

After the prologue Sri Nyayatirtha informs that he was inspired to write a play on Kālidāsa by Dr. Gaurinath Sastri, the then Principal of Sanskrit College, Calcutta and that most of the actors are drawn

*The Samāroha, an annual feature, has given to the Sanskrit world many an original work on Kālidāsa as also affording it an opportunity to witness the stage-performance of Kālidāsa's plays by trained troupes from different parts of the country.

from the staff of that very College. The play introduces through an Interlude in Act I three Princes Narendra, Samarendra and Mathureśa alongwith one Kūrmanātha. Narendra is happy that he has found out a young blockhead with a defective speech. He had seen him earlier in the course of a morning walk cutting the root of the very branch of the tree on the fore-part of which he was seated. Knowing his fall to be inevitable, he was somehow made to climb down. A big fool, he could not understand, though told, as to what wrong he was doing himself. The Princes feeling humiliated at the hands of Vidyāvatī are itching to avenge their insult. And for this they would like to use Kūrmanātha, the blockhead as a tool. After getting his concurrence for marriage, they tell him that a Princess is a suitable match for him. He would get lots of money if he were to marry her. There is only one condition. He should keep mum till marriage. "The Princess likes discussion. You should participate in it (the discussion) by gestures only and not utter a word. If she were to raise one finger, you should raise two; if she were to raise two, you should raise one and draw a circle with it," he was told. Kūrmanātha nods his head in assent. The Princes then decide to go to Vidyāvatī's father, the ruler of Daśapura, whom they find a lot upset because of repudiation by his daughter of many a well-behaved and scholarly eligible match. They are of the view that he may not disapprove of discussion in silence, his only consideration being to secure a match for Vidyāvatī. They dress up like Brahmins to camouflage their identity. Young Kūrmanātha is also properly dressed up. With this ends the Interlude. The Act proper starts with the soliloquy of a royal attendant Sudāsa who gives out the information that the Assembly hall has been properly set for a disquisition. After his exit the ruler of Daśapura accompanied by the chamberlain, is ushered into the stage. He has agreed to the discussion being held *ex silentio.* At his command, the chamberlain invites the guests to take their places in the hall. Enter the Princes with Kūrmanātha and Vidyāvatī with her friend Taḍillatā. The ruler of Daśapura addresses the citizens gathered to witness the discussion. He knows that the silent discussion may not satisfy them but then, he explains to them that such a step has become necessary at the insistence of the kith and kin of the eligible match, though it may not satisfy them. If in the course of the discussion either side were to break silence it would automatically stand defeated. He assigns the duty of explaining the gestures of Vidyāvatī to her teacher Somaśarman. On behalf of Kūrmanātha, Narendra takes this responsibility upon himself. The discussion begins. Vidyāvatī raises the first finger with the gem-studded ring on it. Somaśarman explains that what the Princess wants to ask is : There are numerous stars in the sky; the world is full of a variety of things. Who is that one who creates, sustains and destroys all of them? Kurmanātha, true to his tutoring earlier, raises two fingers. Narendra explains this as meaning that it is not one, it is two, Īśvara and Prakṛti. Vidyāvatī shakes her head and once again raises the fore-finger which is explained by Somaśarman to mean that Īśvara is non-distinct from Māyā or Prakṛti, so it is only one entity in reality and not two. Kūrmanātha draws a circle with two fingers. Narendra explains this as meaning that Śakti or Māyā of the possessor of Śakti could be taken to be one only if both of them were to produce the same effect which in reality they don't. A spider does not produce anything other than a cobweb while God creates all the different things. So two (distinct) entities may have to be accepted. At this Somaśarman expresses helplessness to carry on the discussion in silence. A suitable reply could be given to Narendra but not without words. Vidyāvatī garlands Kūrmanātha. Amidst scenes of gaiety all round, the Act comes to an end.

The Second Act too begins with an Interlude wherein Sudāsa informs Taḍillatā of the running away of Kūrmanātha on the honey-moon day itself, giving rise to the suspicion that he does not like Vidyāvatī though both of them are quick to point out that they had noticed the attraction of the bride and the bridegroom for each other. The conversation between Sudāsa and Taḍillatā is marked by pungent humour : Kūrmanātha, the bride-groom being described as desirous of drinking the face of the Princess like water and Vidyāvatī, the bride being described as looking at the face of the groom like a bitch looking at a piece of flesh. The Interlude is followed by the Second Act proper where Narendra is shown asking Kūrmanātha as to what he has understood in his encounter with Vidyāvatī and Kūrmanātha replying that he has understood everything; with one finger she (Vidyāvatī) had thrown the hint that she wanted to punch his one eye. He raised two fingers and threw the hint that he would punch hers both. She is a woman and I am a man. She was defeated. At that time Sudāsa who had been looking for him appears. He wants to take him along with him. Kūrmanātha indulges in many a foolish prank. Ultimately at Narendra's behest, he agrees to leave for his in-laws' house with Sudāsa. At this enter Vidyāvatī and her friend. Vidyāvatī is assailed by serious doubts about the learning of the man she has just married. She confides in her friend that though she was all attention for Kūrmanātha's recitation of the Mantras, she could not notice accurate pronunciation of them by him. Her friend says that it appears inconceivable. Anyway, the point could well be decided that very night itself. As soon as she finishes, the ruler of Daśapura enters and enquires of his daughter if she is happy with her marriage with Kūrmanātha. Vidyāvatī keeps mum. The Daśapura ruler then advises her to develop love for him (her husband). She says that she is feeling uneasy on account of a bad dream that she had seen in early hours of the previous night. She had found herself being bound and thrown into a billowy ocean by her father, teacher Somaśarman, and an astrologer who had made his appearance there, (after a conversation with him at the end of which it was decided that her death should lead to good). After this, she had found herself placed on a sandy beach by a divine lady with a protruding tongue and with a hand wielding a sword with bright sheen and smiling; she consoled her and disappeared. The Daśapura ruler tells her that the dream, as she has narrated, should ultimately result in good. At this the chamberlain announces the arrival of Kūrmanātha. The Daśapura ruler asks him to bring him in and himself moves to another room. Kūrmanātha enters and bows to Vidyāvatī who slightly moves away from him. He is about to sit on the floor. Vidyāvatī's friend asks him as to why he wants to sit on a low seat. The blockhead retorts whether he should sit on her head. The friend takes it to be a joke. Next, Kūrmanātha asks Vidyāvatī whether his father-in-law was married or not. The friend again takes it a joke. Vidyāvatī however gets suspicious. 'Is he a big fool', she asks herself. She places before him a riddle and asks him to solve it. The riddle is 'Who is that being who proves untrue the principle of Logic that there is no smell in water by feeling it in that; who has four big feet but still is slow in speed.' For long he looks on speechless. Vidyāvatī's friend then puts the riddle in a simpler form : who is the being who has long neck and is bereft of hair, whose feet are weak, whose belly bulges out, who eats thorns and wild growth and who (can) stand, even though walking in a desert, intense heat. Kūrmanātha looks through the window and seeing a camel cries out *uṭṭaḥ, uṭṭaḥ, uṭṭaḥ*. Vidyāvatī feels really miserable at this. She is pained that the man who has married her cannot even pronounce the word *uṣṭra* correctly. She feels that her evil dream has come true. The friend thinks that Kūrmanātha is indulging in boyish pranks. He probably does not like her presence. Saying this she leaves. Kūrmanātha then addresses Vidyāvatī as *piye*. Vidyāvatī gets furious at this. She feels insulted, humiliated and cheated. She asks him if he has anything particular to say : *asti kaścid vāgviśeṣaḥ* ? If not, he should move away from her. Kūrmanātha, though a fool, feels the pinch of the insult. Cut to the quick he says that what has one to do with learning if it does not inculcate devotion to husband ? Does the fool have no feeling of love ? Has he no feeling of respect or disrespect ? It is better for him to end his life. Saying this he runs away from her.

Vidyāvatī deeply laments her lot. The Daśapura ruler enters at this and the miserable lady falls at his feet unconscious. With this comes to an end the Act.

The Third Act begins with the scene of Kālidāsa seated on a platform in a corner of a forest on the banks of the Narmadā. Under the instructions of his guru, he went over to the path of Sādhanā instead of the one of ending his life after he was repudiated by his wife. By the power of the Mantra given to him by his guru his stammering has almost disappeared but he has still not achieved his desired goal. He closes his eyes and prays to the benign goddess for her Darśana. Opening his eyes he looks around and finds the night to be terrible, the sky to be overcast and the date to be that of Āmāvasyā. The hooting of the she-jackals pains his ears. Inspite of this he has made up his mind not to slacken his determination. Either he is to win the Mother's favour or end his life. Firm in his resolve he sings a song in praise of the Mother. After the song he goes into Japa-Samādhi at the end of which he offers water. All of a sudden appears the sound of thunder. Kālidāsa falls unconscious. Slowly light illumines the quarters and appears goddess Kālikā. She awakens Kālidāsa who considers himself really lucky. He asks her to bestow on him knowledge, pure knowledge. The Goddess agrees. She blesses him with the treasure of speech and a name, Kālidāsa, indicative of attainment of knowledge through her. With this she disappears. Kālidāsa asks her to forgive him in that he has asked from her *artha* and *kāma* and not *svarga*; after having seen her who can bestow heaven and emancipation. At this enters Vidyāvatī with her friend and the chamberlain. The chamberlain informs that since she repudiated her husband Vidyāvatī passes her days in practising austerities only. She has just one ornament, the gem-studded ring on her finger. She has come to the Narmadā for bath because of some special importance of it on that day. He asks Taḍillatā, Vidyāvatī's friend to conduct Vidyāvatī through a pucca road and not a muddy one. Taḍillatā notices a person dead or about to die. She wants to avoid him. The chamberlain tells her that the person getting up from the earth has proceeded towards the river. He is neither dead nor is nearly dead. Taḍillatā says that everybody feels confused in darkness. May be, he is a demon, a goblin or a human being. So she would not go by that path. Kālidāsa notices the near end of the night and a lady with her entourage coming to take bath. 'Let her first finish her bath, he would have it afterwards', says he. He is reminded at that time of his marriage with a Princess and his repudiation by her because of his foolishness. He remembers her last words *asti kaścid vāgviśeṣaḥ*. He cries aloud *asti kaścid vāgviśeṣaḥ*. By the grace of the Mother Goddess he has the *vāgviśeṣaḥ*. He then comes out with his verses which begin with *asti* (*asty uttarsyāṁ diśi*), *kaścit* (*kaścit kāntāvirahguruṇā* and *vāk* (*vāgarthāv iva samprktau*). He says he would compose three poems which would begin with these words and would make an offering of them to that lady if ever she were to cross his eyes. Vidyāvatī on her part is surprised at the words *asti kaścid vāgviśeṣaḥ*. She knows these to be her last words to her husband. And none else was present when she had uttered them. Stricken with remorse, she is unable to proceed on and falls unconscious. The chamberlain then approaches Kālidāsa for help. He first feels the pulse of the unconscious Princess and then notices the gem-studded ring on her finger which she had raised at the time of the discussion. He feels certain that she is no other than the daughter of the Daśapura ruler. He whispers into Vidyāvatī's ears the words : *asti kaścid vāgviśeṣaḥ*. Vidyāvatī opens her eyes, marks the clear speech, begs forgiveness of Kālidāsa for the wrong done to him, encircles her feet by her hands and entreats him not to forsake her. Kālidāsa asks her to wait a while till he finishes his bath as a part of his rigours. With these words he goes out and the Act too comes to an end.

In the Introductory portion of the Fourth Act, a character Sumanyu is shown catching hold of Kālidāsa for carrying the palanquin of King Vikramāditya, one of the four original carriers of which having suddenly fallen ill. In spite of Kālidāsa's protest that he is a Brahmin having come to the river for bath, he is not taken seriously. Kālidāsa tells him that he would explain everything to the King. Sudhanya, another character, tells him that genuine Brahmin can secure his release from the King but then he (Sudhanya) would have to lose his job. Being newly-married he would perish along with his wife. This has its effect on Kālidāsa. Says he unto himself, 'Is he also newly-married ? Like me his fortune may also take a turn (for the worse).' Sumanyu, the first character, thinks that he is frightened by his words. That is why he has agreed to accompany them. Sorrowful Kālidāsa resigns himself to his fate. He does not know as to when he would be able to see his wife again.

The Interlude to Act IV begins with the scene of a garden. Enters a lady gardener (*Mālinī*). Under the orders of King Vikramāditya, the garden has been reserved for Kālidāsa's stay. The lady gardener looks after Kālidāsa who treats her as his sister. He recites to her his poems. Still he feels restless. The pangs of separation from Vidyāvatī afflict his mind.

Enters Kālidāsa. He informs her that the King has appointed him a member of his assembly of nine jewels. The lady gardener is all praise for the King in that he has bestowed honour on a new (younger) poet like Kālidāsa in spite of the experts like Vararuci in the line. Kālidāsa remarks that there should be nothing surprising in it. The morning sun is liked more than the rays of the mid-day sun, the half-blooming lotus is better than the umbrella-like one, a plant with its fresh foliage going up attracts the heart much more than a full-grown tree. Mālinī suggests that this could well be his ideal in the depiction of his heroes and heroines. She tells him that she quite realizes his writhing pain. Kālidāsa asks her not to speak any more about it. He tells her that he is passing his time somehow in separation from his beloved by seeing the union of the trees and the creepers and the pairs of the fawns, the peacocks and the bees. Mālinī at this switches over to another topic. She enquires of Kālidāsa as to why he does not send a letter to Vidyāvatī. Kālidāsa says it won't help; it won't satisfy his beloved, for long has there been no contact of him with her, he even does not know her whereabouts; he had met her only for a moment on the banks of the Narmadā. The talk about his wife proves too much for him. He falls unconscious. Mālinī pours water on him and brings him back to senses. Behind the curtain is heard the sound of musical instruments and noise. Kālidāsa gets up and wants to know from Mālinī as to why there should be so much of noise. Mālinī tells him that it is due to the Yātrā of Mahākāla where artificial ghosts, demons and goblins as also puppets of various kinds are dancing. Both Kālidāsa and Mālinī go out to enjoy the festival.

With this begins the Fourth Act with King Vikramāditya, the Court jester, Vararuci and Amarasiṁha on the stage. The King speaks of a large number of pearls in an ocean remaining in water, away from the sight of the people and a large number of flowers withering away unnoticed in forest lands after they had spread their fragrance. Addressing the Court, he narrates an interesting incident. A man caught to carry his palanquin heard from him the words *kṣaṇaṁ viśramyatāṁ jālma skandhas te yadi bādhati,*[1] 'you take rest, O despicable fellow, if you feel pain in your shoulder' and feeling hurt said : *na tathā bādhate skandho yathā bādhati bādhate* 'my shoulder does not give me as much pain as *bādhati* does.' How wonderful! Even a palanquin-bearer finds fault with his words! The jester takes it as an evidence of rudeness on his part. He says that he would pound his head with his stick. The King stops him and says : 'Why should you say so ? If a King were to violate speech either through pride or ignorance, should a learned person keep silent like a fool just because he is poor ? Should he not correct the King ?' The jester does not retract even at this. 'An attendant correcting a King deserves a slap,' says he. The King

1. p. 119.

does not agree with him. Correction in word is to make one understand the mistake. In no way does it warrant punishment. Vararuci is all appreciation for the palanquin-bearer. Keeping up the thread of narrative the King informs the court that he got down from the palanquin as soon as he heard the palanquin-bearer's words. He wanted to know as to who he was. He gave out his name as Kālidāsa and came out with his (the King's) praise in the verse:

राजंस्तव यशो भाति कैलासहरहासवत् ।
कुन्दचन्दनवच्चारु शरच्चन्द्रमरीचिवत् ॥[1]

"Your fame shines, O king, like the laughter of Śiva on Kailāsa. It is as charming as the Kunda flower or the sandalwood or the rays of the autumnal moon."

The jester grabs this as an opportunity to create some humour. I also have an eulogy, says he, and comes out with the following one:

राजंस्तव यशो भाति रण्डामुण्डितमुण्डवत् ।
अस्थिखण्डपयोभाण्डलाजमण्डद्विजाण्डवत् ॥

"O King, your fame shines out like the shaven head of a widow, a piece of bone, a milk-bowl, starch of fried rice and an egg of a bird."

The King continuing says that after he heard his eulogy from Kālidāsa he invited him to his court. After the King finishes, enters Kālidāsa. The King asks Vararuci to move forward to the front seat so that Kālidāsa could sit on the one occupied by him. Vararuci says that there is no difference between the front and the back seats. A jewel, wherever it is, whether in a room or a forest or the full-grown breasts of the ladies, has the same value. Kālidāsa has his own views on it. "Qualities get admiration in their proper place and not otherwise," says he. Vararuci expresses his appreciation of the poet in Kālidāsa. At this the Vidūṣaka also likes to say something that may reveal the poet in him. The king says well let poetry be today's pastime. He utters the line *nahi sukhaṁ duḥkhair vinā labhyate*. The others are to supply the first three lines and a part of the fourth one.

Vararuci, the Vidūṣaka (jester) and Kālidāsa supply the lines one by one. Kālidāsa's lines are highly appreciated by the King. Vararuci at this tells him of an interesting incident. He had derived immense joy from the reading of Kālidāsa's poem, the *Kumārasambhava*. To indicate its

1 & 2. p. 121.

tenderness he had placed it on an unbaked pitcher. Kālidāsa mistook it as an indication of a work of an immature person and began to destroy it from the end onwards. Fortunately he returned not long thereafter and dissuaded him from doing so. There is no loss to the work from cantos I-VII. The king asks Kālidāsa to rewrite the lost portions. Kālidāsa promises to try it. He informs the King that he has composed another poem, the *Raghuvaṁśa* in the meantime and has started work on still another one, the *Meghadūta*. If the King were to permit, a particular portion of his new play the *Abhijñānaśākuntala* could be put on boards. The King readily agrees and the fifth Act of the said play is staged. There is a change of scene after this. The King conveys his orders to the Chief Minister for honouring Kālidāsa and other poets. At this Kālidāsa says that if he (the King) is really pleased with him he could remove from his heart a thorn that had been afflicting it all along. He tells him that he had married the daughter of his vessel, the ruler of Daśapura. As soon as she discovered that he was a fool she repudiated him. For three years he carried on hard penance. After this the goddess appeared before him and granted him a boon. Immediately thereafter, he was united with his wife. As soon as the couple came together a royal attendant took him away to carry a palanquin. The King is sorry to know all this.

Well, he is instrumental himself in his separation from his beloved ! He calls for the Daśapura ruler and comes to know from him that he has no idea of the whereabouts of his daughter in spite of thorough search; he has, however, heard a rumour that she, lost in the thoughts of her husband, is living in a holy place. Kālidāsa falls unconscious on hearing this. Vararuci and Amarasiṁha ask him not to lose heart. In his own words they tell him not to fall a prey to sorrow like an ordinary man; what difference would there be between a tree and a mountain if both of them were to quake in the wind :

न पृथग् जनवच्छुचो वशं वशिनामुत्तम गन्तुमर्हसि ।
द्रुमसानुमतां किमन्तरं यदि वायौ द्वितयेऽपि ते चलाः ॥

Kālidāsa regains himself shortly and seeks permission of the King to go round the country in search of his wife. The King confers on him the title of Mahākavi and allows him to go. He also introduces him to the ruler of Daśapura. "He is your son-in-law, for whom your daughter is staying in some distant holy place away from her home", says he to him. The beaming Daśapura ruler embraces him who in turn bows to him. The King asks the people to wait a while before he comes back after leaving instructions for the preparations for Kālidāsa's journey. He goes out. From behind the curtain is heard a lot of noise. It is announced that a demoness has entered the royal court. Terror strikes the people. The Vidūṣaka hides himself under the throne. The demoness reassures the people. She says she has one riddle; *samasyā*. If it could be solved in a couple of days she would do no harm to anybody and go back quietly. Else, she would swallow all of them one by one. The riddle is :

इहैवास्ति ततो नास्ति ततोऽस्ति नेह वर्तते ।
इहास्ति च ततोऽप्यस्ति नास्तीहापि ततोऽपि न ॥

Vararuci finds it difficult. He wants time to solve it. So does Amarasiṁha. The demoness says that none other than Kālidāsa will be able to solve it. Saying this she goes out. Enters the King. The Vidūṣaka comes out from under the throne and tells the King that a demoness had appeared there. She had mentioned a riddle and had said that Kālidāsa could alone solve it. The King is rather surprised at this. He is unable to make out as to from where the demoness could descend on the court. He thinks of propitiating Mahākāla for the protection of his country from the unfortunate visitation. He feels rather uneasy with the news of the demoness as also his royal duties. With this comes to an end the Fourth Act.

The Fifth Act, the last Act of the play, opens with a scene on a Himālayan terrain. A lady forest-dweller enters the stage singing and dancing. She has a friend in a character called Balāhaka. She prays for the success of his mission. She hears the indistinct sound of the foot-steps and hides herself. Enters Vidyāvatī talking to herself. She is feeling miserable at her condition. She thinks that she has committed a great crime in repudiating her husband. There is no way left for her except to court death. She does not know the path. She only goes on at the indication of the forest-dwellers approaching her. She moves out. The lady forest-dweller comes into the open. She takes the lady she has seen to be either a Princess or a Queen. She calls out to her friend Balāhaka and mentions about her. Balāhaka tells her that according to the information supplied to him by other spies she is the daughter of the ruler of Daśapura. He asks her to take her to her cottage while he would inform the King. The lady forest-dweller enters again and confirms her being the daughter of the Daśapura ruler. She says that she has looked after her well. She has been offered all courtesies, water, fruits and the like. Balāhaka feels relieved at this and asks her to keep her in good humour lest she goes out. Exit the lady forest-dweller. Balāhaka then hears the sound of somebody's foot-steps. He stations himself in a corner. Enters Kālidāsa. Talking to himself he says that he has covered the entire country, from Kashmir to the shores of the ocean, from Gujarat to Orissa. Broken and tired, he has failed to trace his beloved. He has slackened his efforts and is now staying quietly on a hilly region. He thinks the path stretching in front of him to be leading to death. He then discounts the talk of death. "I will not be happy even in death", says he. In Kashmir, he had been treated like a king and offered all courtesies. Still, suffering from the pangs of separation as he was, he could not have peace of mind. After a moment's pause, he refers to the wife of the king of Karnataka and remembers her bold statement that 'the three—the one from a lotus (Brahmā), the one from the river bank (Vyāsa) and the one from an ant-hill (Vālmīki) are the poets and the teachers of the three worlds. We bow to them. If the modern ones were to attract the mind by their poetic or prose compositions she would place on their heads her left foot :

एकोऽभून्नलिनात्ततश्च पुलिनाद्वल्मीकतश्चापरे
ते सर्वे कवयस्त्रिलोकगुरवस्तेभ्यो नमस्कुर्महे ।
अर्वाञ्चो यदि गद्यपद्यरचनैश्चेतश्चमत्कुर्वते
तेषां मूर्ध्नि दधामि वामचरणं कर्णाटराजप्रिया ।।

When she, the Karṇātaka Queen (Karṇaṭarājapriyā) had heard of his poetry she had differently interpreted her words with the result that her *darpokti* had got transformed into *vinayokti*. 'Their left foot I put on my head' was her ingenious interpretation *teṣam vāmcaraṇaṁ Karṇaṭājarājapriyā nijāmūrdhni dadhāmi*. And with this interpretation she had honoured him. Unique really is her devotion to learning. She is learning incarnate indeed! His Vidyāvatī also is like that. He has no idea as to whether she is alive or not. As he is saying this he happens to listen to a song where a lady most poignantly expresses her sorrow at the separation from her husband. She longs to see him. She asks him to appear before her and give her a fresh lease of life. Kālidāsa is surprised to hear this. Who could be singing like this ? It is the very painful story of his wife! He thinks he should send a message to his loving wife through a cloud of whom he had been thinking for quite some time. He asks the cloud to go to his beloved who would be forgetting the tone-combinations, though composed by her own self while she would be putting the Vīṇā in her lap with its unclean garments, the tone-combinations where his name would figure. She would be hard put to play on the string wetted with tears :

उत्सङ्गे वा मलिनवसने सौम्य निक्षिप्य वीणां
मद्गोत्राङ्कं विरचितपदं गेयमुद्गातुकामा ।
तन्त्रीमार्द्रां नयनसलिलैः सारयित्वा कथञ्चित्
भूयो भूयः स्वयमपि कृतां मूर्च्छनां विस्मरन्ती ॥

'My love, where are you' ? Saying this he falls unconscious. Balāhāka approaches him quickly and consoles : "Who are you" asks him Kalidasa. "I am the Yakṣa present in your very mind" replies Balāhaka. "But how could you recognize me, "asks Kālidāsa again. "Your messenger cloud (Balāhaka) told me all about you", replies Balāhaka, concealing his identity of being a spy of the Daśapura ruler. "O Yakṣa if you really are my friend present in my thoughts, then let me know as to where my beloved is" says Kālidāsa. "She is very close to you" replies Balāhaka. Kālidāsa asks him to show her to him without delay. Not even a moment's wait he can stand. At this enters King Vikramāditya, together with the chamberlain and the Vidūṣaka. Kālidāsa utters the last verse of the *Meghadūta* : *etat kṛtvā priyam anucitaprārthanāvartmano me*, etc. and says that his poem, the *Meghadūta* may also come to an end. The King asks Kālidāsa who is very much surprised to see him to embrace him. He informs him that he has come to seek his assistance to ward off the fear of a demoness who wants the solution of a riddle. Kālidāsa solves it there and then. His explanation of *ihaivāsti tato nāsti tatoi 'sti neha vartate*, etc. is :

राजपुत्र चिरं जीव मा जीव मुनिपुत्रक ।
जीव म्रियस्व वा साधो व्याध मा जीव मा मृथा: ॥

King Vikramāditya feels greatly charmed at Kālidāsa's genius. He wants to do him a good turn. He asks Balāhaka to bring in the Daśapura ruler alongwith his daughter which Balāhaka does. He asks the Daśapura ruler to unite Vidyāvatī with Kālidāsa forthwith. He holds Kālidāsa by hand and asks him to accept Vidyāvati, who has renounced everything for him, who is devoted to him, who is his very life-soul. Kālidāsa then recounts him the entire story, from his repudiation by Vidyāvatī to his being forced to be a palanquin-bearer. He is grateful to Vikramāditya for having accepted him a member of his court. Vikramāditya asks the Daśapura ruler to unite the hand of his daughter with that of his son-in-law which he readily does. The lady forest-dweller garlands both. The Daśapura ruler says that he will know no peace of mind till the union of the two is properly celebrated in Ujjayinī. Vikramāditya gives his concurrence for this and announces the appointment of Kālidāsa as a member of his Council of Ministers.

Balāhaka enters at this and informs all present that the lady-gardener attending on Kālidāsa has been put under arrest and is being brought there for judgement. Kālidāsa and Vikramāditya feel pained at a lady being put in chains. Balāhaka tells them that she had assumed the form of a demoness and struck terror in many a heart. The police has the clue to this. Vikramāditya praises her art of acting and orders that she be produced before him immediately. The lady gardener in chains then enters along with a police man. Vikramāditya orders her release. She bows to the King and to Kālidāsa. She tells the King that she had not done anything out of selfish motive. Vikramāditya appreciates her devotion to Kālidāsa. It was she who had set the King on to tracing Kālidāsa which ultimately led to his union with him. Without the fear of demoness the element of urgency would not have been there. The King appreciates the lady's sharp intelligence. After a humorous interlude, Kālidāsa expresses his unhappiness over the arrest of the lady gardener. The lady says that even her arrest has led to her happiness in that she now finds Kālidāsa with Vidyāvatī in front of her. The King tells Kālidāsa that he would listen to all the poems that he (Kālidāsa) had composed when he was on a pilgrimage. After this Kālidāsa utters the Bharatavākya which closes the play.

Critical Appreciation

From the detailed story as given above it would appear that the playwright has kept up the basic elements of an old anecdote quite intact while introducing some innovations. The momentary coming together of Kālidāsa and Vidyāvatī on the banks of the Narmadā and the demoness episode are his major innovations which give quite an interesting turn to the story. The introduction of a character Balāhaka—the name Balāhaka itself is interesting and seems to have been inspired by the Balāhaka, the cloud of the *Meghadūta*—as the spy of the Daśapura ruler and his lady assistant, the forest-dweller, is also interesting. Popular tradition takes Vidyottamā called Vidyāvatī in the play (the reason for the change in name is not clear) to be the daughter of king Vikramāditya. The playwright, however, mentions her as the daughter of a Daśapura ruler—he does not give the name of the ruler who is always mentioned as Daśapurarāja—as the vessel ruler of King Vikramāditya. The names of the three Princes defeated in the Śāstrārtha by the Princess Vidyāvatī are all imaginary. Tradition does not record them. Despite playwright's best endeavours to be consistent all through, inconsistency has crept in at certain places, e.g., when Kālidāsa listens to a song (from behind the curtain) which, he thinks brings out the pangs of his wife, he, instead of trying to find out the source of the song, thinks of sending a message to his beloved through a cloud. It appears the playwright is in undue haste to introduce into his work the point of a message being sent through a cloud. It is apiece with his spirit of introducing into his work everything connected with Kālidāsa. Some of the scholars are of the view that it is Kālidāsa himself who, in the form of the Yakṣa, sends a message to his beloved. If that be so, a message by him to Vidyāvatī through a cloud must find a mention in the play irrespective of whether there is any dramatic justification for it or not.

While weaving the plot, the playwright has fitted into it very skilfully even such anecdotes as have nothing to do with Kālidāsa. In popular anecdote, a new recruit as a palanquin-bearer was just an ordinary labourer. Our playwright makes him Kālidāsa. According to the *Bhojaprabandha* it was King Bhoja whose palanquin he was made to carry and not of the King Vikramāditya. A verse attributed to the Karṇāṭaka queen and found in anthologies too has been included by the playwright into his plot. Kālidāsa is shown to have met her (Karnāṭaka queen) in the course of his wanderings and humbled her pride though he could not help being deeply impressed by her learning which *poignantly reminds him of his wife, who too was equally learned.* There is a very delicate touch here. The playwright has eminently succeeded in bringing into sharp focus by his adroit handling of the Karṇāṭaka queen incident, the mental agony of Kālidāsa: he has met another learned lady but is unable to meet his equally learned wife, he does not even know whether she is alive or not. In anguish, he cries out :

हा हन्त ! ममापि दयिता विद्यावती तथैव गुणशालिनी । न जानामि सा नामशेषा जाता न वेति ।

The popular anecdote of Kālidāsa having a lady-gardener friend, Mālinī, to whom he used to recite his poems and otherwise discuss poetry with her, being a true connoisseur, finds a place in the play, in line with the style of the playwright, as mentioned earlier, of introducing into his work everything connected with Kālidāsa. The Mālinī, also called Mālatī in the work, plays an important part. Assuming the form of a demoness, Rākṣasī, she gatecrashes into the court, scares everybody, mentions a riddle, asks for its solution and points out *inter alia* that none other than Kālidāsa can solve it, thereby putting everybody on top gear in search of him (Kālidāsa). This is an originality *par excellence*

1. p. 187.

of the playwright. In no other play on Kālidāsa, has this role been visualized for her. She is so devoted to the poet that she can take recourse to any means to help him even if it spells grave personal risk for her.

The new minor characters that the playwright has introduced are : Vidyāvatī's friend Taḍillatā, the attendant Sudāsa, the spy Balāhaka and the lady forest-dweller, the Vanacarī, apart from, of course, the Vidūṣaka who provides good humour at places, particularly delightful being the following completion by him of the riddle— *nahi sukhaṁ duḥkhair vinā labhyate* :

घुद्धुत्काररवं निशासु तनुषे फूत्कारवत् क्लेशदं
थुत्कारं सहसे दिवान्यविहगाच्चीत्कारकृत् पेचक !
धान्यध्वंसिकुलं च हंसि यदहो रात्रीषु तद् विन्दसे
त्वं लक्ष्मीप्रियपक्षितां नहि सुखं दुःखैर्विना लभ्यते ॥[1]

"O owl, you produce *ghut, ghut* sound in the night which creates uneasiness like the sound *phut* during the day-time, you, crying aloud have to bear insult from other birds, during the nights you kill flocks of crows. Because of all this, you acquire the status of a bird loved by Lakṣmī. Happiness is not attained without suffering."

The chain of the onomatopoeic words as also the reference to owl cannot but force smiles on the faces of the readers or the spectators, more so when this *samasyāpūrti* is contrasted with that of Kālidāsa reproduced from elsewhere by the playwright :

श्लाघ्यं नीरसकाष्टताडनशतं श्लाघ्य: प्रचण्डातप:
श्लाघ्यं पङ्कविलेपनं पुनरिह श्लाघ्योऽतिदाहोऽनलै: ।
यत्कान्ताकुचकुम्भबाहुलतिकाहिल्लोललीलासुखं
लब्धं कुम्भवर त्वया नहि सुखं दुःखैर्विना लभ्यते ॥[2]

"It is good that you suffered hundreds of blows by dry wood, good that you have been exposed to the scorching sun, good that you were coated with a layer of mud, good again that you got well-burnt in fire since, O you good pitcher, you have attained the happiness of being waved in the tender arms and the pitcher-like breasts of the lovely damsels. Happiness is not attained without suffering."

1-2. p. 122.

The playwright does not depend upon the Vidūṣaka only for humour. He creates it even otherwise. The indistinct and incorrect pronunciation of Kūrmanātha who gives out his name as Kummanātha, his antics when Sudāsa, a royal servant comes to take him to the palace, all provoke laughter. Similarly the description of the mutual attraction of Kālidāsa and Vidyāvatī by Taḍillatā and Sudāsa makes one burst into spontaneous laughter :

तडिल्लता—मया प्रत्यक्षं दृष्टं होमकर्मादिकाले जामाता निर्णिमेषनयनो राजकन्यावदनं पानीयमिव पिपासुर्मुहुर्मुहुः पश्यन् स्थितः ।

सुदासः— मया पुनर्दृष्टं राजकन्यका ईषदवगुण्ठनमध्याद् जामातुर्मुखं मांसखण्डं बुभुक्षिता बन्धनगता शुनीव कुटिलकटाक्षैः पुनः प्रेक्षमाणा स्थितेति ।[1]

It can befit only the lower characters that they should go in for similes of water and bitch in reference to the bride and the bridegroom.

The language of the play is normally correct and idiomatic. It has a classical ring about it. It is only seldom that a questionable form meets the eyes, e.g., *Vidyāvatī—tattaṭe ca bhramaṇārtham ahaṁ jagāma.*[2] The use of Perfect with the first person pronoun jars on the ears even though the event is described to have taken place in dream. The use of the third person pronoun where more properly the possessive pronoun should have been used also looks peculiar; though it is common in the works of the Bengali Sanskrit writers; e.g.,

मदीयशरीरबन्धनं छित्वा मां तदङ्कमारोप्य[3]

for मां स्वाङ्कमारोप्य; मातः कृपामयि देहि तव दर्शनम्[4]

for देहि स्वं दर्शनम्; भो वारिधर, भव मे दुर्दिनसुहृत् त्वदावरणमुन्मोच्य दर्शय

for स्वावरणमुन्मोच्य दर्शय; बला0—तामुपवेशय त्वदीयकुटीरमध्ये,

for स्वकीयकुटीरमध्ये[5]

Occasionally the use of the tense looks improper, e.g., *Sakhī—nānuśayabhājanaṁ bhūyāḥ.*[6] Here the friend is using *āśirliṅ* for the Princess. Occasionally the influence of vernacular peeps out or else how can such words or expressions as mentioned below be justified :

---

1. p. 47
2. p. 76.
3. p. 76.
4. p. 79.
5. p. 185.
6. p. 78.

मनोनीता,[1] मया एताभ्यामेवाक्षिभ्यां[2] दृष्टम्, उत्तिष्ठ मम स्कन्धम्,[3] विदूषकः गिह्रासननिम्ने स्वशरीरं निह्नुते ।[4]

Since the work is on Kālidāsa it was inconceivable that an expression or a phrase or two here and there should not creep into it :

विद्यावती -- नाहं तृणच्छन्नकूपोपमस्य प्रतारकस्य सहधर्मचारिणी भवेयम् ।[5]

cp. शाकुन्तल—क इदानीमन्यो धर्मकञ्चुकप्रवेशिनः तृणच्छन्नकूपोपमस्य तवानुकृतिं प्रतिपत्स्यते ।[6]

In line with the above are the lines from the Kālidāsan verses, some of them with some alterations.

कालिदासः—(Describing the emaciated Vidyāvatī after a chance meeting with her on the banks of the Narmadā) :

(1) तन्वी श्यामा रुचिरवदनाम्भोजकान्तिं दधाना
मध्ये क्षामा नयनकमलप्रापिकर्णावतंसा ।
कम्रौ बाहू विटपललितौ बिभ्रती शुभ्रदन्त-
ज्योत्स्नास्नाताधरपुटदला सैव कान्तास्मदीया ॥[7]

cp. *The Meghadūta* verse :

तन्वी श्यामा शिखरिदशना पक्वबिम्बाधरोष्ठी
मध्ये क्षामा चकितहरिणीप्रेक्षणा निम्ननाभिः ।
श्रेणीभारादलसगमना स्तोकनम्रा स्तनाभ्यां
या तत्र स्याद्युवतिविषये सृष्टिराद्येव धातुः ॥[8]

(2) प्रवर्ततां प्रकृतिहिताय पार्थिवः
पतिव्रता जयति जगत्सुपूजिता ।
सरस्वती श्रुतिमहती महीयतां
न हीयतां कविकुलकर्म शर्मदम् ॥[9]

cp. *Śākuntala* verse

प्रवर्ततां प्रकृतिहिताय पार्थिवः
सरस्वती श्रुतिमहती महीयताम् ।
ममापि च क्षपयतु नीललोहितः
पुनर्भवं परिगतशक्तिरात्मभूः ॥[10]

1. p. 41.
2. p. 48.
3. p. 49.
4. p. 126.
5. p. 78.
6. Immediately before verse 23
7. p. 85.
8. Uttaramegha, verse 22.
9. p. 258.
10. verse 35.

It is common with Bengalis to address any lady as mother may be she is one's own daughter. It was probably due to this that the playwright makes the Daśapura ruler address his daughter as मातर्विद्यावति[1] ।

One of the strong points of the play is its songs. Marked by rhyme and alliteration, they exude a peculiar charm. Lines from two or three of them are being reproduced below by way of illustration :

(1) जय जय विक्रमसूर
निजबलविक्रमदमितरिपुक्रम
विश्वजयक्षम शूर
नृपशतलालितललितकमलपद
वन्दनरतनतवन्दिजनोन्मद
भगवददूर ![2]

(2) नम नम नम गिरिराजम्
सुरनन्दन शिवसुन्दर सितकायम् ।
देवदारुनवश्यामलपल्लव
शोभितनिबिडनितम्बम् ।
भ्रङ्गविराजितमञ्जुलकूजित-
मुखरितविहगकदम्बम्
देवविलासनिकायम् ॥[3]

(3) एष एमि ननु यामि न दूरं
रचयन्निति वचनामृतपूरम् ।
शशधर इव घनजलधरलीनः
कथमसि सहसा दर्शनहीनः ?[4]

The play has a *stotra* too which Kālidāsa sings in praise of goddess Kālikā whom he has been trying all the while to propitiate. The playwright seems to have composed it in a mood of deep reverence and in a moment of rare emotional upsurge. There is a happy matching of sound and sense here, the sounds preeminently reflecting the throbbing of the heart from which they have burst forth straight. The *stotra*, one of the very best in modern Sanskrit poetry, bears nearly full reproduction here :

चलत्कपालकुण्डलां भजे नृमुण्डमण्डनाम् ।
प्रकाण्डविघ्नदानवप्रचण्डकर्मखण्डनाम् ॥

1. p. 50.
2. p. 119.
3. p. 184.
4. p. 187.

चिदम्बरां दिगम्बरां नवाम्बुवाहडम्बरा-
ञ्जनप्रभाविकस्वरां नमामि नित्यभास्वराम् ॥
सुधाकरास्यहास्यभृत् पदाब्जलास्यरङ्गिणी ।
प्रपञ्चमञ्चनर्तकी सदा नटेशसङ्गिनी ॥
सरिद्वनान्तपर्वतश्मशानभूमिपालिका ।
विभातु विश्वमातृका पुरो ममाद्य कालिका ॥[1]

The playwright not unoften permits himself high-flown poetry which reminds us of the ancient masters. As an instance may be mentioned the following which describes the early morning :

अमावस्याध्वान्तं प्रसरन्ति निजान्तं पिशुनय-
न्नदृष्टोऽपि प्राचीमरुणयति भानुः कररुचा ।
शनैश्चक्राम्यर्णी चलति विधुरा सा खगवधू-
र्दिशां हासोद्भासः स्फुटितकमलेषु प्रकटितः ॥[2]

"The darkness of the fourteenth night of the lunar fortnight spreads indicating its end; the sun even though it is not within sight makes the eastern quarter pink by the light of its rays; the separated Cakravākī slowly goes near the Cakravāka; the laughter of the quarters has got itself reflected in the blooming lotuses."

The playwright has a knack of putting things in such a way that they go home straight. When Mālinī asks Kālidāsa to send a letter to Vidyāvatī, he says 'well, it is long, there has been no contact with her.' Will she be satisfied by a (mere) letter ? Is the unwatered earth tilled by mere talk of water (only) :

चिरादकृतसम्बन्धा लिप्या किं तृप्यते प्रिया ।
अदत्तसलिला भूः किं कृष्यते जलवार्तया ॥[3]

The critique on the *Mahākavikālidāsām* will not be complete without a note on the character of Kālidāsa as depicted in it. Though a fool, he is shown here as a tender-hearted person. He may be slow in sense but not insensitive. That is why when Vidyāvatī insults him, he says :

मूक्खस्य (मूर्खस्य) किं पाणयो (प्रणयो) नात्ति (नास्ति) । मानावमानचेतना नात्ति । धिग् धिङ् माम् । मरणमत्तु (मस्तु) ।[4]

1. p. 80
2. p. 83.
3. p. 118
4. p. 79

(Does a fool not have a feeling of love ? the feeling of insult or honour ? Fie upon me.)
Dullwitted, he is aware of the fact that a wife should be devoted to a husband. Very pointedly he says : *kim vidyayā yā patibhakhim na dadāti*; what has one to do with that learning which does not inculcate attachment to a husband ? These words uttered in writhing anguish pierce the heart of even Vidyāvatī, the high-minded lady. Says she :

> किं विद्यया या पतिभक्तिं न ददातीति मूर्खस्यापि वागियं शल्यवन् मथ्नाति मे हृदयम् ।[1]

Though rejected by Vidyāvatī, Kālidāsa bears no illwill for her. He is often lost in her thoughts. The play depicts Kālidāsa as a loving and a devoted husband, a true friend and an affectionate companion. He comes into an intimate contact with the lady gardener, *mālinī*. There is no touch of sensuousness in his love for her. He looks upon her as his sister. King Vikramāditya therefore rightly terms him as the very jewel of his court and the one to be treated as such : *Mahā - na ratnāymano ratnamaeva pariṣadaḥ*[2] and is appointed by him as one of the members of the assembly of nine jewels :

कालिदासः -- महाराजा मां तदीयनवरत्नसभायाः पारिषदपदे वरयन् मामतीवानुगृहीतवान्[3]

and confers on him the title of *mahākavi*. *Maha—Mahākavīty upādhinā satkartavyaḥ Kālidāsaḥ.*[4]

The play strictly follows the dramaturgical rules. It has all the three types of plots, the Sūcya, the Śravya and the Dṛśya or Unmeya. The Sūcya type is represented by the Viṣkambhakas both Śuddha and and Saṁkīrṇa, in the beginning of Acts I, II and IV and Aṅkāvatāra, termed Aṅkāviṣāvatāra in the play in Act IV, the Śravya in the conversation between the characters and the Dṛśya or Unmeya in *janāntikam*,[5] *svagatam*[6], *prakāśam*[7] etc. It records all the three types of acting the *angia*, *the vācika and the āhārya* :

आङ्गिक : कूर्म० -- इत्यङ्गुलिचालनं नाटयति[8]
नरेन्द्रः -- कूर्मनाथं करे धृत्वा[9]
कालि० -- क्षणं मुद्रितनयनो ध्यायन्[10]

---

1. p. 79.
2. p. 126.
3. p. 117
4. p. 124
5 & 6. p. 42
7. p. 43, p. 120.
8. p. 38.
9. p. 50.
10. p. 80.

विद्या० -- नयने उन्मील्य[1]

वर० -- मुखं परावर्त्य[2]

विद्या० -- इति बाहुभ्यां चरणे वेष्ठयति[3]

वाचिक — कालि० -- स्तौति[4]

,, (उच्चैः) अस्ति कश्चिद्वाग्विशेषः[5]

आहार्य -- सर्वे भयं नाटयन्ति[6]

Of the five types of Prastāvanā the play has probably the Avalagita type though it does not strictly answer that. Of the two types of Avalagita (i) a simple introduction of a character and (ii) the introduction of a character by making some point of similarity between the introducer and the character or characters introduced it is the second which comes the closest to the one found in the play. The last verse of the Sūtradhāra which introduces the characters, the three Princes, expresses similarity between the audience and the characters and not between the Sūtradhāra and the characters :

सूत्र०—गीतेनानेन ते कान्ते तरुणेन जडात्मना ।
कुमारा इव नः सभ्या लम्भिता हृदयोत्सवम् ॥[7]

The playwright meticulously follows the five Sandhis in his work the style of which appears to be Pāñcālī an admixture of Vaidarbhī and Gauḍī. It has short and easy sentences in prose and long sentences marked by compounds and excessive alliteration in verse, more particularly, the songs.

Altogether the play leaves a very happy impression on the mind. The playwright has eminently succeeded in achieving the real purpose of a play as enunciated by Kālidāsa :

नाट्यं भिन्नरुचेर्जनस्य बहुधाऽप्येकं समाराधनम् ।[8]

---

1. p. 85.
2. p. 120.
3. p. 85.
4. p. 80.
5. p. 83.
6. p. 126.
7. Prastāvana, p. 37.
8. Malavikāgnimitra, I, 4

6

KAVIKĀLIDĀSAM

Written by Dr. B.K. Bhattacharya, I.A.S., it was published from Calcutta in Śaka year 1890 or A.D. 1968.

It is rather a curious coincidence that the two plays on Kālidāsa, the *Kālidāsacaritam* and the *Kavikālidāsam* were written by administrators who carried on their literary work alongwith their heavy administrative duties. Dr. Bhattacharya was the Chairman of the three State Transport Undertakings of West Bengal at the time he wrote the play, while Sri Velankar was the Post Master General of Bhopal. Both these celebrities have shown by their example that no amount of official duties or lack of literary or intellectual environment can come in the way of production of literary works provided there is the will to do that.

The main motivating force for Bhattacharya to compose his play, as he himself expresses it in the Preface to it, was 'to convey an idea of Kālidāsa's literary virtues'. He has spurned the myths clustering round Kālidāsa's name. He cannot persuade himself to believe in the time-worn traditional account of Kālidāsa, "a simpleton originally, acquiring learning through goddess Kālī." He leaves no one in doubt on this score when he says in as *categorical* terms as possible that he wholeheartedly agrees with those who declare that the various legends are apocryphal and that the man who was thoroughly versed in grammar, rhetoric, prosody, astronomy, geography, scriptural literature as well as philosophy could not have become learned overnight due to a semi-miracle. The plot of the play is based on pure imagination. The imagination is, however, based on the account of the poet sustainable historically, an account based more on probabilities than on myths as the conversation between the Naṭī and the Sūtradhāra would bear out :

नटी :—अहो मन्दभाग्यमस्माकं यन्महाकवेरितिहाससम्मतं जीवनचरितं नास्ति एकमपि ।
सूत्रधार :— अतो नवीनकविना स्वकपोलकल्पितं जीवनालेख्यमङ्कितम् ।
परन्तु तेन किंवदन्तीः परिहाय सम्भाव्यतैव समाश्रिता ।

The play opens with the scene of Kālidāsa proceeding to the court of Vikramāditya in search of livelihood. Sarasvatī, the goddess of learning, has asked him to compose beautiful poetry but he is unable to do so due to his abject poverty. He has heard that Vikramāditya helps the learned. So he is going to him. On the way he meets a young Brahmin Vararuci who is also going to Vikramāditya for the same purpose. Both Kālidāsa and Vararuci pick up conversation and make friends with each other. Both indulge in mutual praise, with which ends the first Act.

The next Act introduces King Vikramāditya on the throne in the company of his daughter and courtiers. He tells the learned assembly that he has seven jewels in his court. If only three more were to be added to them, they would, being ten in number, symbolize the ten quarters. Varāhamihira, the astrologer and one of the jewels of Vikramāditya's court, at this tells him that instead of the three only two would suffice, the King himself serving as the tenth one like the nine constellations, Nakṣatras, with the sun in the middle. He further tells him that astrologically his period is favourable and that he should be able to secure the other two jewels before long. Mañjubhāṣiṇī, the King's daughter, supports his words. As the conversation is on, Kālidāsa and Vararuci enter the court. After introducing themselves, they recite their compositions. The King is extremely pleased with them, especially with the poetic compositions of Kālidāsa which whet his appetite for listening to poetry. He asks all of his jewels to come out with their compositions one by one which they do, though all of them are not poets. After they have finished, Vikramāditya nominates Kālidāsa and Vararuci as his two new jewels. Thus his desire of having nine jewels in his court is fulfilled.

In the third Act Mañjubhāṣīṇī is shown reciting something. She has obtained permission from her father for learning to compose poetry from Kālidāsa. She regrets that she has not been able to acquire the requisite proficiency in it even after three years. She feels that she may do so by going through the master-poet's compositions. Kālidāsa is going on with his *Ṛtusaṁhāra*. She then recites a verse from it. Just then drops in a friend of her, Kasturikā, who cuts many a joke at her expense, also hinting at the love that the Princess has developed for Kālidāsa. After she (Kasturikā) leaves, enters Kālidāsa. He tells her (Mañjusbhāṣiṇī) that he is now writing the description of the spring season. Mañjubhaṣiṇī expresses her great satisfaction at his description of the rainy season which she says, excels even that of Vālmikī. Kālidāsa has great admiration for his predecessor and does not agree with her in this. He then tells her that the *Ṛtusaṁhāra* is almost over and that his next compositon is going to be the *Kumārasambhava* which includes in the title the reference, though covert, to Kumāra, the brother of Mañjubhāṣiṇī. On a query from her he tells her that the *Vikramorvaśiya* which he would take up subsequently will perpetuate her father's memory. He further informs her that he has decided to compose a poem under the title *Raghuvaṁśa* to commemorate the victories of Raghu, her father and grand father. He is, however, sad at the news of the Svayaṁvara of Mañjubhāṣiṇī announced by Vikramāditya. To him, Mañjubhāṣiṇī is a source of inspiration. He cannot write poetry if she is away from her. At this Mañjubhāṣiṇī tells him that she will keep away from the Svayaṁvara and that, if her father agrees, her sister Mandālikā who is equally young and attractive will go to the Svayaṁvara-sabhā. Kālidāsa feels greatly relieved at this. Just at that moment enters the King. Mañjubhāṣiṇī apprises him also of this resolve of her. The King is furious at this. He feels that Kālidāsa has betrayed his trust. He has enticed his daughter though he was asked only to teach her poetic composition. He orders his externment from his kingdom for a period of one year. Mañjubhāṣiṇī first cries instinctively but then consoles herself with the thought that for her the time for firm resolve and hard penance has come and that it does not become her to give way to nervousness. She sings a song to beguile her time and with it closes the Act.

In the Fourth Act, Kālidāsa is shown sitting in a Rāmagiri hermitage. Eight months of his exile are over. Being away from the din and turmoil of Ujjayinī, he has got time enough for his literary pursuits. He has almost finished the *Kumārasambhava*. Lost in self-introspection, he is ruminating over his rather uninhibited description of the love of the Divine Couple, Pārvatī and Śiva in the *Kumārasambhava*. He has described their love after the manner of the humans. How can human imagination go beyond the ways of the humans, argues he. He is convinced that in spite of his misgivings the *Kumārasambhava* would please the Primeval Parents.

In his exile Kālidāsa is accompanied by his devoted friend

Vararuci who looks after him in all possible ways engaging him at times in interesting conversation. While talking to him Kālidāsa happens to look at a cloud clinging to the peak of a mountain. Hardly is he able to control his emotions at this. He addresses him and makes an offering of fresh Kuṭaja flowers to him. Lost in his thoughts, he recites a couple of verses by way of a message to his beloved at Ujjayinī which he asks him to carry to her. He tells Vararuci that he had forgotten all about himself and his surroundings and was talking to his beloved through verses in Mandākrāntā metre having reached Ujjayinī mentally. Vararuci asks him to compose a full poem in Mandākrāntā metre to which Kālidāsa readily agrees. Vararuci leaves at this and Sānumatī enters. The simple forest-dweller had developed love for Kālidāsa during her frequent contacts with him. When Kālidāsa tells her that he would be composing a poem where he would give expression to the pangs of separation suffered, the realization dawns on her that he does not reciprocate her love and that he is in love with another lady. She feels let down. She is painfully reminded of some of the earlier incidents which she had mistaken as indications of the developing feeling of love for her in Kālidāsa. Kālidāsa protests his total innocence though he feels sad at his actions. As dejected and forlorn Sanumatī leaves, his thoughts revert to Mañjubhāṣiṇī. He recites a verse (which occurs in his *Meghadūta*) and leaves the stage.

The Fifth Act introduces King Vikramāditya in his court. He is unhappy at Kālidāsa's exile and Vararuci's absence. His jewels advise him to go out on Digvijaya to beguile himself. He agrees and orders his Commander-in-chief to take up necessary preparations in that regard. Vetālabhaṭṭa, one of the jewels, suggests that after the King attains victory he may perform the Aśvamedha sacrifice. At this enters Vararuci who conveys the news of Kālidāsa's return to Ujjayinī though at his (Kālidāsa's) very behest he refuses to disclose his whereabouts in spite of persistent queries from the King who does not want to waste even a moment to meet him. The only information that he parts with, much to the annoyance of the King, is that he is staying in a hamlet of a lady gardener at Ujjayinī. He is completely lost in composing poetry. He has completed the *Meghadūta* and is busy composing the *Kumārasambhava* which he would not bring to completion because of the adverse criticism of her lady gardener friend at the free and uninhibited description of the love of the Divine Couple. He has also composed the play, the *Vikramorvaśīya,* where he has described the love of Urvaśī and Purūravas. The explanation that Kālidāsa has remembered his patron in the *Vikramorvaśīya* by using the word Vikrama in the title of his play, the *Vikramorvaśīya*, though there is no character of this name in it, makes the King highly sad and penitent at Kālidāsa's magnanimity in the face of his own harshness. At this stage enters the princess Mañjubhāṣiṇī. Noticing Vararuci's presence she enquires from him the whereabouts of Kālidāsa. Vararuci informs her that he is staying in the house of a lady gardener Puṣpitāgrā. The King tells her that henceforth there would he no bar to her meeting her sweetheart. He tells her that both of them, Kālidāsa and Mañjubhāṣiṇī, would be married soon. Bashful Mañjubhāṣiṇī withdraws at this. After a humorous interlude between the king, the jester and some of the jewels which does not add in any way to the story, the Act comes to an end.

The Sixth Act that follows is introduced in the play in the form of a conversation between some of the citizens of Ujjayinī whose names are given there as Kārtika, Gaṇeṣa, Phālgunī and Vāsava. They are joined towards the end by Vararuci and Puṣpitāgrā, the lady gerdener, in whose hamlet Kālidāsa had stayed incognito for some time after his return from Rāmagiri and with whom he had daily sessions for discussing poetry. The citizens' conversation reveals many an incident that has taken place in Ujjayinī with reference to Kālidāsa and Vikramāditya. Kālidāsa has been married to Mañjubhaṣiṇī, their marriage having been celebrated with great fanfare. Even after two years people remember nostalgically the decoration of the city and the singing and the dancing that had accompanied the happy event. Kālidāsa has composed a new play the *Abhijñānaśākuntala* which is considered his life and soul, though there is doubt among people as to which of his works the *Abhijñānaśākuntala*, a later composition and the *Meghaduta* composed at the time of his exile earlier is greater. There is also discussion between two of the citizens about the impropriety of the protrayal in the *Kumārasāmbhava* of free and uninhibited love of the Divine Couple. Vāsava, one of the citizens, gives a fitting reply to Phālgunī, the other citizen who refers to it. The conversation then switches over to the news of the exploits of King Vikramāditya who is away on Digvijaya. It is also given out that Kālidāsa is describing them through the description of the exploits of Raghu in his *Raghuvaṁsa* which he has started composing. The citizens quote from this work verse after verse in connection with the victories of Vikramāditya over the Baṅgas, Kaliṅgas Pāṇḍyas, Keralas and the Yavanas (though these verses are given in the *Raghuvaṁśa*, in connection with the victories of Raghu). Kārtika, one of the citizens, is sure that King Vikramāditya, on his return will get equal happiness, from the Digvijaya as also the *Raghuvaṁśa*.

Gaṇeśa, another citizen, tells Vararuci, who has joined them now that Kālidāsa is busy writing poetry day and night. Kārtika informs him that there has been no trouble in Mālava during the King's absence. There was some locust invasion on fields but that was brought under control thanks to the efforts of the agricultural experts. Puṣpitāgrā enters at this. An interesting conversation ensues with her. She then leaves for the King's harem. Kārtika also leaves for some work. The other citizens depart to witness a wrestling match being held in the capital's stadium. The Act at this comes to a close.

The Seventh and the last Act is introduced with Mañjubhaṣiṇī singing a song. Kālidāsa enters at this and tells her that like Duṣyanta he has been carried away by her song. An interesting conversation follows this. Mañjubhāṣinī tells him smilingly that she is neither a wild fawn nor a Śakuntalā. She is the daughter of an emperor living in a harem. Kālidāsa says at this that what confounded him was the sadness of the song though it was sweet otherwise. Mañjubhāṣinī asks Kālidāsa as to what for he has come to the harem at a rather odd time. His reply is that who would care for time, odd or otherwise. *lāvaṇyam ākorsayati rasajñaṁ rātrau ca divā ca praṇayaraśminā.*[1] (Charm pulls towards it with the rein of love day and night one who appreciates beauty). Well, he has to tell her something in particular : *asti me kaścid vagviśesaḥ.*[2] Mañjubhāṣiṇī at this remarks that she knows as to how he has won fame as an inventor of riddles. Well, like the word *kaścit* he has obliquely hinted at the composition, the *Meghadūta* beginning with *kaścit.* Kālidāsa taking up the thread futher says that the Kāvya beginning with *vāk* is almost complete. His three Kāvyas convey something that is ordinary. Something special to be conveyed is in his mind only. Mañjubhāṣiṇī then enquires from him as to what new poem he would compose after his completion of the *Raghuvaṁśa.* Kālidāsa says that he would not like to compose a Kāvya after that. Let the *Raghuvaṁśa* remain without a second, *advitīya.* Mañjubhāṣiṇī says at this that the *Raghuvaṁśa* may well be his best poem but she likes most the *Meghadūtya,* the unique creation of his poetic genius. With a smile Kālidāsa replies that the worship offerings made to a deity may turn into some invaluable asset for him. With its unique capacity the worship of love turns the lover into a god and the beloved into a goddess. Mañjubhāṣiṇī, though pleased, feels embarrassed at this. She then switches on to a different topic. She enquires from Kālidāsa as to

1. p. 94. 2. *Ibid.*

whether he has composed a Yamaka Kāvya, called the *Nalodaya* during the exile and another Kāvya called the *Puṣpabāṇavilāsa*. Kālidāsa's reply is that these are the creations of some modern poets; there are many composers who are composing poems in his name with an eye on poetic fame. What a peculiar human instinct! People out to win fame would like to live even by the fame of others. At this the conversation between Mañjubhāṣiṇī and Kālidāsa switches on to Vararuci's poetry which Mañjubhāṣiṇī says has a special fascination for her. Kālidāsa also speaks well of it. Mañjubhāṣiṇī at this asks Kālidāsa the likely period of the return of her father from his victory expedition. Kālidāsa replies that according to his information the expedition is already over. The victorious King should be soon coming back to the capital. Hardly does he finish there enters the lady gardener Puṣpitāgrā. All the three. Kālidāsa Mañjubhāṣiṇī and Puṣpitāgrā then engage in an interesting conversation which is marked substantially by wit and humour. After she (Puṣpitāgrā) leaves enters Kasturikā. The same kind of interesting conversation is carried on with her too She also leaves soon. As soon as she is out, the return of the King and the Prince to the capital is announced. The King comes to the very place where Kālidāsa and Mañjubhāṣiṇī are talking to each other. He enquires in a lighter vein about Kālidāsa's poetic expedition. Mañjubhāṣiṇī informs him that his *Raghuvaṁśa* should be over soon. Kālidāsa says that in it he has described his (the King's) victory expedition in the form of that of Raghu. This extremely gratifies Vikramāditya. He says in the *Kumārasambhava* the poet has mentioned the name of his son, in the *Meghadūta* of his grand son Skanda and in the *Vikramorvaśīya* of his own self in the very title. Through Kālidāsa all of them would become immortalized. He expresses the desire to go through the *Raghuvaṁśa* in his (Kālidāsa's) and Mañjubhāṣiṇī's company. There is no grammatical error, involved figures of speech or be-end and all-endness of metres in his poems. He goes on like this with his eulogy of his poetic compositions which embarrasses Kālidāsa not a little He is grateful to the King and feels lucky in securing for himself his affection. Addressing Mañjubhāṣiṇī, the King says that she too is very lucky because of the love and the glory of her father. Mañjubhāṣiṇī fully agrees with him. She takes pride in being the daughter of a loving father and the wife and the pupil of a great poet. Then follows the Bharatavākya with which the play comes to an end.

Critical Appreciation

From what has been said above, it would be clear that the playwright has tried to raise the structure of his play only on some seminal material. He has rejected the popular stories connected with Kālidāsa The only old material he has drawn upon is that which connects Kālidāsa with King Vikramāditya pointing to his having been one of his nine jewels, *navaratnas*. The rest of the story is born purely of his imagination. There is no tradition of Kālidāsa's love for and marriage with Mañjubhāṣiṇī, the daughter of his patron, the King Vikramāditya. The other characters in the play like the Vidūṣaka, Kasturikā, Puṣpitāgrā, etc. are also imaginary. The various incidents like the chance-meeting of Kālidāsa and Vararuci and their proceeding together to the court of Vikramāditya, the recitation of a Śloka by each of the nine jewels, Mañjubhāṣiṇī's love for Kālidāsa and her refusal to appear at the Svayaṁvara, Kālidāsa's stay incognito in the house of a lady gardener Puṣpitāgrā are all figments of the fertile imagination of the playwright. It was this very imagination which again has enabled him to identify the Yakṣa of the *Meghadūta* with Kālidāsa and Raghu in the *Raghuvaṁśa* with King Vikramāditya. The playwright has so made out the story of the *Meghadūta* that he has given the go-bye to the Yakṣa and supplanted him by Kālidāsa, who described in the work his pangs of separation from his beloved Mañjubhāsiṇī because of his exile ordered by Vikramāditya in a fit of pique, charging him (Kālidāsa) with having enticed her (Vikramāditya's daughter). Similarly, the description in the *Raghuvaṁśa* of the Digvijaya is, according to him, an ingenious attempt on the part of the master-poet to describe the Digvijaya of Vikramāditya. Equally ingenious is his attempt to look for references to the King, his son and the grand-son in his works. The entire play is an attempt to bring out the poet in Kālidāsa. The plot is very weak. Verse after verse is rolled out in it. This over-profusion of verses cannot be explained away by the fact that the play is woven round Kālidāsa, the poet. The play cannot but leave an impression that it is a contrived thing, the naturalness not being its primary quality. Since the work is about Kālidāsa, it was but proper that all of his works should find mention in it but the way they have been put is hardly dramatic. Which work are you writing now, what is going to be your next work, this work is nearly over, etc. are the expressions used for introducing works. These expressions are likely to have little appeal for connoisseurs. True to form, the playwright has not forgotten some of the works attributed to Kālidāsā but considered by later researches as spurious. Books on the history of Sanskrit literature mention these as those written by later writers. But to make Kālidāsa say in the play the same thing looks very funny in the face of the fact that the playwright is writing a play where Kālidāsa himself is one of the characters :

कालिदास:—केनचित् अज्ञातनाम्ना अर्वाचीनेन रचितं नलोदयम् ।[1]

How can Kālidāsa say *arvācinena* ? The history book seems to have taken precedence over the playwright than the play, or even the commonsense. All told, the play, as far as the plot, the delineation of events and the dramatic effect are concerned, appears to be rather a mediocre attempt.

As for language, it is full of mistakes, grammatical or otherwise, e.g. विप्रयूनहि मेंधा,[2] for विप्रयूनोहि मेधा, कदाच for कदाचन (repeated a number of times), एषु रवेर्रश्चिषं प्रार्थये[3] for रवेर्रश्चिः प्रार्थये, नररूपस्य सवितुरादेशो मे शिरसि धार्यम् for आदेशो मे शिरसि धार्यः, उपालम्भसे[5] for उपालभसे, परन्तु मृगणाशब्देन[6] for मृगयाशब्देन, न शक्यामि प्रबोधवचनम् उच्चरितुम्[7] for न शक्नोमि प्रबोधवचनम् उच्चारयितुम्, चित्तं नितरां प्रीत्वा[8] for चित्तं नितरां प्रीणयित्वा, समूलघातं हन्यिष्यते[9] समूलघातं हनिष्यते, भवन्ति निलयानि[10] for भवन्ति निलयाः, मालवसैन्या विक्रमचालिताः[11] for मालवसैन्यानि विक्रमचालितानि ; etc. Occasionally the playwright permits himself non-Sanskrit-expressions too like *kāhinī* for *kāhini*, story, *pangpal*[12] (meaning not clear). Here and there analogical formations such as *tadṛśa* तदृश on the lines of *sadṛśa* सदृश also cross the eye. At quite a few places the construction lacks the Prasādaguṇa and is ambiguous, e.g.,

(1) विस्मयंतेऽङ्गो वित्तेश्वरस्य महती क्रूरता चित्तदीना
दृष्ट्वा महत्त्वं रिक्ताश्रितं चिरधृतो मालवानां नगर्याम् ।।[14]

(2) यथा कुसुमिता लता रमरुचा
हृदो नयनयोर्विभाति सुखदा ।[15]

The only radeeming feature of the play is its fairly good number of songs which are, by and large, racy and crisp. The author's originality is at its best here. He has invented a large number of new metres, as many as 57 of them, and used them in his play. On his own, he has provided names to them also like

1. p. 98.
2. p. 3.
3. p. 13.
4. p. 22.
5. p. 33.
6. p.46.
7. p. 49. Also sees imilar construction, p. 75.
8. p. 63.
9. p. 65.
10. p. 74.
11. p. 84.
12. p. 89.
13. p. 86.
14. p. 66.
15. p. 12.

विचित्रा, निर्माल्य, कल्लोलिनी, वेणुस्वन, शान्तयुति, मणिदीप, वप्रप्रभा, जलतरङ्ग, नीलाञ्जना, कलकण्ठी, सम्मादिनी, etc. Where the new metre had only a slight variation from the older one, a new name varying only in part from the name of the older one has been adopted, e.g., खञ्जक्रांता, शार्दूललसित, etc. At least two of the metres have somewhat a non-Sanskrit-like appearance, e.g., शुभेट्टणभा, Ranranīyata. The rest of them have all beautiful artistic names like :

चम्पककलिका, निर्झरिणी, मदालसा, लीलालास्य, शार्ङ्गनाद, क्रौञ्चीरुत, पम्पाप्लुत, रम्यचारिणी ।

The playwright is keenly conscious of his important contribution to this. He says clearly in the English Preface to his work : "After all, if Sanskrit is to continue to play its unique role in our cultural life, there are bound to be occasions for resorting to new metres and it would be no sacrilege to urge that our accredited prosodists have not said the last word on the subject."

The playwright, it must be said to his credit, is thoroughly imbued with the spirit of Kālidāsa. It appears he has read through his works again and again and fully digested them. It was, therefore, natural that in the course of his composition, words and expressions, prose-lines and verses of the master-poet should unconsciously appear at appropriate places. The playwright not unoften suitably alters them, giving a verse or a hemistitch of it prose garb or a prose line or a passage, a verse form or even otherwise changing a word or two here and there to suit the requirements of his play. He does the same with lines from other works too. The overall effect left on the mind is that of the spontaneous inflow of the lines or words or expressions from older works into that of his but occasionally one cannot help feeling that there is a deliberate effort to stud the work with them. A few instances of the words and expressions and lines from older works occurring in the work are :

(1) समप्राणः समस्वभावश्च सखा मत इति वदन्ति कवयः ।[1]

(2) विक्रम : विचित्रमेतद्यत् प्राकृतजनसेविता श्रीहीना वागेव प्रतिभासंस्कारमारकर्ती द्युतिं धत्ते काञ्चनसंसर्गात्काचमणिरिव [2]

(3) मञ्जुभाषिणी —तत्किञ्चिदपि रसात्मकं वाक्यं विरच्यताम् ।[3]

(4) वेतालभट्टः—अपि च पद्मरागाणाम् आकरे क्व जातु काचस्य सम्भवः स्यात् ।[4]

(5) कालिदासः—त्वं हि मे सचिवः सखीममा प्रियशिष्या च चारुकलाविधौ ।[5]

1. p. 13.
2. p. 14.
3. p. 16.
4. p. 19.
5. p. 34.

(6) मञ्जुभाषिणी:—भवत आशालता कल्पलतेव पर्याप्तपुष्पस्तबका भवतु।।[1]

(7) मञ्जुभाषिणी:—नाहं चापलप्रणोदिता ।[2]

(8) कालिदास:—वररुचे, पश्य पश्य, खलु वप्रक्रीडारतं प्रेक्षणीयगजमिव आश्लिष्टसानुम् अम्बुदम् ।[3]

(9) विक्रम:—कन्यके, किमर्थं वाचं न मिश्रयसि मद्वचंसि ? भूयिष्ठं विषयान्तरे निहितं मनस्ते भवेत् ।[4]

(10) विक्रम:- प्राणाधिके मा गम: कातरत्वम् ।[5]

(11) वासव:—नारुचिर: प्रयासोऽयं परन्तु अस्मिन् त्वदीय: स्थूलहस्तावलेपो मनाग् दृश्यते ।[6]

(12) कालिदास:—अहो सुमधुरं सुकण्ठीसङ्गीतम् । तवास्ति हारिणा गीतरागेण प्रसभंहृत: कवेश्छद्मना दुष्यन्त इव ।[7]

(13) कालिदास:—देवस्यैव दाक्षिण्येन कृतार्थोऽस्मि मन्द: कवियश: प्रार्थी प्रांशुलभ्ये फले उद्बाहुर्वामन इव गच्छेयमुपहास्यताम् ।[8]

Quite a few of the verses from the works of Kālidāsa have been reproduced in the play from the *Ṛtusaṁhāra*, from the *Meghadūtā*, from the *Rāghuvaṁśa* and so on. This was natural in a play pertaining to Kālidāsa.

The larger verses in the play do not generally have the natural flow and cannot be read through with effortless ease. The shorter verses, however, fare better in contrast, some of which, are indeed couched in a very happy expression. As illustrations may be mentioned the following few :

(1) राजन्यानां प्रमोदाय चार्तिनाशाय शर्मद: ।
विग्रहो नितरां श्रेयान् मृगयादेरिति स्मृत: ।।[9]

(2) स्वाधिकारप्रमत्तो य: शिक्षादानच्छलेन हि ।
मनोऽहरत्स्वशिष्याया: कुत्र तेन सम: शठ: ।।[10]

(3) तिलं तालीकरोत्येव छिद्रान्वेषी दुराशय: ।
परीवादेन गच्छन्ति सन्तोषं कुत्र चापरा: ।।[11]

In line with some of the modern plays the playwright has avoided Prakrit. Otherwise he has strictly followed the rules of Sanskrit dramaturgy.

1. p. 36.
2. p. 39.
3. p. 49.
4. p. 73.
5. ibid.
6. p. 80.
7. p. 94.
8. p. 106.

KAVIKULAKOKILAM

This Play in Ten Scenes on the life of Kālidāsa depicts the age-old legend of his having been a fool initially and having got poetic talent through divine grace. Its author, Dr. Mrs. Roma Chaudhuri has been described by the well-known savant Dr. Satkari Mookerji in his Preface to the play as "the greatest woman modern Sanskrit drama writer and a pioneer of the modern Sanskrit drama movement with as many as thirty Sanskrit dramas to her credit which have been staged all over India and also outside many times before appreciative audiences of thousands strong". It was published from the Pracyavani, the Institute of Oriental Learning, Calcutta in 1970. Even while in manuscript it was staged at the Kālidāsa Samāroha at Ujjain in 1967 where it had won the coveted Suvarṇakalaśa Award as the best drama production. The Pracyavani has its own drama troupe of amateurs drawn from different walks of life - teachers, administrators, students and so on.

Theme

The play opens with Kālidāsa's father Sadaśiva Nyāyavāgīśa singing an hymn in praise of dawn in Pauṇḍra, a village close to Ujjayinī after the traditional Prologue where the Stage Manager, after he had announced the title and the authorship of the play, was shown in a stage of high anxiety for arranging for the rather difficult role of the greatest of the poets, Kālidāsa, and his inadequacy in this regard and is assured by the Actress (Naṭī) to feel strong and not to lose heart in view of the full preparations in that connection. He is almost in ecstasy when Kālidāsa enters dancing, laughing and singing. He too sings the praise of dawn.

He is extremely happy. He tells his father, who asks as to why he is feeling so happy, that he has seen a big lotus in a small pond in a corner of the village. This is too ordinary a thing for the father. He can't understand as to why Kālidāsa should feel so excited about it. Kālidāsa, on the other hand, tells that there is every reason for him to feel happy. A seed covered in dark earth has got release-the smallest of the small seeds has grown into a big lotus. He further tells his father that every petal of the blooming lotus pulls him towards it and takes him to a celestial world. He wants for himself a place in the peaceful lap of the Mother Nature which is free from fear, free from restrictions. The father is all wonder at this abstruse talk. He is unable to make out as to whether it is indicative of good or bad. Just as he is busy with these thoughts rushes in a Pandit from the Pāṭhaśālā. Using the choicest of the invectives he asks Kālidāsa to come to the Pāṭhaśālā failing which he would kill him. He tells Kālidāsa's father that Kālidāsa had been absenting himself from the Pāṭhaśālā for more than a week and that he had not gone through even a single line of the texts and further that he had been engaging himself in quarrels and arguments with his class-fellows. He conveys to the stunned father that Kālidāsa is the most foolish, the most incapable and the most wicked of the students. On a query from the father, Kālidāsa confirms all this. The father asks him as to why he should be averse to studies. He replies that the Pandit's teaching produces a burning sensation in his ears and does not touch his heart. He ridicules the Pandit which further infuriates him to the point of telling his father that from that day onwards he stands expelled from the Pāṭhaśālā. He (Pandit) softens a little on a request from the father to allow him just a day to set things right. As the Pandit leaves, the father asks Kālidāsa sternly to be like other students and prosecute his studies with the Pandit. Kālidāsa flatly refuses to do so. He does not yield though pressed hard time and again. The angry father then orders him to be off from there and not to show his ugly face to him. Kālidāsa gets ready to leave for the world outside, to go to the abode of Mother Nature who he thinks is calling him out. At this crucial moment enters his mother. She pleads with her husband to be patient with the son who she feels needs to be brought round and not to be discarded. She requests him (her husband) to keep quiet and asks Kālidāsa to accompany her for a quiet talk. Kālidāsa agrees to this. He gets very emotional and agrees to do whatever she says.

The Second Scene is laid at noon in a garden adjoining the house of Kālidāsa's father. Enters Kālidāsa with a key in hand. An insolent fellow, he thinks himself a sovereign and not a slave of anybody, not even that of himself. He looks upon himself as Mahādeva, superior even to Mother Kālī. He is aware that people call him a fool, a bad person, beyond all control. But he cares a fig for all that. He certainly is not going to go to the Vidyālaya and listen to the crude words of the Pandit. He hears in the meantime his mother calling him to have bath and meals. He then suddenly remembers the promise that he had made to her. She at this enters the garden unable to wait even for a minute. It is getting very hot in the garden outside. Kālidāsa tells his mother that he is not going to attend the Vidyālaya even if it means courting the great sin of breaking the promise. He wants to go only to the Vidyālaya of Mother Nature where he has many subjects to learn. The mother feels absolutely bad at this and leaves in a huff followed by penitent Kālidāsa but soon she is beyond his reach Enters the stage his father with two gentlemen who complain that Kālidāsa had removed from the garden of one fruits and flowers from that of the other. Kālidāsa is not a bit sorry for this. His argument is that they are the property of Mother Nature who belongs to all in common. A thief is one who keeps it to himself. The gentlemen ridicule him for all his strange thoughts and threaten to report the matter to the Town-in-charge and have him put behind the bars. The father is all sorrow for this and does not know what is in store for him.

The Third Scene is laid in Kālidāsa's house. It is morning. Enters the saddened mother of Kālidāsa. She has lost her husband and has suddenly become helpless and penniless. As for her son Kālidāsa, he is uneducated, indolent, quarrelsome and unmanageable, moving about day and night from forest to forest and place to place totally unmindful of making a living for himself. Looking at her misfortune, she begins to cry. Enters Kālidāsa. He enquires of his mother as to why she be in cries. Addressing her as the pious one he tells her that even a drop of her warm tears can set the whole world on fire. The unhappy mother tells him that his sweet words can no longer soothe her; they no longer can provide clothing for her body. What she has seen till that time is public censure for him and sorrow and misery for herself. These words do touch Kālidāsa. He realises nevertheless that it is too late for him to do anything worthwhile—even to go in for education. The mother tells him that there is not even a grain in the house. Some arrangement for food will have to be made immediately. Kālidāsa asks her to wait for a while till he is back after doing the needful and rushes out. The distraught mother feels sorry for her harsh words for her son. She cannot figure out as to how he would manage food, clothing and other necessities of life and goes out crying.

There is a change of scene at this. The next scene is laid at noon in a dense forest. Bewildered Kālidāsa enters it running. He is unable to make out as to how he should procure a handful of rice. He is ready to do anything for this. Just at that time enters a wood-seller bent down with the weight of wood. On a query from Kālidāsa he tells him that the sale of wood is his ancestral profession. With this he supports his family. This gives an idea to Kālidāsa. He too wants to be a wood-seller and requests the man to show him the way the wood is cut. Finding him penniless, the wood-seller takes pity on him and offers him his own axe to cut wood, he having another one at his place. He invites him to his hut where after having rest he proposes to show him happily the way the wood is cut. Tearful Kālidāsa feels deeply obliged to him. Both of them, the wood-seller and Kālidāsa, then leave the stage.

There is further change of scene at this. Enters Kālidāsa the stage at noon weighed down with the weight of wood and feeling tired. Wood cutting needs good effort. He, however, is not averse to it. The earlier laziness has completely left him. His only regret is that he is chopping off with his axe the limbs of the trees, the watchmen of the Mother Village, with their branches spreading out far and wide. But he has no way out. His first duty is towards his impoverished mother who has not had food. He bows to the trees and asks their forgiveness for the injury he is inflicting on them. Suddenly begins to blow there breeze which soothes him. He feels much relieved and rejuvenated. He feels his whole body has had a touch of ambrosia. He tells Mother Nature that he feels defeated and captured. He would like to stay with her all the time. To hell with society and relatives. He closes his eyes and stands infatuated. Enter then two young men laughing loudly. They are out in search of firewood for picnic party which they have not been able to have so far. As they are about to give up, they happen to notice a wood-seller fast asleep. They prod him with a stick. When he is up, they find him to be no other than Kālidāsa, the son of the great Pandit Sadāśiva. To them it is a big joke that the son of the foremost of the scholars should have to turn into a wood-seller. Kālidāsa tells them that they should not behave with him like that. He is illiterate, a foolish person, with no help and support, a veritable blot on the family. Finding no other way he has taken to wood-cutting as profession. One of the two men tells him jokingly that there is a way for him. He should go and marry the learned daughter Vidyāvatī Kamalā of Māṇikyeśvarasiṁha, the ruler of Gauḍa, who intends marrying a great scholar. He suggests, in a lighthearted mood again, that he should present himself at her Svayaṁvarasabhā and ask for her hand. She would definitely select him. The other man also joins in the joke. As they depart, Kālidāsa laments his misfortune. He finds himself the object of ridicule for everybody. He tells Mother Nature that it was for her sake that he had left the Pāṭhaśālā. What has he got by offering himself to her? The Third Scene ends at this.

The Fourth Scene begins in the drawing room of the Princess. It is afternoon. Enters the stage the well-dressed arrogant Princess with her two friends Mālatīmālikā and Ālokalatikā. The Princess is unable to restrain her laughter at the previous day's incidents in the Svayaṁvarasabhā—how the foremost among the scholars were floored by her. While Mālatīmālikā joins in her laughter lauding her superiority over others, Ālokalatikā feels bad that the Princess should have misbehaved with scholars and showed so much of arrogance. Since there is going to be another session of the Svayaṁvarasabhā, it is yet another opportunity for the Princess for enjoyment. She invites Mālatīmālikā to accompany her. Ālokalatikā too does so out of a sense of duty. The curtain drops at this.

The next incident is shown in the Svayaṁvarasabhā. It is afternoon. Some anxious Kings and Pandits are shown seated representing among them the different strata of society affording the Princess a good choice. Each one of them is shown staking his claim to her forestalling the choice of the Princess for her likely fascination for the quality that he possesses, the quality which is evident from his very name. The Kings and the Pandits are : King Vipulavikrama who boasts of his valour and feels so sure of his success that he asks others to leave; Pandit Jñānamārtaṇḍa who on account of his scholarship feels sure to win the hand of the Princess knowing full well that she is looking for a scholar and not a hero; King Kuberakuñjara who is proud of his wealth and is confident that no woman can refuse it and Pandit Bhaktisudhākara who, boasting of his insight into the feminine mind, is certain to win her for himself, the women falling in just for devotion. As they start quarrelling and calling names to one another arrives the Princess Vidyāvatī Kamalā in the company of Mālatīmālikā carrying the garland for the bridegroom in a golden vessel and Ālokalatikā. The Princess asks every one of the suitors present to give his introduction himself in all humility, an account of his looks, qualities, wealth and position. She would then put certain questions to them. One not able to answer them will be instantly expelled from the assembly. Pointing a finger at Vipulavikrama and addressing him as a fat man, she asks him to start first. She makes fun of him when he getting nervous speaks haltingly. She asks him as to who is the bravest of all on the earth. Vipulavikrama saying that it is Bhīma, she ridicules him saying that it is tortoise who carries on it even the holy serpent Vāsuki who has on it the whole earth. She asks him to quit the Palace, there being no place therein for fools. Turning next to Jñānamārtaṇḍa she first makes fun of him at his feeble voice which is, according to her, in line with his feeble frame, and then asks him as to who is the most knowledgeable one on the earth. His mention of Yudhiṣṭhira gets a rebuff from her who points out that it is an ant which can move about freely on the earth, the water and the sky to gather news. Jñānamārtaṇḍa too has to go. It is now the turn of Kuberakuñjara. Addressed as one anointed with oil he is first ridiculed at his nervous speech which is not as soft as is his body. He is put the question as to who is the richest of all on the earth. She rebuts him when he says that it is Kubera and says that it is an insect who stays inside the earth which is the repository of all the wealth and turns him out also summarily. Turning to Bhaktisudhākara she tells him plainly that she is not for *bhakti*, devotion but for *jñāna*, knowledge the pursuit of which is the sole aim of her life. She asks him as to who is the best of the devotees on the earth. She ridicules his answer that it is Hanumān and says that it is a bunch of straw instead, that being always in a bending state. He too has to go out. The Princess laughs arrogantly at the success in humbling all the suitors. She is still unvanquished and unmatched in the world. This fills her with great delight and pride. The doorkeeper enters at this and, announcing the departure of the Princess, calls out to the rejected suitors who are angry and agitated at the insult meted out to them which they would now like to avenge. He advises them not to speak aloud lest it may interfere with their private discussion. He feels that due to the excessive pampering of the parents the Princess has turned arrogant, quarrelsome and of harsh speech and needs to be checked. Some way may have to be devised for this quickly. Jñānamārtaṇḍa of all gets up suddenly and says that the best way of avenging the insult would be to marry her to a confirmed fool. All others agree with him and go out in search of one.

The Fifth Scene is laid in the jungle around Kālidāsa's village. It is morning. Enters the stage Kālidāsa tired and exhausted. He is musing over his lot in that even though born of the family of great Pandits he has now turned into a wood-seller. He realizes that for this he has to blame only himself. For his love of Nature he did not attend school and is now illiterate and ignorant. He cuts short his thoughts and concentrates on selling the wood to arrange for necessary provisions. He notices a big tree in front, climbs up its branch and moving towards its forepart begins to cut it at its root. Enter just then Vipulavikrama and others. They had been on the move for long and failed to spot a real blockhead. As they talk among them Jñānamārtaṇḍa notices Kālidāsa cutting the very root of the branch on which he is perching. Every one feels satisfied that a big fool has at last been discovered. They call out to him to come down by tempting him to marry him to Vidyāvatī Kamalā who wants a learned person for her husband which he certainly is in his having discovered a novel method of cutting which he proudly asserts as his innovation. Kālidāsa is set athinking at this.

Maybe, he is being made fun of. Earlier too two young men had made fun of him and had said that he should marry the Princess. His ego hurt, he decides to marry the Princess to show that he can do so and is not an object to be played with. Vipulavikrama tells him that for the proposal that they have made to him he has only to act as they would like him to. With him signifying his assent the scene comes to an end.

The Sixth Scene is laid in the royal palace. It is morning. Emperor Māṇikyeśvarasiṁha is talking to the Queen. He is extremely worried about the marriage of his daughter. A number of Svayaṁvara assemblies have been held to which have come quite a few Kings and scholars but the Princess has chosen none of them. The Queen asks him not to worry. Destiny will take its own course. The Princess is far too much proud of her knowledge. She has no qualms in insulting even the best among scholars. Their curses would reduce the Palace to ashes. The Queen feels that it is time the Princess is curbed with a heavy hand. The King does not agree with her (the Queen). She is major now and is highly intelligent as also self-dependent. The Queen is in agreement with the King in this but is not able to make out as to the course to be adopted under the circumstances. As the talk is on, the doorkeeper announces the arrival of four respectable gentlemen together with a great Pandit seeking audience with the King. The sudden appearance of the great Pandit means, according to the King, the Lord has listened to his prayer. Feeling likewise the Queen thinks that the son-in-law is round the corner and that they would have him that very day. The gentlemen and the great Pandit are ushered in. Jñānamārtaṇḍa picks up the conversation. He tells the King that they have his well-being and that of his wife and daughter at heart. That is why they have brought with them a learned man as a suitor. Since the man keeps silent at the query of the King about his name and occupation, Vipulavikrama joins in to inform that that is the day of silence for the Pandit prefacing this information with the remark that the topmost of scholars don't pick up conversation with any and everybody any time. He gives out the name of the Pandit as Kālidāsa and says that he is the most respected of the scholars. Since the selection of the groom rests with the Princess, the King calls her in. She is upset, being disturbed in the midst of her deep study. She is surprised to see the very four men rejected by her earlier and informs her father accordingly who asks her to have a look instead at the fifth man who at the very first sight, on account of his unique divine handsomeness, thrills her, though she tries to control her feelings. She says that she would not accept any one as her husband without Śāstrārtha, disquisition. Vipulavikrama informs her that that being the day of his silence the scholar will have the disquisition with gestures. The Princess signifying her assent to this, the disquisition starts.

Addressing Kālidāsa as respected sir, she raises one finger. Pat raises Kālidāsa two fingers. Every one present appreciates this. Vipulavikrama asks Vidyāvatī, who has her face lowered now, to explain herself as to what she had meant by her one finger. She says that what she had meant was to convey the idea that the primary cause of the universe is Brahman. Vipulavikrama carrying on says that by raising the two fingers what Kālidāsa had meant was that the causes are two : Brahman and the Māyāśakti. Every one present proclaims Kālidāsa's victory. The Princess garlands him and the Scene comes to an end amidst all-round joy with the King offering profuse thanks to the four men who were instrumental in arranging the union of his daughter with a worthy husband.

The Seventh Scene is laid in the Palace bed-room. It is night. Enter worried Kālidāsa and bashful Vidyāvatī—both silent. Both are uneasy—Vidyāvatī because she does not know how her husband would talk to her in the honeymoon night and Kālidāsa because of his ill-luck in being placed in a situation when an illiterate person like him, a mere woodseller, comes to be taken by the Princess as the foremost among scholars. While the Princess finding Kālidāsa keeping silent thinks that he is busy solving a philosophical riddle and should not, therefore, be disturbed Kālidāsa rues his weakness and indiscretion in accepting the advice of the Pandits and commiting an unpardonable sin of cheating an innocent lady. Now that she is his wife, it is he who is to start the conversation. It is too much to expect the bashful bride to do that. Just to start, he asks the bride to take rest, now that she must be feeling tired. The sweet and sonorous voice of the groom pleases her the most. She asks him to start a philosophical talk which may serve as an introduction for them. Kālidāsa is simply scared at this and prays to Sarasvatī to appear on his tongue for a while to help him out of his predicament. In the meantime is heard the grunting of a camel. Vidyāvatī gets afraid at this hitherto unheard sound. Kālidāsa tells her that it is that of *uṭra*, camel. Startled, Vidyavati asks him to repeat the word. Kālidāsa does so in its form of *uṣṭa*. The cat is out of the bag for Vidyāvatī. She understands now that she has been cheated through the device of the vow of silence. Her misfortune has placed her in the hands of a blockhead who does not know how to pronounce even a common word like *uṣṭra* correctly. It cannot, however, force her to spend her life with him. At her query Kālidāsa tells her that he is a poor wood-seller, born in a Pandit family and not knowing even a word. While he was striking with his axe at the root of the very branch of the tree at which he was sitting, some gentlemen spotted him and brought him to the Svayaṁvara-sabhā by disguising him as a great

Pandit. That is all about him. The Princess now understands that it is the handiwork of the rejected suitors. They have avenged the insult. As for Kālidāsa, he feels extremely sorry and is stricken with remorse. He has now come to realize that it is a curse to resort to cheating in a matter like marriage. The enraged Princess tells him that there is no use in his asking for forgiveness. The marriage once solemnized cannot be set aside. She calls him names. All of a sudden, darkness descends on Kālidāsa's life. Vidyāvatī says that it is better to die than to cling to a dullard. This cuts Kālidāsa to the quick. He offers to die himself and solicits her permission to do so which she takes as a clever ruse to bring her round which is impossible with her now. She asks him not to show his face to her. Kālidāsa agrees to do that but prior to that he would like her to pardon him which she stoutly refuses even though approached by him again on the ground that in its absence he would continue to burn all his life in a big blaze which, according to her, is what he deserves. She orders him to get out from there in a second. Since Kālidāsa continues there weeping silently, she kicks him, though realizing after a while that she being an Indian woman has done in a fit of anger the most improper thing. She then starts to cry. Kālidāsa asks her not to do that. That is the most befitting reward for him—no punishment, but a reward. He rushes out then, the lone figure in the crowded world, a figure which had the misfortune of being kicked by the wife, to see whether the kick purifies life or not.

The Eighth Scene is laid in a Sarasvatīkuṇḍa, the pond named after Sarasvatī, in a thick jungle. It is night. Enters bewildered Kālidāsa. He is now back to Mother Nature whom he had left earlier for the Palace and for which he had come to the present pass. He blames himself for all that has taken place. The night that he is out happens to be that of Amāvasyā. An hitherto unseen beauty of Mother Nature appears before his eyes, the darkness, the stars, the sound of crickets. He bows to goddess Night and beseeches her to bestow on him peace. He then thinks of praying to Sarasvatī but does not know how to do it. He is ignorant, too small a man to do that. He prays to the Goddess to appear before him. He surrenders himself completely to her. His life is now at her disposal. Let her take it or discard it, or do with it as she pleases. Only she has to appear before him in whatever form she may choose—that of Durgā or Caṇḍikā. He would go on muttering her name and would not leave his seat till she appears. There is heard then the sound of the Vīṇā and the humming of the bees. Appears there suddenly Goddess Sarasvatī. Kālidāsa's joy knows no bounds at this. He does not want anything now—knowledge, contemplation, devotion, salvation, prosperity, divine power—nothing of the kind. The Goddess is pleased with his intense devotion and offers him a boon. There is nothing for Kālidāsa to ask for now. With the sight of the Goddess he has the total fulfilment. An interesting conversation ensues then between the Goddess and her devotee (Kālidāsa). The Goddess asks him whether he wants poetic talent or capability to write which Kālidāsa denies. He had only been longing to have a glimpse of her, says he. Feeling immensely pleased at this, Sarasvatī asks him to have a dip in the pond and bring to her quickly what he finds there. Kālidāsa does as asked and brings to her a lump of earth. The Goddess asks him to repeat the exercise. This time it is a ball of mud. The exercise is gone into the third time and this time it is two things, a lotus and a water lily, one with thorns and the other without them. Kālidāsa asks her as to which of the two she would prefer, a lotus with a hard stalk or a water lily with a soft stalk. On the Goddess saying that she would have both, Kālidāsa offers the former at her right foot and the latter at her left one. While enquiring of the preference of the Goddess, Kālidāsa had used the epithet 'the lotus-eyed one', *paṅkajanetre,* in the Vocative for the Goddess to which the Goddess takes objection, that being appropriate only for ordinary ladies and not the Goddess. She, however, explains it away in her benign manner as being due to the presence of the thoughts of his wife in his mind the only atonement for which, even though not a deliberate indiscretion, could be that he should be *kavikulakokila,* the cuckoo among poets. She blesses him to be the sweetest among the singers of poetry in the world. Overpowered with emotion Kālidāsa prays to the Goddess to stay in his silent voice, his tasteless tongue, his worthless pen to which she agrees saying that she would do whatever he wants.

The Ninth Scene is laid on a jungle path. It is morning. Enters Kālidāsa brimming with joy. What a surprise for him! First a kick from a wise lady and then the Great Blessing from Goddess Sarasvatī—a complete transformation in his life. Now every shrub, every flower bed, every ray of light, every hum of bees, every chirp of birds and every murmuring in the jungle brings in a new feeling in him. He has finished the worship of the divine Goddess of Speech. There is change of scene at this. The next scene is laid in the royal palace. It is morning still. Vidyāvatī is shown stricken with remorse and cursing herself for treating her husband in an inhuman manner. The Queen Mother consoles her. The spies are out all over to look for him. The King also advises her to have a little patience. He is sure that he (Kālidāsa) would be back before long. The Queen advises her not to harbour in her any more the pride of her learning. Remorse leads to penitence and that is the first step in the right direction. The Princess agrees with this. Suddenly is heard a knock at the door. The Princess is reluctant to receive anybody at that hour. The knock persists and is finally accompanied with the words *asti kaścid vāgviśeṣaḥ*, 'is there any improvement in speech' ? This has an electric effect. Thinking that her husband is back, the Princess opens the door. She stands speechless while beaming Kālidāsa steps in. She tells him that she had been thinking of him every minute. But before anything else, she wants all her sins to be forgiven. To Kālidāsa, what she had done to him is not a sin but a favour in that it had opened his eyes. She deserves to be called a teacher. He tells her of what had transpired some time back. Goddess Sarasvatī had said that he is going to be *kavikulakokila* which immensely pleases the Princess who considers herself really lucky in having such a husband She wants that with each of the four words that he had uttered, *asti kaścid vāgviśeṣaḥ*, the words that had opened the doors to their good fortune, he should compose four Kāvyas. Kālidāsa does that there and then and recites a stanza each from each of the Kāvyas, the *Kumārasambhava*, the *Meghadūta*, the *Raghuvaṁśa* and the *Ṛtusaṁhāra*. With charmed Vidyāvatī and happy Kālidāsa the Scene comes to an end.

The next Scene is laid in the Court of Emperor Vikramāditya. It is morning. Enters the Emperor with his Nine Jewels. He is extremely happy that he has nine celebrities with him : the physician Dhanvantari, the astronomer Varāhamihira, the philosopher Ghaṭakarpara, the poet (lit. rhetorician) Kālidāsa, the lexicographer Amarasiṁha, the grammarian Vararuci and the learned scholars Kṣapaṇaka, Śaṅku and Vetālabhaṭṭa, every one of whom is at pains to point out the superiority of his discipline over others. The judgement being left to Kālidāsa by the Emperor, he speaks of poetry being the best of the disciplines. Though all the different disciplines have one aim, they represent in them only the part and not the whole, which poetry alone does . The medical science only frees the mind and the body, astronomy only brings out the importance of the planets and constellations, grammar only increases the capacity to think. The Emperor is all appreciation for this line of Kālidāsa's thinking. Continuing Kālidāsa says that it is poetry which has a free access to all the fourteen worlds, is present everywhere, and is liked everywhere. Reality and imagination have equal importance in it. Imagination, though unreal, is not untrue. It thrills the whole being, from it flows forth a torrent of nectar. Everyone present is agog at Kālidāsa's adumbration of poetry's excellence. The Emperor confers on him the title of *Kavisārvabhauma* and says that he would be *kavikulakokila*. Kālidāsa feels lucky at the signal honour done to him and prays to Goddess Sarasvatī that he should justify his being *kavisārvabhauma* and *kavikulakokila*. He feels confident that with her blessing he would be able to unfold the immeasurable beauty underlying the universe torn by sins and afflictions, illusion and ignorance. The Emperor giving himself over to emotion says : 'Let this dream of yours come true'! Others present also join him in this and with this the Scene and also the play come to an end with the Bharatavākya by Kālidāsa.

Critical Appreciation

The kernel of the theme of the traditional narrative of Kālidāsa : a fool originally having been married deceitfully to a learned Princess who had vowed to marry only the man who would defeat her in disquisition, and gaining knowledge through divine grace, the present writer, has adopted at such but like many other present-day Sanskrit writers, dealing with it has introduced such innovations in the play as the exigency of carving a drama out of it demanded. Towards the close of the play she has brought in Vikramāditya as well with all his Navaratnas, Nine Jewels, another of the few narratives connected with Kālidāsa, thus trying to knit together two different narratives. She could have won encomiums for this if she had succeeded in establishing a link between the two. But as things stand, the two in the play just look disjointed. Upto Ninth Scene it is one narrative. In the Tenth it is suddenly another. Emperor Vikramāditya is brought in, it appears, just for the purpose of the conferment of the title *kavisārvabhauma* on Kālidāsa, as if the earlier one of *kavikulakokila* bestowed on him by Goddess Sarasvatī herself—from which the play derives its title—was not enough. It seems the playwright in her anxiety to present what she knows about Kālidāsa from the traditional accounts paid scant regard to dramatic justification for adding something which cannot but look an unnecessary padding.

As said earlier, the playwright has introduced many innovations in the traditional narratives. In the first one she has changed the name Vidyottamā of the traditional narrative to Vidyavatī Kamalā without any apparent justification. To her father she assigns the name Māṇikyeśvarasiṁha and makes him the ruler of Gauḍa, Bengal, which should agree with her feelings for her native place, she herself belonging to Bengal. Kālidāsa's father she makes a Naiyāyika carrying the title of Nyāyavāgīśa and assigns him the name Sadāśiva. She makes him a native of the village Pauṇḍra near Ujjayinī, again a concoction. The traditional narrative has it that quite a few of the Kings and Pandits were vanquished by the Princess in disquisition, some of whom avenged their defeat by arranging her marriage with a confirmed fool. The playwright, unlike the original narrative, gives their names, coining them in such a way as to go well with the speciality of each. The names are Vipulavikrama, Jñānamārtaṇḍa, Kuberakuñjara and Bhaktisudhākara, they being brave, wise, rich and devoted in the same order.

Ālokalatikā and Mālatīmalikā are again the fanciful names that the playwright assigns to the two girl friends of the Princess whom she introduces in her play, casting them each in a different mould, one a sycophant and the other a dissident, not appreciating the attitude of the Princess towards the learned scholars. The Queen is not assigned any name being called always Mahiṣī, the Queen. Nor is the mother of Kālidāsa who is always styled *Mātā*.

The originality of the playwright manifests itself in ample measure in many of the subsidiary episodes that she introduces in her play. They are Kālidāsa not attending the Pāṭhaśālā, the teacher making a complaint to the former's father and expelling him from it and the latter stubbornly refusing to attend it, Kālidāsa removing flowers and fruits from the gardens of two gentlemen, their getting angry at that and their reporting the matter to his father, the suitors at the Svayaṁvarasabhā quarrelling among themselves, each of them boasting that he would win the hand of the Princess, Kālidāsa meeting a wood-seller in a forest, his gifting away his axe to him and taking him to his place as also teaching him the art of wood-cutting and Vidyāvatī asking Kālidāsa to compose four Kāvyas taking a word each from the four words *asti kaścid vāgviśeṣaḥ* which he had uttered from outside the closed doors at which he had knocked after he had been blessed by Goddess Sarasvatī. In the second narrative the minor episode pertains to the discussion among Nine Jewels about the superiority of the discipline of each and Kālidāsa's nomination by Emperor Vikramāditya as the judge to decide the issue which he does in favour of his own, bringing round, with conclusive and convincing arguments, everybody else to his point of view and winning approbation for that.

The originality of the playwright is noticeable not only in episodes but also sometimes in detail, as for example, in the extreme handsomeness of Kālidāsa depicted by her which impresses even the haughty Princess at the very first sight :

विद्यावती (कालिदासं दृष्ट्वा स्वगतम्) अहो ! अपूर्वदिव्यकान्तिधरोऽयं जनः । दर्शनमात्रेणोद्वेल्लति सहसा मम मनः अनिर्वचनीयभावावेगेन [1]

The impression is so deep that at the very start of the disquisition, she addresses Kālidāsa as *mānyamahodaya*[2] which even the rejected suitors do not fail to mark :

विपुलविक्रमः—आश्चर्यम् ! न मा अस्मान् ईदृशसम्मानसूचक-सम्बोधनेनाहूतवती ।[3]

1. p. 47

2 & 3. p. 48

The major innovation of the playwright lies in the Goddess. She has changed Kālī of the original narrative to Sarasvatī in the present play. In making Kālī the Goddess to confer the boon, the original narrative was in all probability guided by the word Kālī in the name of the poet (Kālidāsa). By making Sarasvatī the Goddess to confer the boon, the playwright, it seems, was actuated by the consideration that for conferring knowledge it is Sarasvatī who could be better fitted than Kālī. It is precisely for this reason that Kālidāsa is made to go to the Sarasvatīkuṇḍa in a dense forest and not to the temple of Kālī as in the original narrative. Even there he is not inspired to pray by the image of Sarasvatī but does so through inner urge only. He approaches her with total dedication which makes the Goddess appear before him. In the original narrative the ignoramus in Kālidāsa on a query from the Goddess as to what he wants is able to utter in tears only the word Vidyā meaning thereby that Vidyottamā had misbehaved with him, in the present play the same ignoramus on a query from Sarasvatī says in a spirit of total devotion that he just does not want anything, having had the fulfilment with her sight only. In the original narrative it is incongruous that the omniscient Goddess should miss the true import of the words of Kālidāsa and misunderstand him in wanting *vidyā*, knowledge from her and granting it to him. In the play it is incongruous that an ignoramus like Kālidāsa should first think of Goddess Sarasvatī and then start praying to her, more so, to possess an elevated sense of not thinking of any mundane thing when face to face with her. The original narrative, everything said and done, has an element of naturalness in it which the touched-up narrative of the playwright lacks. The devotee in the playwright puts herself in place of Kālidāsa and makes him behave as she would have behaved if she ever could have the opportunity of seeing the Goddess in person. The entire bearing of Kālidāsa as described in the play does not go well with his description as an illiterate wood-seller. This includes the sense of discrimination in him in offering a soft lily to the left foot of the Goddess on the ground that the left portion in the case of women is superior to the right one and the lotus to the right foot. The same can well be said of Kālidāsa's reciting a beautiful verse even before he has been blessed with poetic talent by the Goddess. A full-length conversation between Kālidāsa and the Goddess has been included in the play by the playwright which is her innovation.

As has been stated earlier, the playwright has kept all the main strands of the original narrative intact. This includes Kālidāsa's cutting the same branch of the tree on which he was perching, an evidence *par excellence* of his foolishness. He had, therefore, to be depicted a big fool. This is what the playwright seeks to do but does not meet with much success. She has not been able to project that picture of Kālidāsa which may agree with his form of a total fool which he should be on the evidence of the incident as described above. Her Kālidāsa talks of high philosophy at times as when he mentions to his father that each petal of a lotus has a spontaneous attraction for him and that he does not want anything else in life except to find a quiet place in the lap of Mother Nature prompting the latter to comment :

कथं तरुणबालकस्य मुखे ईदृशी निगूढतत्त्वकथा ?

The playwright makes Kālidāsa a great lover of Nature who gets simply lost in it and who can read a message in the most subtle of its movements, something incompatible with a fool. The feelings surging in his mind after marrying the Princess also seem incompatible with his presentation of a total fool indulging in the most irrational behaviour of cutting the very branch to its root on which he is sitting. He is shown stricken with remorse for deceiving an innocent Princess. The incompatibility becomes much more pronounced when in the first night after marriage Kālidāsa is made to speak the following faultless words to the Princess :

भद्रे ! विश्रामं लभस्वात्र सुखेन । मन्ये श्रान्तक्लान्ता हि जाता त्वम् ।[2]

which elicit the following comment from the Princess ;

(स्वगतम्) अहो ! प्रसन्नगम्भीरो हि तस्य मनोहरः कण्ठस्वरः । श्रवणमात्रेण मनो मे नृत्यति सजलजलदमालावलोकनतृप्तमयूरवत् ।[3]

The same Kālidāsa a few minutes later is shown as not being able to speak even the simple word *uṣṭra.*

The playwright sometimes indulges in overdoing. The Princess getting disturbed at the grunting of a camel in the dead of the night is one thing but to show her as completely scared is another:

विद्यावती (भीता कम्पिता च) अहो अहो ! किमेतन्नाथ, किमेतत् ? ईदृशो विकटकर्कशो निनादो न मया श्रुतपूर्वः कदापि । वेपते मे हृदयम् । कम्पन्ते हस्तपादाः । घूर्णति च मस्तकम् ।[4]

Similarly, to show the Princess devoted to scholarly pursuits is one

1. p. 9.
2. p. 50.
3. p. 51.
4. *ibid.*

thing but to make her request her husband to talk of philosophy in the honeymoon night is another :

तत्र ममैका प्रार्थना अस्यामनिन्द्यानन्दनन्दितायां रजन्यां रजन्याम् — ब्रह्मतत्त्वमूलिका मधुरा दर्शनकथा तु भवत्वद्य मङ्गलमञ्जुलनिशीथे अस्माकं प्रथमपरिचयसूत्ररूपा ।[1]

This is carrying the love of letters a little too much. The playwright has made an ingenious alteration in the sequence of the words *asti kaścid vāgviśeṣaḥ*. In the traditional narrative it is the Princess' who utters them from behind the closed doors when Kālidāsa announces his arrival. In the present play it is Kālidāsa who utters them when the Princess, again from behind the closed doors, asks him, not knowing as to who he is, as he had been knocking persistently, as to what he has to do with her. It is from these words that she recognizes that it is Kālidāsa who is on the other side of the doors. In the drama context the words could mean : "There is something special to convey". That indeed is. Kālidāsa is to tell the Princess all that had transpired between him and the Goddess, which has completely transformed his life. This change has far greater appeal than the one in the original narrative.

As for the language of the play, it is generally grammatically correct. The style is racy and fluent, though more poetic. The same idea is conveyed generally in many different words, in different similes, different metaphors in quick succession. The playwright seems to be an highly emotional person and her emotion explodes at the slightest opportunity. A seed sprouting forth sends Kālidāsa into ecstasy. Says he :

कालिदासः (सहसा भावाविष्टः) — अन्धकारमृत्तिकाभ्यन्तरप्रोथितं बीजमद्य मुक्तिमलभत । चतुर्दिक्स्थकठिनकठोरवेष्टनीं भित्त्वा चतुर्दिक्स्थघनघोरतिमिरं छित्त्वा चतुर्दिक्स्थकृष्णकुटिलक्लेदं तीर्त्वा तत् क्षुद्रातिक्षुद्रं बीजमद्य परिणतं विशाले विपुले शतदले । पितः किं नैष परमानन्दजनकः संवादः ? परमाश्चर्यजनकं संघटनम् ? परमाशाव्यञ्जिका वार्ता च ।[2]

Kālidāsa in the forest is simply carried away by Nature. His words adequately reflect his feelings :

जननि, प्रकृतिजननि ! पराजितोऽहं बन्दीकृतश्च । ततः स्थास्याम्यत्रैव शाश्वतकालम् । दूरे यान्तु मम समाजपरिजनाः । तिष्ठतु केवलं मम प्रकृतिजननी मम मोहिनी मायाविनी पल्लीजननी — केवलं सा, केवलं सा, केवलं सा ।[3]

1. p. 51
2. p. 8.
3. p. 26.

Kālidāsa regretting his indiscretion at deceiving an innocent Princess and ruining her life compares his action with similar horrible ones, one by one :

पद्मवने मत्तकरिप्रवेशादपि भयानको हि ममान्यायप्रवेशस्तस्याः प्रज्ञाप्रसन्न जीवने, केलीकुञ्जे अशनिपातादपि कठोरो हि मम निष्ठुरनिपातस्तस्य। आनन्दरम्यजीवने, पूजाप्राङ्गणे धूलिकणस्थितेरप्यशुचिस्तस्याः पुण्यधन्ये जीवने मम कुटिलास्थितिः ।[1]

Kālidāsa's begging of forgiveness of Vidyāvatī gets the following rebuff from her which is sought to be made more forceful by just the repetition of words :

(सरोषम्) न न न, कदापि न, कदापि न, कदापि न । नाहं क्षमिष्ये त्वां क्षणमात्रमपि आजीवनम् । न न न, कदापि न, कदापि न, कदापि न ।[2]

The emotional explosion reaches its peak when Kalidasa prays to Sarasvatī, fully conscious of his inadequacy for the same :

किन्तु, किन्तु, मूर्खोऽहं मूढोऽहं क्षुद्रोऽहं तुच्छोऽहम्—न जाने मन्त्रं तन्त्रं वा, न जाने जपं तपो वा, न जानेऽर्चनं वन्दनं वा ।
निश्चितमहं पृथिव्या दीनतमो हीनतमः क्षुद्रतमस्तुच्छतमश्च जनः—
तृणादपि दीनतरः कीटादपि हीनतरः वालुककणादपि क्षुद्रतरः जलबुद्बुदादपि तुच्छतरः ।
तथापि अकारणकृपाकारिणि ! घोरपापितापितारिणि ! करालक्लेशक्लेदहारिणि ! जननि !
दयस्व मयि, दयस्व दयस्व; क्षमस्व मम सर्वापराधान्, क्षमस्व क्षमस्व. त्रायस्व मां
सङ्कीर्णसंसारात्, त्रायस्व त्रायस्व ।[3]

The play has a good sprinkling of nice stanzas, juicy and delectable. One of the men noticing Kālidāsa in the forest turned into a wood-seller praises him with the tongue in the cheek which for its felicity of expression has an appeal all its own :

ऊर्मिस्त्वमुत्तालतमो रसाम्बुधेः
प्रसन्नधारामृतनिर्झरस्य ।
पीयूषखण्डोऽमृतकुण्डवर्ती
क्व भूतले ते तुलनाऽखिले स्यात् ॥[4]

1. p. 54
2. p. 55
3. p. 58
4. pp. 27-8

The picture of Vidyāvatī's father worrying for her marriage is drawn very vividly by the playwright in the following stanza :

> कामं स्नेहास्पदमनुपमं कन्यकामातृपित्रो: ।
> कामं चिन्तास्पदमपि तयोराविवाहात्तथापि ।
> रक्षा यावन्न भवति दृढा तावदर्थोऽर्जितोऽपि
> चिन्ताभारं जनयति सतां जागती रीतिरेषा ॥[1]

The playwright has divided her play into Scenes, instead of into Acts. These Scenes with the changes of location in some are fairly long and can easily pass for Acts. It is difficult to explain as to why the playwright has adopted the above technique. Maybe, it was due to an urge to appear a little different from the established practice.

The play has instances of all the three types af acting : Āṅgika, Vācika and Āhārya.

आङ्गिक : (1) तत: प्रविशति बालक: कालिदास: नृत्यन् हसन् गायंश्च करतालिका-योगेन[2] (2) हस्तसंज्ञया बोधयति[3] (3) ललाटे कराघातं कृत्वा[4] (4) पश्चाद्धावन्[5] (5) काष्ठानि भूमौ निधाय कृताञ्जलि:[6] (6) काष्ठभारनत: कालिदास:[7] (7) नतमुखी[8] (8) अङ्गुल्या विपुलविक्रमं निर्दिश्य[9] (9) मूले स्थित्वा शाखाया अग्रभागं छिन्दन्[10] (10) एकामङ्गुलीं प्रदर्शयति[11] (11) मस्तककण्डूयनपर:[12] (12) वृक्षादवरोहति[13] (13) उत्थाय[14] (14) सहसा कालिदासस्य पदलुण्ठिता[15] (15) द्वारे पुन: कराघात:[16]

वाचिक : (1) सोपहासम्[17] (2) उपहासभरेण कालिदासमनुकृत्य[18] (3) क्षीणस्वरेण[19] (4) अनुकरोति[20] (5) प्रकाशम् उच्चै:[21] (6) बहि: सुगम्भीरस्वरेण[22]

आहार्य : साग्रहम्,[23] आश्वस्त:,[24] आश्चर्यान्वित:,[25] भावाविष्ट:,[26] सस्नेहम्,[27] चिन्तान्वित:[28],

---

1. p. 44.
2. p. 6.
3. p. 7.
4. p. 16.
5. p. 17.
6. p. 24.
7. p. 25.
8. pp. 29, 31, 66.
9. p. 33.
10. p. 40.
11. p. 48.
12. p. 34.
13. p. 42.
14. p. 90.
15. p. 67.
16. ibid.
17. pp. 10, 20.
18. p. 17.
19. p. 19
20. pp. 29, 30, 34.
21. p. 43.
22. p. 67.
23. pp. 2, 45, 55.
24. p. 3.
25. pp. 8, 23, 24.
26. p. 8.
27. ibid.
28. p. 9.

सावेगम्,[1] विस्मितः,[2] लज्जितः,[3] सक्रोधम्,[4] निर्भयः,[5] व्याकुलः,[6] कठोरः,[7] सरोषम्,[8] उद्धतः,[9] रुष्टा,[10] अधैर्या,[11] सगर्वम्,[12] गम्भीरा,[13] साहसभरेण,[14] सदम्भ,[15] सोल्लासम्[16] उत्तेजितः,[17] सानन्दम्,[18] हताशा,[19] सलज्जम्,[20] करुणाविगलितहृदयः,[21] विनीतो लज्जितश्च[22] आनन्दविह्वलः,[23]

The Prastāvanā of the play does not fit into any of the five varieties of it mentioned in the works on Rhetorics.

The ultimate objective of the play, as is clear from its title, is to show Kālidāsa acquire the capability of a great poet. As the theme stands, this acquisition is occasioned by the insult meted out to him by his newly-married haughty but scholarly Princess-wife who drives him to desperation and appeal to the Goddess of Learning who takes pity on him and blesses him with it. Princess's marriage with Kālidāsa is the key point, the seed, the Bīja, which leads to the final consummation of the acquisition of the poetic talent by the latter. Though it is difficult to rationalize the Sandhis in the play as it stands, it may well be pointed out that the seed of the plot is noticeable in the taunting remarks of the two gentlemen who run into Kālidāsa in a forest and notice him in having turned into a wood-seller, though son of the learned Pandit, a Nyāyavāgīśa. The gentlemen make fun of him by saying that he (Kālidāsa) is so intelligent that he should attend the Svayaṁvarasabhā of Vidyāvatī who is keen to marry a great scholar, to beg for her hand. This is the first reference, though jocularly made, to the possibility of Kālidāsā's marrying the Princess. This could be the Mukhasandhi. His discovery by the four rejected suitors and their persuading him to marry the Princess is the other such reference. This could be the Pratimukha Sandhi. The consummation of the marriage could be the Garbha Sandhi. Kālidāsa's insult by Vidyāvatī and his expulsion from the Palace in a hopeless condition and praying to Goddess, though not asking for anything at her

---

1. pp. 9, 63.
2. p. 9.
3. ibid.
4. ibid.
5. p. 10.
6. pp. 11, 16, 26, 51.
7. p. 10.
8. pp. 12, 13, 29, 32, 37, 54, 55.
9. p. 12.
10. p. 22.
11. p. 30.
12. p. 33.
13. p. 34.
14. pp. 35, 36.
15. p. 37.
16. p. 38, 39.
17. p. 41.
18. pp. 45, 49, 68, 74.
19. p. 47.
20. p. 49.
21. p. 51.
22. ibid.
23. p. 60.

sight even when prodded by her repeatedly which could have the possibility of the negation of the objective could be the Vimarśasandhi. The volunteering of the Goddess to bestow on Kālidāsa the capability of being the foremost of the poets, the *kavikulakokila*, getting pleased with his self-abnegating devotion could be the Nirvahaṇasandhi. This could be the order of the Sandhis as they peep out of the work.

As for the style, it is pleasant, though repetitive, as hinted at earlier. The author is in the habit of using the word *śrīla* in place of the usual *śrī*, also combining it at times with *śrīyukta* :

(1) श्रीलश्रीयुक्तमाणिक्येश्वरसिंहमहोदयस्य[1] (2) श्रीलश्रीयुक्ता विद्यावती कमला[2]
(3) अह्लयात्र श्रीलराजकन्याम्[3] (4) श्रीलकालिदासः न करोति वाक्यालापम्[4]
(5) श्रीलश्रीयुक्तकालिदासः[5] (6) श्रीलश्रीयुक्तविद्यावती कमला[6]

The language is generally correct. There are pitfalls, no doubt but mercifully only a few. These are the use of the word *gacchita* for *gata* in *gacchitadhanacauryāparadhalipto niścitam*, the use of *prakāṇḍa* in masculine in *paṇḍitaprakāṇḍāḥ* in violation of Amara's clear indication of its neuter gender : *prakaṇḍam udghatallajau* and the use of *siddhī* withī in *macchakti-siddhī mama sadhanā vā.*

Occasionally the vernacularism is noticeable in the work as

(1) निजापराधान् अन्येषां स्कन्धोपरि स्थापयितुं चेष्टसे ?[7]
(2) भवन्तः सर्वे केवलं प्रकृतिजनन्या भारप्राप्ताः सेवकाः[8]

The playwright has carved out a beautiful work of art from the time-honoured theme imparting to it enough of her originality and imprint, which do not fail to impress a discerning critic.

1. p. 28.
2. Ibid.
3. p. 46.
4. p. 47.
5. p. 48.
6. Ibid.
7. p. 19.
8. p. 20.

8

KĀLIDĀSAKĀVYASAMBHAVAM

A small work in three scenes by Shri Mathura Datt Pandey, it was published in Vol. XVI, Nos. 3-4, May-August, 1979 of the *Viśvasaṁskṛtam* of Hoshiarpur. As the title suggests, it traces the origin *(sambhava)* of the poem *(kāvya)* in the present instance, the *Meghadūta* of Kalidasa. It is based on a reference in Mallinātha's commentary on the *Meghadūta* in explanation of the dereliction of duty on the part of the Yakṣa, the duty being to gather fresh flowers every morning for Kubera's worship of Śiva. One day a bee appeared from one of the lotuses at sunrise and stung Kubera. This led to the Yakṣa being charged with dereliction of duty and being cursed by Kubera to undergo exile for a year. It was during the exile that the Yakṣa living in the Rāmagiri hills noticed a cloud clinging to the peak of, one of the hills in the month of Āṣāḍha, the beginning of the rainy season and decided to send a message through it to his beloved in far away Alakā high on the Himālayas.

Our playwright adopts the story as above as the theme of his play introducing into it certain changes, the most basic of which is that he makes Kubera the maternal uncle of Kālidāsa, calling him Kubera Sharma and the Megha (cloud) named Megharāja, his son. The beloved in this case is Mālinī, the gardener woman or could it be the river of that name personified as a woman, with whom, according to one of the traditions, Kālidāsa had an affair and to whom he would recite his poems to elicit her opinion on them, she being that expert a connoisseur.

The first scene of the play is laid in the house of Kubera Sharma. While he is offering a lotus to Śiva in the course of the morning worship, his finger is stung by a bee. He infers therefrom that Kālidāsa had gathered the flowers the previous evening. A bee in one of the lotuses would have got enclosed in it at sunset and appeared from it in its opening up at sunrise. He calls out Megharāja and asks him to convey to Kālidāsa his orders that he, Kālidāsa, should leave his (Kubera Sharma's) house immediately and not to show him his guilty face for one year. He spurns Megharāja's entreaties for withdrawal of these orders and sticks to his decision adding that that is the certain remedy for his infatuation for Mālinī which made him so neglectful and that either he should leave her and go abroad or she be married to someone else.

The Second Scene is laid on the banks of the river Alakā with the sky overcast. Mālinī is surprised to see Kālidāsa early morning. On her query he informs her that he had gathered the flowers for his maternal uncle's worship the previous evening itself, keeping himself free to be with her in the morning when the clouds would be on as inferred by him by the dancing of the peacocks, the jumping out on ground of the frogs and the southern breeze. It begins to rain in the meantime. The couple greets the first rainfall of the season with a song. The song over, Mālinī's friends appear. In a spirit of mirth and merriment, they go out and appears there Megharāja who conveys to Kālidāsa his maternal uncle's order telling him of the circumstances which had led to it and his desire to see him. Guilty Kālidāsa does not want to face his uncle. He does not want to leave immediately. Megharāja tells him that his mother has interceded on his behalf. He may not have to leave immediately. That may wait till the end of the rainy season. As for delimiting the period of exile to one year, Megharāja is able to convey only this much that his father did not spell out its reason. He only said that it would do good. He knows Kālidāsa's talent and his attachment to Mālinī. During this period the kings of the South would patronize him.

The Third and the last Scene is laid at the expiry of the period of the year on the Citrakūṭa hill where on the bank of the river Payoṣṇī, Kālidāsa is shown looking at the cloud. He remembers his being with Mālinī on the bank of the river Alakā on the appearance of the first cloud the previous rainy season. One memory follows the other as in a Kaleidoscope. With each one of it Kālidāsa writes a stanza, a reproduction from the *Meghadūta* and recites it. He remembers the warbling cātaka, the geese and the breeze while writing and reciting : *mandaṁ mandaṁ nudati pavanaś cānukūlo yathā tvām*, etc. He remembers Mālinī and writes as also recites *tanvī śyāmā śikharidaśanā* and so on till at the end of the remaining four months he could be with Mālinī once again. He writes and recites finally the stanza : *śāpānto me bhujagaśayanād utthite śārṅgapāṇau nirvekṣyāvaḥ pariṇataśaraccandrikāsu kṣapāsu*. With this the Scene is over and with it is the play.

Critical Appreciation

It was a novel idea to dramatize the small incident as described by Mallinātha and to trace the *Meghadūta* therefrom. There is no Yakṣa here, no Yakṣi, not even Kubera in his from of the Lord of the Yakṣas. There is nothing divine or semi-divine here. Every character is a human being. Mālinī, the gardener woman derives her name from a river of that name. Even Megha, the cloud of the *Meghadūta*, is presented here as a human being, though the playwright could not remove himself totally away from his phenomenal character, its appearance before Kālidāsa to announce his father's order being marked with thunder : *gaganamaṇḍale stanitaṁ bhavati.*[1] This probably has been done to impart a realistic touch which could be useful from the dramatic point of view. In this play, it is Kālidāsa himself who is made to go into exile and it is his memory of Mālinī which flows in verse form thus giving rise to poetry. Not all verses are from the *Meghadūta*. One, *sthitāḥ kṣaṇaṁ pakṣmasu tāḍitādharāḥ* [2] in memory of Mālinī drenched in rain is from the *Kumārasambhava,* which is sought to be traced in the play to the origin of poetry as such. Hence the title : *Kālidāsakāvya-sambhavam.*

Before passing on to the discussion on other aspects of the work, one may well pause and ponder as to what purpose the playwright had in mind in making Kubera the maternal uncle of Kālidāsa, unless it were to be assumed that for inflicting pain and anguish it is maternal uncles who could be more fitting as recorded in Indian tradition in many instances. The name Kubera Sharma—the addition of Sharma to Kubera—could be for confirming the humanness of the character, though in line with making peculiar changes like that of Alakā from a city to a river or that of Mālinī from a river of that name to a woman, if that be the case, is scarcely likely to sink to the mind.

For the stage the playwright has introduced a novelty. Kālidāsa while writing or reciting the composition is to be presented on the stage with a spotlight while the memories surging in his mind are to be shown in paintings as backdrop.

Occasionally the playwright uses such expressions in his work as are drawn as such or with such modification as would suit the context, e.g., in *asmin dvirephe koṣagata eva kamalinī dinamaṇivirahākulatayā saṅkucitā*[3] the use of *dvirephe koṣagate* is evidently inspired by the use of it in a Subhāṣita : *ittham vicintayati koṣagate dvirephe hā hanta hanta nalinīṁ gaja ujjahāra. So is dakṣiṇadiśātaḥ mandaṁ mandaṁ sagandhaḥ pavanaś*

1. p. 25.
2. p. 27.
3. p. 21.

cāvahat[1] and *ānanasparśalobhat*[2] by Kālidāsa's *mandaṁ mandaṁ nudati pavanaś cānukūlo yathā tvām vāmaś cāyaṁ nadati madhuraṁ cātakas te sagandhaḥ*[3] and *ānanasparśalobhāt*[4] respectively. Once a while he just puts in prose what Kālidāsa has said in verse, e.g.,

कालिदास: :— पश्यामि कथमेते त्वत्पक्ष्मस्था वर्षाबिन्दव: प्रथममधरताडनात् क्षणं गर्वान्विता: पुन: कर्कशोरोजनिपातचूर्णिता गतगौरवा वलीषु स्खलिताश्च नाभौ विलोवन्ते । (किञ्चित्स्थित्वा) मालिनि ! यथा त्वयाऽहमनुकम्पित: स्वोपस्थित्या तथैवेमौ कन्दराबहि:स्थौ रक्ताशोक: केसरश्चानुकम्पनीयौ ययोरेकतरस्तव वामपादाघातं वाञ्छति, अन्यश्च दोहदव्याजेन गाण्डूषामृताय स्पृहयति ।[5]

Cp. Kālidāsa :

स्थिता: क्षणं पक्ष्मसु ताडिताधरा:
पयोधरोत्सेधनिपातचूर्णिता: ।
वलीषु तस्या: स्खलिता: प्रपेदिरे
क्रमेण नाभिं प्रथमोदबिन्दव: ।।[6]
रक्ताशोकश्चलकिसलय: केसरश्चात्र कान्त:

एक: सख्यास्तव सह मया वामपादाभिलाषी
काङ्क्षत्यन्यो वदनमदिरां दोहदच्छद्मनाऽस्या: ।।[7]

As for the language in the play, it is fairly correct and idiomatic. The only aberration : *kin tu pitṛpādaiḥ pravāsakālaḥ prāvṛṣāntaparyantaṁ niścitaḥ*[8] could well be a typographical error for...*prāvṛṣo' ntaparyantam.* In certain instances the vernacular diction does peep out : *kṛtaṁ tu tad eva mayā yet tair anumitam,*[9] *kathaṁ niḥsambalaḥ ekākī yāsyāmy aham.*[10]

Everything said and done, the play is a nice little attempt full of originality and creativity and perhaps the only one of its kind in evolving a play with suitable modifications out of the incident leading to the incurring of wrath by the Yakṣa—in the present instance by Kālidāsa—of Kubera or Kubera Sharma of gripping interest and consequently deserving of serious notice.

---

1. p. 23.
2. p. 24.
3. *Meghadūta*, Pūrvamegha, verse 9.
4. ibid., Uttaramegha, v. 24.
5. p. 23.
6. *Kumārasambhava*. v. 24.
7. *Meghdūta*, Uttaramegha, verse 15.
8. p. 26.
9. p. 25.
10. ibid

to once more attract tourists. The cleaning of beaches damaged by tides, floods or winds, and of paths used in ecotourism must also be counted as indirect damage. It is necessary to calculate the extent of probable tourism occupancy reduction resulting from damage to other related sectors, such as access roads, water and sanitation systems, power availability and communications systems.

Any decrease in tourism activity also implies a diminished demand for related services such as the use of restaurants, nightclubs and taxis. One last type of indirect damage that must be taken into account by the tourism and other sector specialists is the increase in insurance premiums that companies often charge in the wake of a disaster in anticipation of a possible recurrence of such extreme natural phenomena. The increased premiums could lower the income and operational profitability of tourism establishments. In the case of cruise tourism –so popular and common in the Caribbean– certain additional estimates must be carried out.

Since cruise liners schedule their ports of call well in advance, it is possible to estimate the income each of those tourism sites would have been likely to post had the disaster not occurred. Any natural event that damages port infrastructure, natural resources or commerce in a tourism destination can cause immediate cancellations by cruise ships. Interviews with national authorities, businessmen in the sector and representatives of the cruise lines can allow the analyst to project how long it will be before the ships are likely to return, thereby making it possible to calculate the corresponding (indirect) loss in income.

MACROECONOMIC EFFECTS

We have already noted that officials in many countries in the region register tourism as part of accounts for other sectors; tourism satellite accounts are not yet common practice or might not be sufficiently updated or broken down by activity or region. In addition, the heterogeneous nature of tourism means that many of its components fall within the sphere of other sectors, such as infrastructure, communications, commerce and the like. Despite such potential obstacles, and in light of the economic weight of tourism in the Caribbean and increasingly in Central America, Mexico and elsewhere in the region, it is necessary to conduct a separate assessment of tourism's macroeconomic impact.

Such an analysis must include calculations of how a disaster's impact on the sector would affect economic output, external accounts, and public finances, with proper attention given to the effects on public and private investment, employment and women.

Effects on Economic Activity

Forecasts of how tourism would have performed in the year in question, had there been no interruption in activities due to the disaster, are normally available in national planning offices, central banks or sector agencies. The tourism specialist should compare this information with estimates on decreases in income as estimated in the part on indirect losses, and then estimate a new economic output (contribution to GDP) for the tourism sector after the disaster.

Special care must be exercised to ensure that these estimates do not lead to double accounting should other specialists include tourism activities in their sectors. (In the cases of small Caribbean economies in which income from tourism is high, potential duplications are unlikely). It should also be noted that tropical storms and hurricanes that cause damage to the sector in the Caribbean usually occur during the low tourism season.

Therefore, indirect losses due to drops in occupancy rates and the subsequent effect on GDP are not necessarily significant, unless the reconstruction period for damaged infrastructure is very long.

Effects on the External Sector

International inbound tourism has a special impact on the external sector. If the relative weight of tourism in the economic activity of the affected country is significant, any drop in tourism activities due to a disaster will imply major

9

ASTI KAŚCID VĀGVIŚEṢAḤ

Published in the *Saṁskrita Pratibhā,* the Sanskrit journal of the Sahitya Akademi, New Delhi, Volume IV, Part I, 1984 it is an one-Act play by Sri Maheshwar Shastri N. Joshi.

It opens with a King on the throne together with his retinue. He is shown discussing with his minister the marriage of his daughter. The minister hesitantly makes the proposal that she could be married to his son. The King calls for the daughter to know her view. She summarily rejects the proposal throwing *inter alia* a broadside against the minister that even the dogs have begun to aspire for the throne. In response to the King's specific query as to whether she likes the minister's son or not she says that it is only an ill-starred woman who would do that, and the Mālatī creeper would not hang on a Nimba (Margo) tree. Her remarks deeply hurt the minister but he keeps his cool, withdraws the proposal on the ground that he is a servant of the royal family and the matrimonial relationship between his son and the Princess would not be in order, though he could not but express himself in favour of knowledge going well with humility. With him withdrawing from the scene, in a huff, the King conveys his unhappiness to his daughter in rejecting a number of Princes and heaping humiliation on several royal families in the name of knowledge. He tells her that he is getting old and is anxious that she should be married off. The Princess disagrees with his suggestion to marry the minister's son. The question of her marriage she leaves to fate. With this ends the First Scene.

The Second Scene opens in a forest with the minister, cut to the quick at the arrogance of the Princess, out to teach her a lesson.

He notices a man cutting from the root that very branch of the tree on which he is sitting. To him, he is the right man for the Princess. He takes him along with him telling him that he would marry him to a Princess and that he has only to keep mum when she is with him and that he should not answer any of her questions, should she put them to him; he himself taking care of them being by his side, which should be enough to remove his fear or apprehension. He puts him on the horse back and leaves.

The Third Scene is again laid in the royal court. The minister enters with the same man whom he had met in the forest, a young cowherd, whom he introduces, as a valiant Prince, well-versed in lores from Burma who could be a suitable match for the Princess who is then called in to give her opinion. The minister satisfies the Princess who comes with her friend Vāsantī that the young man is quite at home in Śāstras and arts but being given to few words, is observing silence. The Princess carried away by the handsomeness of the young man which had appealed to the King too at the very first sight is inclined to accept scholarship in him. Through Vāsantī she conveys her consent to marry him. Overjoyed the King orders for the preparation for the marriage. The minister, finding his plan succeeding, withdraws from the scene thus bringing to an end the current Scene.

The place of the Fourth Scene is the royal harem with minister exulting over his success. With his exit are shown on the stage the bride and the groom with Vāsantī and other ladies around. At Vāsantī's request the Princess gives a song after which the elderly ones among the ladies pronounce blessings. Exit the Princess after it. Vāsantī with other ladies takes the young man along laughing.

The place of the Sixth Scene again is the harem. The young girls drive the young man in while he is all wonder at its grandeur and high walls, the curtains, the beds and other swan-marked things heard in stories. Due to marriage festivities for three or four days, he was feeling tired and wanted to take rest, which alone he could not have though fed to the full. Avoiding the well-laid bed which he thought was meant only for kings or royal personages, he sleeps on the floor with his turban under his head. At this enters the Princess who has the first shock of her life in finding him sleeping on the floor, her second shock being his loud snoring. She makes three attempts to awaken him, first two more subtle and delicate and the third more direct by pouring scented water on him, which awakenes him post haste. She shows him then a painting with Kṛṣṇa with Gopīs in Rāsa dance which does not interest him. He continues to look at another one with a bull fight. With her suspicion about the identity of the person aroused, she asks him as to who really he is. His telling her in all sincerity that he is a cowherd who has come there at the instance of the minister is the third and the greatest shock for her. Cheated and angered, she with a mouthful of invectives asks him to be off at once. Insulted and humiliated, the young man vows not to show his face to her again and goes out.

The next Scene is laid in a forest. The young man is all sorrow for his illiteracy which drove him to such a pass. He notices a sort of a figure at a distance. Approaching it, he finds it that of goddess Kālī. He falls at Her feet and prays Her to have pity on him. Repeating ॐ काल्यै नमः he begins to practise penance.

The Seventh and the last Scene of the play is laid again in the harem with the Princess playing on the Viṇā and singing with tearful eyes a song of separation. Vāsantī joins him at this. Through the conversation between the two the information is imparted that the Princess, very much reduced, is pining for her husband and regretting her action in turning him out which is not the way the Aryan women do. Vāsantī cansols her saying that her husband would come back to her. She helps herself with the milk that the former gives her along with fruits. She prays to goddess Sarvamaṅgalā as her only recourse before going to bed. Exit Vāsantī. There is a knock at the door. She is all joy to listen to the words that her dear one has come and that she should open the door. She rubs her eyes and considers herself lucky. When the request to open the door is repeated, she proceeds a few steps but retraces them quickly. If he were to be the same old fool, what has she to do with him? If she were to turn him away, she would relapse into sorrow. She then decides to put him the question *asti kaścid vāgviśeṣaḥ*? is there any improvement in speech? The young man repeats the same. There is an attempt at composing verses beginning with each word of the sentence making the Princess run to him and fall at his feet. She begs forgiveness of him and rushes out to inform her father who comes along with her and wants to know as to how he could acquire learning. The young man tells him of the incident of his seeing the idol of Kālī. Since he could not win her favour even though practising penance for long, he told her that he would chop off his head and offer it to her. The goddess at this appeared before him and granted him his request of command over speech calling him her *dāsa*, servant. Since the goddess had called him her *dāsa*, said the King, he would be known by the name of Kālidāsa. He blesses him that his fame will spread all over the world and pronounces the Bharatavākya with which the Scene as well as the play come to an end.

Critical Appreciation

The play, as can be seen from the summary of its theme as given above, is evolved, apiece with many other similar attempts, out of, as the tradition would make out, the words uttered by the learned Princess to the fool whom she had been tricked into marrying and whom she had turned out unceremoniously but who had reappeared, now a poet by the grace of the goddess Kālī, and composed three of his masterly poems beginning with each of the words uttered by the Princess. The author follows in the main the traditional account with the only difference that he makes the very minister of the King take revenge on the conceited Princess for her having turned down his (minister's) proposal for her marriage with his son. As for the silent disputation in the royal court with gestures properly interpreted by the humiliated Pandits out to take revenge, he has said just nothing. He retains only that portion of the account where a person being an ignoramus is shown cutting the very branch of the tree on which he is perching. The instruction to him to just remain quiet while in the palace of the King is also retained. So is retained his humiliation at the hands of the Princess though for a different reason. There is nothing of the mispronunciation of the word *uṣṭra as uṣra* on hearing the grunting of a camel as evidence of his being a fool. The fool of the play is a cowherd boy who confesses his being so and does not disclose his identity at the instance of the minister who had brought him along to the distraught Princess, when asked by her after she had noticed him, sleeping on the floor with his turban as the pillow and snoring like a rustic. As for the grace of Kālī, he gives an altogether different explanation. Having been insulted and humiliated and feeling hopelessly miserable, the young rustic had left for the Vindhyas. There he came upon the image of Kāli. To propitiate her he engaged himself in severe penance. When this did not help, he got ready to chop off his head and make an offering of it to her. The goddess then appeared before him and offered him a boon. He asked for the mastery over speech. So be it, my servant, said the goddess and disappeared. Since she had called him her dāsa : तथास्तु मम दास, that became the reason of his being called Kālidāsa. This is as far as the name goes.

The playwright introduces in Vāsantī, the friend of the Princess, a new character. She acts as her mouthpiece, confidant and companion. The traditional account has no such character. To show the Princess as stricken with intense remorse on turning out her husband in a fit of anger, though he might have been a fool, is also the playwright's innovation. This shows him superimposing on the characters the age-old deep-rooted picture of a woman totally devoted to a man once she takes him her husband, though only by a quirk of circumstances, as in the present case, of which she just became a victim.

The playwright makes the fool a very handsome person who wins appreciation from the Princess and her friend. As a matter of fact, this is one of the reasons and of course a very potent one at that for the Princess accepting him as her husband. Though he had been made out by the minister to be a very learned man, well-versed in different lores and consequently a man of few words, profundity in learning lending appropriateness to economy in words, the Princess could convince herself of his being learned even in the absence of any ostensible evidence to this effect, he observing silence, on account of his handsomeness which generally is accepted as its natural concomitant :

राजदारिका—अहो पमस्य पुंस: । प्राय: पाण्डित्यमपि सन्निहितं भवेत् । यत:, यत्राकृतिस्तत्र गुणा वसन्ति ।[1]

At the first sight, she feels attracted towards him. That is why the bluntly outspoken and rude girl just falls in for the person being presented to her and her gullible father as a learned man. There is no attempt even to test his learning. However, the trick played on her in the play to which she unknowingly slips, is the same as figuring in the traditional episode.

Again, in the traditional episode it is her rejection one by one of the Pandits that makes them take revenge on her by contriving her marriage with a fool. In the present play it is her caustic remarks that turn the minister revengeful. Her remarks touched him to the core making him repeat them when he vows for revenge and when he achieves it by making her and her father agree to the marriage and finally in a mood of exultation when the marriage had been actually solemnized and, as far as he was concerned, the life of the proud Princess resolved to marry only a learned person was ruined for ever by marrying an unlettered rustic cowherd. To equate the desire of the minister to marry his son to the Princess in his (minister's) very presence with the desire of the dogs to occupy the throne: *Rājadārikā—vilakṣaṇaḥ khalu kāla upasthsitaḥ yad utō śvānaḥ simhāsanam adhiroḍhum icchanti*[2] or of a woman, marrying his son as a Mālatī creeper resorting to the Margo tree; *mālatīlatā nimbavṛkṣam avalambate*[3], was provocative enough to make the minister return evil for evil. Every playwright has the right to introduce certain innovations even while accepting the basic structure of the traditional episode. The only consideration should be that they should not look odd. It is to the credit of our playwright that his innovations -and there are quite a few of them as can be seen from above—do not look odd.

1. p. 44
2-3 p. 40

In the traditional episode, the grace of Kāli comes to the fool accidentally, he pronouncing the words *vidyā vidyā* (unable to utter the full name Vidyottamā) seeking to convey at the goddess's query as to why he was crying that Vidyottamā had misbehaved with him and the goddess taking his words to mean that he wants *vidyā* and is crying for that and granting it to him. In the present play, the rustic young man is shown genuinely struck with remorse at his being unlettered, the sole cause of his humiliation being that his very wife had discarded him, and his being possessed with the firm resolve to acquire it through the grace of the goddess to the point of offering his head to her should he fail to achieve it. This shows a degree of intelligence on his part not agreeing well with the incident of cutting the very branch of the tree on which he was perching, an evidence *par excellence* of his being a fool, retained by the playwright from the traditional episode. The same can also be said about his desire not to sleep on the royal bed in consciousness of his humble birth.

Except certain modernisms like *hasantyaḥ santi*[1], *paśyann asti*[2] the language of the play generally retains the classical flavour. Even making allowance for printing errors which disfigure the entire write-up, there are certain expressions which may be difficult to justify. The word *prakāṇḍa* being *niyataliṅga* has always to go in neuter, vide Amara *matallikā macarcikā prakāṇḍam udghatallajau, paṇḍitaprakāṇḍāḥ*,[4] may, therefore, be difficult to accept. In *tava gītaṁ śrotum vāñchatā manasy asmakāṁ balavatī khalu cirād eva vijṛmbhate*,[5] if the idea is desire, the word should have been *vāñchitā*. *Pāritoṣaka*[6] used twice in the work[7] should have been *pāritoṣika*. The omission of *muk* in *cintayānāyāḥ*[8], the correct form is *cintayamānāyāḥ*, is indefensible in Paninian Sanskrit though the form is not rare in the epics and the Purāṇas. *Kim api vigraha iva*[9] should have been in order here or just *kim api* would have been all right : *sāmānye napuṁsakam*, which means the word *vigraha* should have been avoided. Causal in *garhayamāṇaḥ*[10] is unnecessary. There are three such expressions :

(1) किन्तु खलु तस्य पण्डितमणेन मणेनमिधेयम[11]

(2) द्वारकापतिनकदारक[12] :

(3) पतित्वेनमुररीकृत्य[13]

---

1. p. 40.
2. p. 48.
3. I.3, 27
4. p. 43.
5. p. 45.
6-7. p. 56.
8. p. 53.
9. p. 51.
10. p. 55.
11. p. 40.
12. p. 41.
13. p. 51.

which do not make any sense most probably because of the typographical mess. In *mamāpi hṛdaye evam eva manyate*[1] the Locative also probably owes itself to it. It must have been *mamāpi hṛdayam*. So is the case possibly with *asya* used with *mūrteḥ*[2] which must have been *asyāḥ* in the manuscript, such monstrosities being unimaginable from an author whose diction otherwise is fairly good. The same could possibly have been the case with the sentence *ete khalu...vividhāsu paraṁ pravīṇāḥ*[3] where something like *vidyāsu* has been left out after *vividhāshu* in composing. However, the same cannot be said about *apadhvasta* in *mā spṛśa mām, apadhvasta, niḥsara*[4] It should either have been *apadhvasto bhava* or *apadhvaṁsasva*. The Imperative Second Person Singular of *dhvaṁs* can in no case be *dhvasta*. Similarly *iṭ* in *vasitum*[5] cannot be ascribed to typographical error but *o* in *avoci* : *punarmilanam acirad bhaviteti mayā*[6] *'voci*[7] can be, the correct form of it is *avāci*. Not ascribable to typographical error again, but not entirely indefensible; Bhaṭṭojīdīkṣita having quoted an earlier instance of *prārthayanti śayanotthitaṁ priyāḥ* where *arth* is used in Parasmaipada, is the form *prārthayam*.[8]

The play has a song too which on account of its flow and pleasing alliteration has a charm of its own. It has an aberration, however, in its sixth stanza in the line *vadanākhye mama pātre vartī me khalu netre*.[9] The idea could be : These eyes of mine are set in vessel called face. If that be so, *varti* or *vartī* would just be indefensible. It should be *vartinī*. Further, being in dual it cannot be combined in Sandhi with the following *ime*. If *varti* is the word and the meaning is wick, the expression should have been *vartī* ime, Sandhi being still not admissible, vide Pāṇ. *idūded dvivacanaṁ pragṛhyam* (1.1.11) and *plutapragṛhyā aci nityam* (6.1.125).

It is natural for an author dealing with Kālidāsa to be imbued with his spirit. Expressions from his work would naturally come to him which may be difficult for him to resist to weave into his composition. The same is the case with our author who in using such expressions as *eṣā tantrīḥ nayanasalilair ārdrayantī tiṣṭhati*,[10] *mama bhāgadheyāni pṛccha*,[11] *tarhi siñca me tilodakam*,[12] *asti me tad āmūlāc chrotuṁ kautūhalam*[13] has the following lines of Kālidāsa at the back of his mind : *tantrīm ārdrāṁ nayanasalilaiḥ sārayitvā kathañcit*,[14] *vatsa te bhāgadheyānl pṛccha*,[15] *anyathā 'vaśyaṁ siñcataṁ me tilodakam*,[16] *āmūlāc chrotam icchami*.[17]

---

1. p. 44
2. p. 48
3. p. 43
4. p. 49
5. ibid.
6. p. 56
7. p. 46
8. ibid.
9. p. 46.
10. p. 52.
11. ibid.
12. ibid.
13. ibid.
14. *Meghadūta*, Uttaramegha, verse, 23.
15. *Abhijñānaśākuntala* (Ed. B.H.U., Varanasi, 1976), p. 553.
16. ibid., p. 464.
17. ibid., p. 440.

Occasionally the playwright so structures the sentence that though grammatically correct, it lacks symmetry, e.g., ete *mahābhāgāḥ vidyāyāyāṁ bhagavān Budhaḥ, vāggmitāyāṁ Bṛhaspatiḥ, kāvyakalāyāṁ ca sākṣāt Śukra eveti manye.*[1] Here the young fool comoutlaged as a learned scholar and poet is referred to in plural : *ete* while Budha, Bṛhaspati and Śukra with whom he is compared are left without an honorific.

Barring some of these aberrations the expression is fairly correct and idiomatic with a genuine ring, e.g.,

(1) मन्त्री—देव विवाहो नाम दैवायत्तः। यत्र दैवसङ्कल्पः, तत्रैव भविष्यति। अलमनया चिन्तया।[2]

(2) राजा—वत्से, नैतत्त्वयि शोभते। कियन्तो वा राजसुतास्त्वया न निराकृताः ? केवलं विद्याराहित्य निमित्तीकृत्य कियन्ति च राजकुलानि न तिरस्कृतानि ? अहन्तु वृद्धोऽस्मि। जनन्या विना वर्धितां त्वां वीक्षमाणस्य मे हृदयं दुःखक्रकचेन द्विधा विदीर्यते। त्वं तु तावत् प्रत्यहं राजपुत्रान् तिरस्कुर्वाणा मम चिन्ताचितां तन्तनोषि।[3]

(3) आम्, मन्त्रिणामेव कुतन्त्रमिदम्। विद्यायां बुधः, वाग्मितायां गुरुः, काव्ये शुक्र इत्युक्त्वा नूनं स मामभ्यवञ्चयन्।···बुधः गुरुः शुक्रोऽस्तीति सोऽवादीत्। किं तु त्वं तावत् शनिः संवृत्तः। येन हतो मे भाग्यपर्वतः।

निस्सर गोपापसद। तव सकाशात् कलङ्कितं राजकुलं नः। अपेहि, श्वः यदि यत्र कुत्रापि तव मुखं दृश्यते तर्हि न त्वं भविष्यति। राजकुमारीं लब्धुं कथमपि तवाभिलाषः। हम् कुक्कुरः समुपवेष्टुमिच्छति। काकः नैवेद्यं भोक्तुं कङ्क्षति!! बकः हंसीमालिङ्गितुं प्रवर्तते।[4]

The play presents a fine study of the principal characters, the Princess and the cowherd, particularly of the latter, which is marked by fine sensitivity. Conscious of the royal lineage, the Princess just cannot stand the proposal of the minister to marry his son to her. She takes it sheer audacity on his part. She is too conscious of her being a Princess to even entertain the idea. To the thought of marrying the son of a servant—the minister after all is a royal servant, though of a high category—is an anathema to her. The same proud Princess is carried away at the youth and consents for the marriage. The marriage over, she is like any other bride, shy, coy and anxious, her first two attempts to wake up her sleeping husband by the jingle of the bracelets and the stroke of the lotus revealing it more than anything else. It is when these delicate attempts fail that she resorts to the extreme step of pouring scented water on him. That he is awake is no consolation to her. His rustic speech injures her more than anything else and confirms the suspician aroused in her earlier by his queer manner of sleeping (he was sleeping on the floor), his uncouth

1. p. 43
2. p. 49
3. p. 40
4. p. 43

snoring and his intent preoccupation with a painting of bull fight in preference to that of Kṛṣṇa in Rāsa dance with Gopīs which she was pointing to him. His telling her that he is a cowherd makes her lose her patience. She is all fire spitting venom at the frightened hapless young fellow. "Don't touch me, be off from here," roars she. Having turned him out she pines for him, loses her sleep and feels guilty. That moment she is just a wife, the embodiment of traditional Indian wifehood who deifies husband, quality or no quality. When Kālidāsa after acquiring learning comes to her, knocks at her door and calls her out, her joy knows no bounds. She leaves the bed, moves forward a few steps. Then the thought overtakes her : If he were as dull as before, she would have to have the same on her hands. If she were not to open the door, the happiness that is hers now would go away from her. Torn between these contrary feelings she stands quiet for a while and prays to her family deities and then puts the question, the question that is to decide her fate, seemingly overcoming her emotion giving preference to the love for learning over the love for her sweetheart *asti kaścid vāgviśeṣaḥ*, is there any improvement in speech ? Her question well answered, she runs to her husband and begging forgiveness falls at his feet. She is all joy that her husband loves her : *kin nu khalv abhimatataraṁ loke 'smin syāt satīnāṁ nāma, yat patīnāṁ snehabhāvād anyat.*[1]

The playwright has presented, as can be seen from above, the picture of a young bride in high spirits who has got a husband of her choice and liking longing to meet him to offer him her love but meeting instead a dullard rustic. So all her hopes are dashed to the ground. The playwright has also successfully brought the gradual transformation in her character : The rude Princess turning into a coy bride, passionate and excited, the coy bride turning into a fiery woman, the fiery woman mellowing into a pining wife, the pining wife turning into a firmly principled lady, the principled lady turning again into a wife, just a wife.

The depiction of the character of Kālidāsa, the cowherd of earlier days, also shows the delicate touch of the playwright. When the minister approaches him and tells him that he would marry him to a Princess his innocent remark is that why should he play a joke on him. Even when coaxed by the minister, he is unsure of himself and somehow agrees to do his bidding. Entering the harem after the marriage he is struck with its grandeur. The playwright brings out the true rusticity in him by making him guess about its cost : *asya gṛhasya nirmāṇe kiyad vā dhanaṁ dattaṁ ? Lakṣam uta koiṭh,*[1] how much money was spent on its construction ? A lakh or a crore ?. He is wonderstruck at the curtains, the beds, the lamps, practically with everything there. The playwright shows a keen insight into the working of the mind of a person unused to such things. The

1. p. 55. 2. p. 47.

insight becomes keener in depicting the hesitation of the rustic in sleeping on a well-laid bed forgetting that he now is the husband of a Princess :

युवा—अहं तावदस्यां हंसतूलिकायां स्वपिमि । नहि नहि, राजानोऽत्र स्वपन्ति, राजपुरुषा वा, न पुनर्मादृशाः । अतोऽत्र न शये । अहं तु भूतले शयिष्ये ।[1]

It is a fine study of the mental make-up of a person, his behavioural pattern, whatever the situation. The rustic cannot persuade himself to believe that he too can sleep on a cosy bed. Even feeling the floor cold enough, he prefers to lie on it :

अहो शीतलं कुट्टिमम् । अत्रैव शयिष्ये उष्णीषमेव उपधानं भविष्यति ।[2]

This behavioural pattern finds realistic depiction when the Princess coming to know that he is a cowherd falls unconscious. The poor fellow, the rustic, is just stupefied at this, afraid, nervous, confused. He had not asked for what he was getting :

युवा—[सभयम्] भर्तृदारिके, उत्तिष्ठ । भोः, आगच्छत, सर्वे आगच्छत [इत्युच्चैः शब्दायते]···न कोऽप्यागच्छति । [रोदिति] अहं तु मन्त्रिवचनं सत्यमिति मत्वा समागतोऽस्म्यत्र । किन्त्वत्र विपदीदृशी समापतिता ।[3]

With the Princess unceremoniously turning him out : *nirvidyānāṁ tvādṛśāṁ jīvitāt maraṇam eva varam,*[4] it is better for unlettered people like him to die than to live, *nissara gopāpasada,*[5] get out, O you wretched cowherd, he feels cut to the quick : *viśeṣeṇa dhikkṛto 'smi.*[6] He is sorry for himself : *dhiṅ me śūkaranirviśeṣaṁ jīvitam,*[3] fie upon my life in no way different from that of a pig. He vows that he would not show his learningless face to her : *vidyāvikalaṁ mama mukhaṁ nahi te darśayiṣyāmi.*[8] His remark in the forest after departing from the Palace that there is no happiness for an uneducated person, so much so that his very wife after accepting him as her husband in front of the great god of fire forsakes him, sums us his writhing agony :

साक्षादेव देवदेवस्य जातवेदसः सम्मुखे पतित्वेन मामुररीकृत्य विद्याविकल इति पाणिगृहीताऽपि त्यजति ।

To offer justification as it were for the composition of the three major works of Kālidāsa and their beginning with the words *asti kaścit* and *vāk* the traditional episode makes the Princess put the question to the erstwhile fool, now turned a great poet, *asti kaścid vāgviśeṣah ?* is there

1. p. 47.
2. ibid.
3. p. 49.
4-6. p. 50.

any improvement in speech ? The question goes very well with the defectiveness in speech noticed by her earlier in the young man pronouncing *uṣṭra* as *uṭra*. One version of the traditional episode has it that Kālidāsa also answered back in the very words which satisfied the Princess. In the present play what the playwright has done is that he has made the poet start with the words *asti kaścit* and *vāk* there and then itself :

(नेपथ्ये) अस्ति कश्चिद्वाग्विशेषः । अस्ति...कश्चिद्वाग्विशेषः । मधुरोऽयं पदविन्यासः । अस्ति...अस्ति...अस्ति...उत्तरस्यां (गायति) दिशि देवतात्मा हिमालयो नाम नगाधिराजः । पूर्वापरौ··· (हं...हं) तोयनिधी...वगाह्य...स्थितः पृथिव्या...इव मानदण्डः ।

which could be certainly convincing to the Princess that there is definitely *vāgviśeṣa* in him. This is an innovation for which the playwright deserves full plaudits. Since the union between the two, the Princess and Kālidāsa depended upon the satisfactory answer of the question *asti kaścid vagviśeṣaḥ*, it assumed pivotal importance. It is therefore but meet that it should have been taken up as the title of the play.

The work under study is on the whole an enjoyable piece in evolving a play of absorbing interest out of the traditional episode wherein the author succeeds eminently.

1. p. 54.

10

ASTI KAŚCIDVĀGARTHĪYAM

It is yet another play based on the traditional episode of Kālidāsa: his being originally a fool, married to a learned Princess who had resolved to accept only a learned person as her husband, through the machinations of revengeful rejected Pandits, whom she had turned out in sheer desperation; his (Kālidāsa's) acquiring learning as also poetical capabilities by the accidental grace of goddess Kālī, his return and being asked the question *asti kaścid vāgviśeṣaḥ* and his composing the three Kāvyas each beginning with each of the words of her question. The episode has inspired so many writers of the modern period, most probably on account of its melodramatic content, that a full corpus of literature has grown round it. Since the crucial question of the Princess presupposes the whole turn of events, it has been adopted as the very title of their plays by at least two writers who have proceeded to treat the traditional episode, each in his own way, introducing into it such innovations as they deemed fit.

In the traditional episode there is an attempt in some way to seek justification for the three major works of Kālidāsa beginning with particular words as also for his name which should have evidently something to do with goddess Kālī, in addition to finding justification, which could only be through a supernatural process, for the extraordinary talents of a writer which have kept the world spell-bound for the past two thousand years or so. Popular imagination wove a story round him which, apart from anything else, has the greatest dramatic quality, the quality of suspense. For once Kālidāsa is a hopeless creature, illiterate, unintelligent and turned out by his newly-wedded wife. Fortune smiles on him suddenly. The man who could not pronounce the common world *uṣṭra* properly becomes one of the greatest of the poets of the world.

The story has been so woven that it has scope for the depiction of a number of emotions : arrogance, vengefulness, deceit, anger, desperation, despondency and joy which makes it particularly suitable for a drama. It is therefore no wonder that it has caught the imagination of so many of the playwrights who have tried their hand at it.

Asti Kaścidvāgarthīyam is a play in five Acts by Dr. Krishna Kumar, former Head of the Department of Sanskrit, Garhwal University, Srinagar who has already established himself as a creative and critical writer of eminence.

Theme

First Act : Vidyottamā, the daughter of Sudarśana, the King of south Kosala has taken the vow that she would marry only that young man who would defeat her in disquisition. Many a learned person tried their luck at it but met with no success. Turned out of the disquisition hall, they returned dejected and pained. One of these, Dhūmraketu, resolved to avenge the insult in collusion with an initially hesitant and reluctant Govardhana who had also suffered humiliation like him to hatch a plot for the marriage of the arrogant Princess with a fool. The two of them noticed a young man near the village Devagrāma hewing wood in a forest along with his mother. Son of the great Naiyāyika Śivadāsa, he had been very brilliant initially but had lost his brilliance due to a chance head injury. In spite of his mother's entreaties he persisted in cutting the very branch of the tree on which he was perching and fell on the earth with a thud injuring himself in the process. Concluding that there cannot be a better fool than him, the twosome tempted him with the proposal of marrying him to a Princess and took him to the capital of Sudarśana after tutoring him suitably.

Second Act : The twosome dressed up the young man named Kālidāsa but calling himself Kariyā as a scholar and introduced him as well-versed in all lores with the name of Darśanācārya who as they said was Head of the Department in a University. They further said that as he was observing a vow of silence till the middle of the full moon night some three days thence—he had come earlier since that day happened to be auspicious according to astral calculations—he would participate in the disquisition with gestures only. Carried away by the handsomeness of the young man the Princess agreed to the proposal. Thus started the silent disquisition The Princess raised the ring finger of the right hand. The so-called Ācārya raised three of the same. Govardhana interpreted the gesture of the Princess to signify that the cause of the creation is one. The three fingers of the Ācārya he interpreted to mean that they are three : Īśvara, Jīva and Prakṛti. To Vidyottamā's remark that she had another question too in her gesture, Dhūmraketu said that what she had meant to ask was whether for the wellbeing of the kingdom and its proper running it is only one being, i e., the king who is required. By raising the three fingers the Ācārya had answered that, no, all the three, i e., the king, the officers and the subjects would be needed for that. As the Princess wanted to test the young man further, she put to him another question by raising her five fingers. The Ācārya first raised the same number of his and then the fist. Govardhana interpreted the gesture of the Princess as her query as to whether the creation is composed of five elements. The Ācārya's gestures he interpreted to signify that he first agreed with the Princess but added by raising the fist that they, the elements, together lead to creation. Dhūmraketu on the basis of Polity put a different interpretation on the gestures of both. The Princess's gesture he interpreted to mean her query as to whether five types of forces would be necessary for defence though the Śāstras mention them to be only four. The Ācārya seemed to signify his agreement with her with this addition that they (the forces) could succeed only if they act in proper co-ordination under one unified command. The questions of the Princess having been satisfactorily answered, she garlanded the Ācārya and accepted him as her husband.

Third Act : The marriage ceremony over, Vidyottamā waited with her friend Ilā with longing. She felt surprised to see the sign of foolishness on the face of the so-called Ācārya when brought to her by her friends and attendants, whom he had regaled earlier with his queer movements of hands and feet. His disinclination to speak even at the sweetest of the moments she first attributed to the vow of silence and waited somehow till the midnight when, as had been pointed out by the deceitful Dhūmraketu and Govardhana, the vow of silence was to come to an end. When ultimately he did speak, he spoke in such a rustic manner that she became totally dumbfounded. On coming to know as to how the cheats had contrived the whole thing, she flew into rage. In spite of the so called husband's persistent entreaties, she turned him out saying that she could belong to a learned person only adding that she would wait for him and when he would come after completing his education she would put him the question : *asti kaścid vāgarthaḥ* ? It is on his satisfactorily answering it that she would allow him entry in her room.

Fourth Act : Though Vidyottamā had turned out the helpless husband, she being an Indian woman, had got stricken with remorse. She searched for him. She would always talk of him to her friend and confidant Ilā. She was sorry that she had misbehaved with him, something the Aryan women don't do. One day in the Plantain grove, the Kadalīmaṇḍapa, in the course of the conversation between the two friends Vidyottamā and Ilā, it was revealed that a poet named Kālidāsa had attained great fame. Along with poems he had written plays also which Vidyottamā had procured all the way from Ujjayinī at great effort and expense. She mentioned them, the *Ṛtusaṁhāra*, the *Meghadūta*, the *Mālavikāgnimitra*, the First Act of the *Abhijñānaśākuntala* and reproduced a number of quotations from them for pinpointing in them one quality or the other. At Ilā's suggestion that the stage performance of one of the plays be arranged in the royal theatre, Vidyottamā said that that was precisely her own view as well. Her father had invited the great poet. The performance of the play under the direction of the playwright himself could be more lively. Hardly had she finished, Irāvatī, an attendant informed that Kālidāsa had reached the outer gate of the city and would be brought from there on the royal road down the harem for girls to the main gate of the palace in procession. The girls heard the welcome cries and went out to have a look at the great poet. Vidyottamā took out a few flowers from her vase and gave them to Ilā. They both then left for the harem for the girls.

Fifth Act : This Act is laid in the bed room of Vidyottamā where she and the wood-carrier had got together ten years earlier with the only difference that the decoration was not as good as at that time. On a table were placed the works of Kālidāsa. Both Vidyottamā and Ilā looked out of the window to see Kālidāsa's procession. The whole city, as a matter of fact, the whole kingdom seemed to have come out to welcome him. As the procession approached near, Ilā recognized the poet to be the same wood-carrier. She showed him to Vidyottamā who was hardly able to control herself and was on the point of falling into swoon. Just at moment Irāvati came in and informed that the poet first wanted to meet the Princess. Thinking that he was the wood-carrier who had won fame by acquiring learning somehow, she ordered the closure of doors of the bed room and asked Ilā to open them only after she had got a proper answer to her question : *astī kaścid vāgarthaḥ* Ilā did as asked, opening the door after the satisfactory answer. After coming, the poet, on being asked by the Princess as to how the transformation had taken place, told her the whole story as follows :

"Coming out of the bed room of the Princess he had gone out to the same forest from where Dhūmraketu and Govardhana had picked him up. A fierce storm appearing there at that time uprooted a Śaka tree a thick branch of which hit him on the head which took away his dullness. With brightness appearing again, he went to the Gurukula of the celebrated teacher Vāmadeva where after pursuing studies for five years he started composing poetry. While there he would always be thinking of Vidyottamā who is the spirit behind his charming heroines. He has completed two dramas, the *Mālavikāgnimitra* and the *Vikramorvaśīya* as also the first Act of the *Abhijñānaśākuntala*. He has also composed a lyric on six seasons. The question of the Princess would always be a ringing in his mind. He had, therefore, started composing the *Mahākāvyas*, the *Kumārasambhava* and the *Raghuvaṁśa* each beginning with the words *asti* and *vāgarthaḥ* respectively. With the word *kaścit* he has composed the lyric the *Meghadūta*. Before composing it he had proceeded on a pilgrimage to Uttarākhaṇḍa in the Himālayas. He had gone as far up as to Kedāranātha. Taking the north-westerly direction he had reached Daśārṇa passing through the hilly regions of Rāmagiri, the Māla area and the river

Revā. After crossing Nirvindhyā he had reached Ujjayinī where he had offered prayers at the temple of Mahākāla. From there he had reached Kurukṣetra after crossing the Gambhīrā and the Carmaṇvatī. From there he had gone over to Kanakhala and Māyāpura and further on to Kedāra temple after crossing a number of rivers and their confluences arriving ultimately at Uṣīmaṭha. On his way back he had reached Gaurīmaṭha where he had worshipped goddess Kālī for a few days. It was at this temple that he had seen a dream wherein he had visualized himself a Yakṣa and Vidyottamā a Yakṣī making love to him. Coming back from the Himālaya he had gone up the Rāmagiri hill and had found its top covered all over by clouds. Pining in separation from Vidyottamā he had sent a message through the cloud to Alakāpurī where he had fancied her to be in the form of a Yakṣī."

After narrating his account where he had spoken in detail, sometimes in answer to Vidyottamā's queries and sometimes otherwise, of the many places near Kedārnātha, the streams of the Gaṅgā, each with a different name, their sources and a whole lot of holy places around, Kālidāsa told the Princess that he would go now to the royal court where her parents and the members of the State Council would accord him welcome. He would go next to Devagrāma to meet his mother. At this the Princess in tears told him that his mother had come to the city in search of him. In spite of her repeated requests she had not agreed to stay with her and had left one night quietly. Disconcerted Kālidāsa then heard some noise outside. On the attendant reporting that an old woman in rags looking for her son calling him out as Kariyā was being followed by noisy children, Kālidāsa thought that she must be none other than his mother and wanted to go out. Just at that moment under the orders of the Princess the old woman was brought in which led to the union of the mother and the son and the daughter-in-law and the mother-in-law. The Chamberlain at that moment gave a message from the King for coming to the court for which all of them got ready. Kālidāsa together with Vidyottamā touched his mother's feet and sought her blessings which she said they always had. She then uttered the Bharatavākya which brought the play to an end.

Critical Appreciation

Like other playwrights dealing with the traditional theme, the present playwright has given it a new orientation. Of the many innovations introduced the one, the formost at that, pertains to the sentence the Princess is supposed to have uttered. In the traditional episode it is *asti kaścid vāgviśeṣaḥ*. The present playwright has made it *asti kaścid vāgarthaḥ* possibly, because he did find the third word of the sentence going well with the beginning of the third Kāvya, the *Raghuvaṁśa* which starts with the word *vāgartha*. In the episode it is only the *vāk* portion of the third word which is possible of connection with the beginning of the Mahākāvya, the *viśeṣa* portion remaining high and dry, presenting a sort of anachronism. With *viśeṣa* substituted with *artha* it is possible to bring in more aptness into the incident of beginning each Kāvya with each component of the sentence. The attempt is ingenious, though not very convincing. If each word is taken up in each of the Kāvyas as such, *asti* as such, *kaścit* as such, why should then the third one, the dual of *vāgarthaḥ*, be the singular of *vāgarthaḥ:* If this cannot present an insurmountable difficulty, it should similarly present none in the omission of *viśeṣa* in the case of the episode. Again, the question *asti kaścid* has *svāvasya* in it. The Princess's question : 'Is there any improvement in speech ?' goes very well with the defectiveness noticed in it by her earlier, which was the cause of Kālidāsa's expulsion. *Asti kaścid vāgarthaḥ* lacks it. It just means : Is there any meaning in speech which does not have much of relevance in the context under notice. Further, in the episode the question follows the approach of Kālidāsa to the Princess after acquiring learning. In the play it appears much before that. It is while expelling the dullard that the Princess says that she would wait for him and if he would came back to her after acquiring learning she would ask him the question. This takes away somewhat from the sequential naturalness.

The second major innovation pertains to the acquisition of learning. In the traditional episode Kariyā acquires it just through the accidental grace of goddess Kālī. In the present play a whole set of new incidents has been introduced to lead to this consummation. Since the brilliant Kālidāsa had lost his brilliance in an accidental head injury that he had received when he was three years old, he is made to regain it after his expulsion through a similar accidental hit on the head by a thick branch of a tree. He is then made to pursue his studies in the Gurukula of Ācārya Vāmadeva for five years and thus acquire learning. He being the son of the famous Naiyāyika Śivadāsa of Devagrāma who died while the young one was just three years old, is all the imagination of the playwright. So are two Pandits Dhūmraketu and Govardhana, Pārvati, the mother of Kariyā or Kālidāsa, and Ilā, the friend of the Princess. The name Sudarśana for the King is also the playwright's creation.

The other innovations of the playwright pertain to Ilā's presence at the time of Kālidāsa's expulsion and her persistent pleading with the Princess against it, accepting him as such and allowing him a chance to learn by arranging his education, the pining of the Princess for him regretting her action and procurement of the works of Kālidāsa from Ujjayinī, referring to them appreciatively with quotations from them in her discussion with Ilā. Kālidāsa's journey to Uttarākhaṇḍa, the northern region, covering all the places as described in the *Meghadūta* before undertaking the great work is also a novelty peculiar to this play. So is his invitation to help in the direction of one of his own plays and his ceremonial bringing in to the city amidst tumultuous welcome. The finale comes with the union with the mother and the reception at the court.

One of the significant features of the play is that it shows Kālidāsa a well-established poet even before he meets Vidyottamā the second time. His verses are already sung in towns and cities. There is nothing of the kind in the traditional episode. Another notable feature is the introduction into the play of the two-fold interpretation of the questions and their answers, one connected with Philosophy and the other with Polity which too the traditional episode does not have.

Though the original episode is rather small, the playwright has a fairly lengthy play out of it by dilating on a few things and by introducing many an innovation as detailed above. The very dialogue between Dhūmraketu and Govardhana, the former coaxing the latter to join his plan and the latter resisting, the former boiling with anger and the latter pacifying him, but ultimately joining him occupies the major portion of the First Act. Similarly, a fairly lengthy portion of the Third Act is taken up in Ilā's recounting her sad story of how her parents were butchered by Śakas and how the timely arrival in Vidarbha of Vidyottamā's father, an ally of Vikramāditya Śakāri had saved her. A better part of the Fourth Act is occupied with Vidyottamā's description of some of the salient features of the works of Kālidāsa punctuated with appropriate quotations from each. A substantial portion of the Fifth Act is taken up as in the *Maghadūta* which is ascribed to Kālidāsa himself in the present with the description of the route which he is said to have followed in his onward journey to the North with a graphic description of the places on the way on the lines of the *Meghadūta* in addition to minute as also picturesque delineation of the places high up on the Himālayas showing the playwright's intimate acquaintance with the terrain.

All the winding dialogues and the detailed mention of the places and regions, though dramatically not very ept, have, however, one advantage. They afford an opportunity for the full play of the descriptive talents of the author. The most remarkable of his descriptions is that of the Himālayan region where the poet in him bursts out again and again. As an instance may be mentioned his description of the Mandākinī studded in part with a reproduction of an old verse :

परितोऽत्युच्चैः शुभ्रहिममण्डितशिखरेभ्यः प्रस्रवन्तीनां तरलमौक्तिकावलिद्युतिविडम्बिनीनां जलधाराणां प्रपातैः समृद्धसलिला मन्दाकिनी स्वच्छन्दोच्छलदच्छजलैः हर्षविहितस्नानाह्निकानां भक्तानां मन्दतां भिनत्ति ।

Equally poetic is the description of Uṣīmaṭha :

प्राकृतिकसौन्दर्यनिधिरेव सा स्थली । एकतस्तु गिरिजया पयोधरघटसमविनिसृतैः पयोभिः

1. p. 2"0.

परिषिच्यमानानां देवद्रुमाणां हरितनीलपङ्क्तयो ऽपरतश्च देवपूजनार्हाणां लेखनीयत्वग्धारकाणां भूर्जपादपानां शुभ्रावल्यो दर्शकानां दृष्टीराबध्नन्ति । अत्र च यक्षवधूवेणीभूषणप्रसूनमञ्जरीप्रसवयितृणां पारिजाततरूणामरुणाभकिसलयसम्मिश्रहरितपत्राणि मरकतमणिजटितगारुडरत्न राशय इवाभान्ति । ग्रन्थिपर्णकृतप्रणयानां मृगमदमृगाणां समासादनेन समधिगतसुरभिषु शिलातलेषु प्रणयिभिः सह संविशद्भिः यक्षतरुणैः कल्पतरुपल्लवेषु गौरीपतिचरितानि लिख्यन्ते गीयन्ते च ।[1]

How graphic is the description of the sudden appearance of clouds and the outbreak of the storm :

सहसा पूर्वस्यां दिशि कामिनीकृष्णकुन्तलसवर्णानां सघनानां घनानामाडम्बरेण सकलं नभोमण्डलमभिव्याप्तम् । परितश्च निबिडेनान्धेन तमसाऽऽवृताः सकला दिशः :⋯तदानीमेवापतितः प्रचण्डो झञ्झावातः । भीषणो दुःसहश्च प्रभञ्जनस्तरूणां स्थूलान् दृढांश्च स्कन्धांस्तृणानीव प्रकम्पयितुमारेभे ।[2]

The playwright has a good command over his expression which is generally appropriate and idiomatic. There are, however, certain aberrations one of the more prominent of which pertains to his frequent use of Perfect with reference to the speaker himself in violation of Pāṇini's prescription for it only in *parokṣa* when the incident/incidents is/are not a matter of direct experience on the part of the speaker vide *parokṣe liṭ* (3.2.115), e.g.,

गोवर्धनः—परं त्वं तु तत्र कलहे प्रवृत्तो बभूविथ,[3] कालिदासः—प्रथमं...तावदहम्... उत्तरपश्चिमामाशां प्रतस्थे,[4]...गिरितटान्यतिक्रम्य दशार्णदेशं...,अहं कुरुक्षेत्रमाससाद,[5]... कनखलं सम्प्राप्य,[6]...गौरीमठनामकतीर्थमधिजगाकं,[7] विद्योत्तमा—नहि, नहि, न मया तया (तथा ?) सौभाग्यशालिन्या बभूवे ।[8]

The second pertains to the use of Parasmaipada in place of Ātmanepada either the root being Parasmaipadin, e.g., *ākrośate*[9] and *ākrośamāṇā*[10] *or ākrośamanā*[11] in place of *ākrośati* and *ākrośantī, ākāṅkṣamāṇam*[12] in place of *ākāṅkṣantam*, or Parasmaipada being specifically enjoined in certain conditions, e.g., *pravahamānā*[13] where Pāṇini specifically enjoins Parasmaipada by *prād vahaḥ* (1.3.81). In an isolated case of *jijñāsati*[14] Parasmaipada is used where Pāṇini specifically enjoins Ātmanepada by

---

1. p. 204.
2. p. 178.
3. p. 23.
4. p. 195.
5. ibid.
6. p. 197.
7. p. 198.
8. p. 203.
9. ibid.
10. p. 36.
11. p. 131.
12. p. 214, 216.
13. p. 208.
14. p. 201.
15. p. 81.

jdṛñāśrusmṛāṁ sanaḥ (1.3.57). The third pertains to wrong use of gender. *Avadhi* which is masculine is used in the feminine. e.g , *asyām ovadhau.*[1] *paribandha* which is masculine is used in neuter, e.g., *paribandhaṁ naṣṭam.*[2]

His other anomalies consist of his use of *pratyekasya*[3] which should have been *pratyekam*, that being Avyayībhāva; *sañjvālayitum*[4] which should have been *sañjvalayitum*, *jval* being *mit* by Pāṇ Gaṇasūtra *ghaṭādayo mitaḥ*—the *mittva* in the case of *jval* and a few others (by Gaṇasūtra *jvalahvalahmalanamām anupasargād vā*) is optinal only when they are not preceded by a preposition—leading to the shortening of the vowel, vide Pāṇ *mitāṁ hrasvaḥ* (6.4.92); *āśrayiṣiṣṭa*[5] which being the Aorist form should have been *āśrayiṣṭa*; *parisiñcanārtham*[6] which should have been *pariṣecanārtham*, *num* to *sic* being admissible only when followed by *śa*, vide Pān. *śe mucādīnām* (7.1.59); *sammilanam*[7] which should have been *sammelanam* with Guṇa by Pāṇ. *pugantalaghūpadhasya ca* (7.3.86).

The work has a number of syntactical irregularities as well, e.g.,

(1) काल्युपासकेन मे भर्त्रा देब्या प्रसाद इति मत्वा सुतं कालिदासाभिधानेन समलङ्चकार (the correct term should be समलञ्चकार) ।[8]

(2) बादकी वीणाया मुरजस्य च स्वरान् साधयन्ति ।[9]

(3) पश्य दीर्घिकाया रामणीयकम् । सा च प्रफुल्लपुण्डरीकेन्दीवरकोकनदसुमनोविभूषितं स्वच्छसुनीलसलिलालङ्कृतम् ।[10]

(4) इयं चापि मां सहचरी स्थाने स्थाने परिभ्रान्ता ।[11]

(5) विन्ध्याद्रेर्विशीर्णां रेवां कुकुभसुरभिणश्चानेकान् गिरितटान्यतिक्रम्य दशार्णदेशं समाससाद ।[12]

The author is caught napping in at least two places in the use of Sandhi which is very wrong : *śirocālanam.*[13] *prabalo prahāras tu.*[14]

In a work in modern period it is not uncommon to have some reflection of vernacular expression. The present work is no exception to it. The expressions दुर्बला एव क्षमाया रागमालपन्ति,[15] अलमेतै: किन्तु परिन्त्वत्यादिभि:,[16] तव कथनमाचरिष्यामि,[17] वृद्धा तदुपरि पट्टिकां बध्नाति,[18] चैतन्यमधिगत: स:,[19]

1. p. 73.
2. p, 63.
3. p. 14.
4. p. 415. Bhaṭṭojidīkṣiṭa has offered justification even for such forms : *kathaṁ tarthi prajvālayati unnāmayati* ; *ghanantat takarotīti ṇau.*
5. p. 16.
6. p. 58.
7. p. 202.
8. p. 40.
9. p. 60.
10. p 124.
11. p. 175.
12. p. 195.
13. p. 89.
14. p. 91.
15. p. 24.
16. p. 25.
17. p. 26.
18. p. 36.
19. p. 42.

(=होश में आने पर), मत्स्यकेव छटपटायमाना,[1] नागरिकास्तु···मनोरञ्जनं लभन्ते,[2] अन्या चेयं वार्ता,[3] एवमन्यन्निवेदनम्,[4] ततश्च ससमारोहं संस्कारो विधीयते,[5] धूम्रकेतुगोवर्धनौ पुनरपि जयकारानुद्घोषयतः,[6] ईषत्तु धैर्यं धारय,[7] कियती रजनी व्यतीता,[8] एकस्य दिनस्य तु वार्ता का क्षणमप्यवस्थानमसम्भवम्,[9] शाकुन्तलं नवनाटकविधया वर्णितम्,[10] निवेदनमेकम्,[11] पृच्छामि किम्न[12] ?
do have on them a shadow of the vernacular ones.

The author has skilfully interwoven some lines or expressions from earlier works particularly from those of Kālidāsa either as they are or with suitable modifications. The line *na jūne vidhis tasyaikaṁ subhagaṁ sukṛtinaṁ varaṁ samupasthāpayiṣyati*[13] cannot but bring to mind the *Śākuntala* line *na jāne bhoktāraṁ kam iha samupasthāsyati vidhiḥ.*[14] *priyajanasaṁvibhaktaṁ duḥkhaṁ sahyavedanaṁ bhavati*[15] has been taken up as such from the same work.[16] *Vipad vipadam anusarati*[17] and *kṣata eva prahārā nipatanty abhīkṣṇāḥ*[13] are the same with some changes as from Bāṇa and Viṣṇuśarman respectively where they are *satyo 'yaṁ janapravādo yad vipad vipadaṁ sampat sampadam anubadhnātīti*[19] and *kṣate prahārā nipatanty abhīkṣṇam.*[20] *hṛdayadaurbalyaṁ vimuñca*[21] easily shows the presence in the mind of the author of the *Gītā's hṛdayadaurbalyaṁ tyaktvā.*[22] *sarve janāḥ kuśalinaḥ sukhinaḥ santu*[23] is a quotation from an old work in inverted commas with the addition of *janāḥ* and *sukhinaḥ.* Vidyottamā's *hṛdaya ! alam uttāmya*[24] is the same as Śakuntalā's *hṛdaya mā uttāmya.*[25] *gamanāya padam udvahati*[26] does carry on it a reflection of the *Kumārasambhava's nikṣepaṇāya padam uddhṛtam udvahanti.*[27] So does *kāntāsammitopadeśa eva yuktatamaḥ*[28] of Mammaṭa's *kāntāsammitatayopadeśayuje.*[29]

Occasionally the playwright just uses Hindi words with Sanskrit terminations, e.g., *pākhaṇḍibhiḥ,*[30] *jholakaḥ,*[31] *mañcikā,*[32] the last meaning a table.

The playwright also goes in for onomatopoeic words a couple of times, e.g.,

---

1. p. 50.
2. p. 67.
3. p. 58.
4. p. 73.
5. p. 83.
6. p. 84.
7. p. 87.
8. p. 100.
9. p. 118.
10. p. 149.
11. p. 153.
12. p. 169,
13. p. 19.
14. Kā Gr ,p. 453.
15. p. 37.
16. *Kā Gr.*, p. 463.
17. p. 42.
18. p. ibid.
19. p. *Kādambarī*, Nirnaya Sagar Press, Bombay, 1916 p. 146
20. *Pañcatantra*, II. 178.
21. p. 50.
22. p. II. 3.
23. p. 59.
24. p. 87.
25. *Abhijñānaśākuntala, Kā Gr.*
26. p. 97.
27. V. 85.
28. p. 117.
29. *Kāvyaprakāśa*, I.—2
30. pp. 7., 197.
31. p. 35.
32. p. 139.

ह्लादिनी तडतडकडर्कदिति श्रूयते,[1] नेपथ्ये दारुच्छेदजन्यः कटकटेति ध्वनिः,[2] द्वारदेशे खटखटेति ध्वनिः,[3] खटखटायिते च द्वारे,[4] सहसा सुदूरे···तडकडर्दिति निर्घोषः समुत्पन्नः[5]

The deformed speech put in the mouth of the dullard wood-carrier running for considerable length is a great coinage of the author showing in full measure his imaginative faculty even in creating a language. First it occurs when Kālidāsa or Kariyā of the time is cutting the branch of the tree on which he is perching and the two Pandits Dhūmraketu and Govardhana meet him and the second time after the marriage when he pleads for himself in the face of the severe reprimand of the Princess. It will not be out of point to mention here a few of the specimens for the better appreciation of the connoisseurs :

(1) होय पंडते! तुअं सच्चे कत्थेअसि । परं हं करोमि किं ? मम तु जानु एव फुट्टः ।[6]

(2) कथं न ? होय पंडते जया तुमं कत्थेअसि, तथा ह करोमि । ममं करेसि विवाह ।[7]

(3) किं कत्थेअसि एकस्स विस्सविद्दालस्स अचारः, ई किं वत्थु ?[8]

(4) किं कत्थेअसि ? आरपुत इति किं वत्थु, हं न जाणे । हं तु मातर् पुतो भवेमि तुमं जाणेओ ।[9]

(5) कत्थेमि हं तु। हं तु मातर् पुतो,। तस्सा सारधे गरामे वसेमि । वणे काट्ठे छिन्देमि, आपणे विकरय करेमि । मातर् रोट्टिका करेदि, हं खादेमि ।[10]

Interestingly, for reasons best known to him the playwright presents the translation, of the contrived speech in Bhojpuri, in contradistinction to the Sanskrit matter which is done in Hindi. May be, he feels the translation of this also should look different so that it is just marked out.

The playwright is very strong in his prose which is very descriptive at times. It mirrors the entire situations and captures the feelings and emotions in their entirety.

The playwright has developed a style which effectively portrays what goes around mirroring particularly the feelings and emotions of the characters, in short, crisp sentences. As a specimen is reproduced below the paragraph which reflects the worry, the anxiety, the helplessness of the distraught mother when her only son does not stop cutting the branch of the tree while sitting on it :

वत्स ! एवं स्थितेन शाखाकाष्ठं कस्मात् छिद्यते ? नीचैरवरोह । देहि अवधानम् । हा ! न कर्णे कुरुतेऽयं मे वचः । शाखां कृन्तत्येव । ...अचिरादेवायं पतिष्यति खलु ।

---

1. p. 14
2. p. 130.]
3. p. 87.
4. p. 171.
5. p. 180.
6. p. 35.
7. p. 50.
8. p. 10.
9. p. 102.
10. p. 105.

मूर्खोऽप्येष एतयैव सार्धमात्मानं पातयित्वा पाणिपादे भङ्क्ष्यति । हा पुत्र ! सावहितः शृणु । विरम, विरम । हा ! अयं तु कथमपि न विरमति । हन्त ! एवंविधस्य विद्वद्वरेण्यस्य ईदृशो मूर्खः पुत्रः ।[1]

As one more specimen could be reproduced Vidyottamā's outburst at the helpless wood-carrier who tearfully solicits her to live with him now that she is his wife, which portrays most forcefully her anger, her hatred, her detestation of the rustic symbolizing the Great Deceit she had been subjected to :

रे वज्रमूर्ख ! धूर्त ! मामात्मना सह नेतुकामः । असह्या कल्पनाऽपि । त्वमितः सत्वरमपसर । यावत् पितृचरणा वृत्तमेतन्नैव विजानन्ति राजकर्मचारिभिश्च त्वं वधस्थलं न नेनीयसे तावदेव त्वमितो बहिर्याहि । निर्गच्छ ।···अहो···नैव निर्गच्छसि । आकारयाम्यहं भृत्यान् । त एव त्वां सार्द्धचन्द्रं भर्त्सयन्तस्ताडयन्तश्च नगराद् बहिः प्रक्षेप्स्यन्ति ।[2]

Though the playwright has introduced a number of characters the play revolves, as in the traditional episode, round two characters, Kālidāsa and Vidyottamā, the others playing only a peripheral role.

The playwright has first depicted Kālidāsa as Kariyā, a foolhardy wood-carrier and later as Kālidāsa, a poet of great fame, who is very much attached to his lady-love in spite of her having ill-treated him. As rustic, he is innocent and honest to the core which even the imperious Princess in her calmer moments concedes. She admits that he had no intention to deceive her. There was no artificiality about him, he was the same man inside or outside. When cornered by the Princess he blurts out the entire story as to how he was picked up by the Pandits Dhūmraketu and Govardhana and brought to the Palace on the promise of marrying him to a Princess. He also gives his own interpretation of the gestures in the Śāstrārtha. By raising one finger he thought the Princess wanted to punch his one eye. By raising the three fingers he wanted to convey that he would punch hers both as also wrench off her nose. As a simpleton he is not able to understand as to why the Princess should address him as Ācārya or Āryaputra. He even suggests that if the Princess is not prepared to live with him he would go back to his village and live with his mother. He even pleads with her not to turn him out, now that he is her husband. As Kālidāsa he always remembers her. Even though very harshly treated by her, he does not nurse any rancour for her. As a matter of fact, she is the spirit behind his poetic creations. It is she who is behind her immortal characters, Śakuntalā and the Yakṣī.

As for Vidyottamā, she is a lady of firm conviction. She resolved to marry only that man who would defeat her in scholarly disquisition, the

---

1. p. 30. 2. p. 112.

Śāstrārtha. Once defeated, she marries the person introduced to her as Darśanācārya. She waits for him impatiently after the marriage and wants him to take the initiative in love-making while he sits stoically and does not do so. 'Is the initiative to come from me, a lady'; she asks herself. Finding the so-called scholar reticent even after midnight when his vow of silence as given out by the deceitful Pandits was to come to an end, she is forced to engage him in conversation. First she thinks the so-called scholar is playing a joke on her by speaking to her in rustic language but when finally the cat is out of the bag, she is beside herself with rage. She calls out to Ilā and gives the young dullard the severest of the reprimands going to the extent of kicking and slapping him. All the pleas of Ilā to be patient with him fall flat on her. The fool is summarily turned out and, as shown in other adaptations of the traditional episode, she pines for him later.

As a lover of letters she procures the works of Kālidāsa who had risen to great fame as poet. She discounts the suggestion Ilā impliedly conveyed that the same could well be her husband, his name also being Kālidāsa. Ultimately the same happens which she had not imagined. Destiny smiles on her. Kālidāsa being brought to the city in procession is none other than her own sweetheart. Both the husband and the wife unite after a lengthy conversation tracing the genesis of each work and the presentation of them one by one by the former to the latter. The consideration that the latter (the Princess) shows to Kālidāsa's mother bespeaks her nobility. She remembers nostalgically her affectionate hug when she first met her on her coming to the city in search of her son.

As a play *Asti Kaścidvāgarthīyam* ranks as one of the finest of the attempts of its kind. The theme in the play is well evolved and has a highly innovative touch which imparts to it absorbing interest. The very fact that the play has been staged twice, once in 1967 in the Govt. Post-Graduate College, Pithoragarh and the second time in 1973 in the Thakur Devi Singh Visht College, Nainital speaks volumes for its stageworthiness. The playwright deserves full plaudits for presenting to the Sanskrit world this creation of beauty which certainly is a joy for ever.

11

VIDYOTTĀMĀKĀLIDĀSĪYAM

Written by Acharya Ram Kishor Mishra, it is a Mahākāvya in twenty-one cantos woven round the traditional account of Kālidāsa : his being an ignoramus originally, entrapped into deceitfully marrying a learned Princess who vowed to tie the nuptial thread to a man learned enough to humble her in scholarly disquisition, the Śāstrārtha, through the machinations of a rejected scholar who arranged between the Princess and him (Kālidāsa) a Śāstrārtha in signs to be interpreted by him (the scholar) with intention of teaching the Princess a lesson for her arrogance, the Princess soon discovering her so-called husband to be a dud, his being turned out by her from the palace unceremoniously, his acquiring learning thereafter and returning to her, his knocking at her closed doors and her asking him the question *asti kaścid vāgviśeṣaḥ*: Is there any improvement in speech and his composing three of his works each beginning with each of the words in the sentence culminating in their happy reunion. This narrative being very popular among them, a number of modern writers have based their works on it. Strange though it may seem, except the present one, all of them happen to be dramas. The present work was published by the author himself in 1984.

Theme

The Mahākāvya opens with the King of Kāśī trying hard to obtain a son. Once he shows his palm to a palmist who predicts that he would have a daughter after ten years. Very learned, she would immortalize his name. Her fame will spread far and wide. Married to a fool she will later turn into a poet's wife and a poetess herself. This pleases the King who tells his wife all about it. She goes to the temple of Gaṇeśa and prays there for off-spring (Canto I). The Queen having become pregnant in due time the King performs Puṁsavana and Sīmantonnayana rites wherein he feeds Brahmins and his kith and kin. Women sing songs. Some knowledgeable person marks the Queen's steps, the other one examines her palm and still another horoscope. Some predict a son for her, some daughter. The Queen gives birth to a daughter in the early hours of a Sunday. The King is happy at this but not the Queen. She wanted a son. The King tells her that it just does not matter whether it is a son or a daughter. He orders festivities in the kingdom. On the eleventh day of her birth, the girl is given the name Vidyottamā. A darling of her parents, she indulges, upto the age of five, in all sorts of pranks. The King, his name Śāradānanda, engages a number of teachers to teach her different lores like Grammar, Literature, Lexicons, Polity, Erotics and Dance. At the age of sixteen her fame spreads through the whole of Kāśī. The King then thinks of her marriage. Coming to know of the King's desire through friends, she takes the vow that she would marry only that man who would defeat her in the Śāstrārtha which delights the King. The vow having been well-publicised in the kingdom, attracts a number of people young, old and middle-aged, Mishras, Pathaks, Acharyas, Dwivedis, Trivedis and even Chaturvedis, poets, prose writers, dancers, singers and experts in Polity and Erotics. They all fail to defeat the Princess in the Śāstrārtha. In a situation like this one Bhairavanātha, a prominent scholar of India, even though 52 comes forward at the instigation of scholars smarting under defeat to engage the young Princess of 18 in Śāstrārtha which the King fixes for the following day. He, however, gets worried at the thought of his daughter becoming the wife of an old man. He goes to her to tell her of his anxiety. He feels sorry for the vow undertaken by her. Throughout the long conversation between the two she maintains her composure and is the least worried. She is confident of defeating the old man (Canto III).

The Śāstrārtha starts the next day. The topic is : Which of the two, *bhāgya*, fate and *karman*, action, is more powerful ? It is *bhāgya* according to Bhairavanātha and *karman* according to Vidyottamā. The example of Rāma having to go to forest cited by Bhairavanātha for the inexorability of fate is countered by Vidyottamā by citing another example, that too of Rāma, in supporting the force of *karman*. Rama could obtain Sītā by breaking the bow which is *karman*, action. If it were fate, Rāma or any one else could have got her, even without the breaking of the bow. To Bhairavanātha's other instance of Satyavān having got Sāvitrī without effort in support of the forcefulness of fate Vidyottamā's reply is that even there *karman* or action is present; Sāvitrī had put in efforts to find out Satyavān for her. And then comes Vidyottamā's argument of arguments. She cites Bhairavanātha's own example in proving the superiority of action. He has come to have Śāstrārtha with her to have her for him which is *karman*, action. If it were fate, he need not have come for the Śāstrārtha and would have her any way. Bhairavanātha has no answer to this. He concedes victory to Vidyottamā. Now, what Vidyottamā had been doing so far was that whomsoever she would defeat in the disquistion, she would put him to some service or the other. In line with that she asks Bhairavanātha if he is ready for it.

He agrees but advises the Princess to desist from such a course. With the victory of Vidyottamā over Bhairavanātha, her fame spreads far and wide. With all the scholars so far approaching her for Śāstrārtha having been floored, the people in the Court begin to have doubts about Vidyottamā ever getting married (Canto IV). Such also is the feeling of her mother. She is happy when she hears of her daughter's victory but feels depressed when she thinks of her marriage. One day she comes to her and tries to persuade her to give up her vow to which she (Vidyottamā) does not agree. As for her husband, she would get him in due time. On that score she has no worry. She assures her mother that in case she is unable to find a husband in terms of her vow, she would choose one from among those defeated. This statisfies the mother. In the meantime, an attendant informs the Princess that she has to get ready for Śāstrārtha scheduled to take place after eight days and conveys to her the King's message that she should start necessary preparations for it. There could be questions on Philosophy. The attendant is unable to say as to who is coming for the Śāstrārtha. The Princess tells her mother that Śivanātha, the Ācārya of the Gurukula or one of his learned pupils wants to engage her in Śāstrārtha. An aged Śivanātha wants to marry her the young one. But then such is the vow. The mother again tries to persuade her, in view of the possibility like the above, to give it up to which she does not agree. She assures her that she would wed a young man (Canto V). Now the story of Bhairavanātha is that he goes to his teacher Śivanātha who infers from the former's remark that nothing is well with scholars and people like him in Vidyottamā's rule of scholarship that he has suffered defeat at her hands. He tells Śivanātha that he has all regard for Vidyottamā's scholarship but the way she treats her vanquished adversaries is what he is against. One among them she has appointed a door keeper, the other one to serve breakfast, still the other one to serve food. Him she has made the stable supervisor. He suggests to Śivanātha, upset at the insult to scholars, to arrange her marriage with a fool which he alone can do. Śivanātha agrees to do so and asks Bhairavanātha to look for one. Bhairavanātha goes out and comes across a person cutting the very branch of the tree on which he is sitting. He does not listen to Bhairavanātha asking him not do so lest he should fall down with the same. He advises him to come down for he has something to do with him. On hearing it he jumps down in spite of Bhairavanātha asking him to come down slowly lest he should injure himself. He does injure himself by jumping down but is soon all right. He tells Bhairavanātha that he lives in the house of Princess Vidyā. From Bhairavanātha's bearing he makes him out to be an Ācārya. He laughs at Bhairavanātha's query about his family for the purpose of arranging his marriage with the Princess. He informs him that he had lost his parents when he was five. His father was, as he has heard, of the Bhāradvāja Gotra and of the Miśra sub-caste. His mother had the name Kālī and father Kālīnātha. Him they had given the name Kālidāsa, known more among the peole as Mūrkha, fool. He accompanies Bhairavanātha to the Gurukula on the understanding that he would be married to a Princess and is produced before Śivanātha who assures Bhairavanātha of marrying him to her and thus rescue the scholars from ignominy. (Canto VI). After tutoring him to keep silent and making him comprehend the signs, he takes him to the Court of the King of Kāśī to engage the Princess in Śāstrārtha. The Princess asks him (Śivanātha) if he, even in his advanced age, is stricken with lust in thinking of marrying a young lady of eighteen. No, no, says he. He already has six sons and one daughter from his two wives and is satisfied on that account. It is his pupil who would have the Śāstrātha with her. He is the young man Kālidāsa who at the very first sight impresses the Princess with his handsomeness and silence which Sivanātha explains is due to his having undertaken a vow. According to Śivanātha he would answer all her questions in gestures which he, Śivanātha would explain. To the Princess disinclined for this type of Śāstrārtha, he says that she has inflicted defeat on a number of scholars which could mean her remaining unmarried. It carries social stigma inviting public calumny. Already people say all sorts of things about her. People connect her insult of scholars with her illicit relationship with a servant in the Palace to satisfy her lust. They also speak about her falling in the hands of a dullard. That is why, in the absence of scholars, he says, he has persuaded the silent young man to go in for Śāstrārtha. Keeping her youth in view Śivanātha advises the Princess to think of having a husband for her, for a woman without a man is no good. Vidyottamā agrees to have the Śāstrārtha with the philosopher Brahmacārin, who, though unwilling, agreed for marriage on the persuasion of Śivanātha. In the Śāstrārtha, Vidyottamā, raises one finger. The fool thinking that she wants to pierce his one eye raises two. Śivanātha's explanation of the two signs is : The Princess's one finger means that Brahman is one. The fool's two fingers mean that he has two aspects, without form and with form, *nirākāra* and *sākāra*. Next the Princess raises five fingers. The fool thinking that she wants to slap him, raises the fist. Śivanātha's explanation of the two signs is : Five fingers mean that there are five Bhūtas, Beings. The fist means that these five together are responsible for creation. The answers having satisfied the Princess, she concedes defeat. The King of Kāśī announces her marriage the same night to which he invites all his courtiers, soliciting their blessings for the couple which they offer in full (Canto VII). Kālidāsa leaves for the royal palace with a marriage party of Pandits who indulge in all sorts of loose talk about him as also the Princess. The poor dullard in all his bright dress and ornaments is an object of ridicule for them, more so, with the possibility of his becoming the ruler of Kāśī in the time to come. The Princess, reaping the fruit of her insult to the Pandits in the discovery in due time in marrying an ignoramus, is an object of derision for them.

The party reaches the well-lit palace. The King gives away rich gifts to its members and the womenfolk of noble lineage sing traditional marriage songs. The party, after being received ceremonially, is treated to a sumptuous feast which is followed by the wedding ceremony to the accompaniment of the songs by ladies of noble birth. With all the traditional rites like the Seven Steps having been gone through, Vidyottamā and Kālidāsa are declared man and wife. This having been achieved, Śivanātha leaves back for the Gurukula along with his pupils while the newly-weds leave for their palace. The King and the Queen are happy to see their daughter with their son-in-law. The only desire of the King now is to have a son born to them to inherit the throne of Kāśī (Canto VIII).

In their room in the palace with its one bed and two chairs the Princess beckons to Kālidāsa to come to the bed. He, however, sits on the chair and does not budge from it on the ground that he not being a Prince, is not fit for the royal bed. He likes to sleep on his poor charpoy. The Princess tells him that the honeymoon night is not to be spent alone, the two-some have to be together in it. She asks him to look into her eyes and notice the streak of passion in them which the poor fellow is not able to mark. He has not read the Kāmaśāstra, the text on Erotics, the science invented by Vātsyāyana. The Princess is ready to teach him that if he were only to come to the bed. She has the feeling that he knows only Philosophy and not Erotics. She invites him to her to drink deep at the joy of life, to engage in love making. While Vidyottamā is passionate, Kālidāsa is not. All of her wooing of him as also efforts to turn him on fall flat on him. While this is on, a camel grunts. The Princess asks Kālidāsa as to whose grunting it is. That of *uṭra*, camel, says he. He begs apologies of her on being asked as to why he has mispronounced *uṣṭra* for the slip of the tongue. She asks him to trace the word *uṭra* with the rules of Grammar. On his telling her that he does not know Grammar, she asks him to talk of Śāstra, in case he has no interest in love making and to quote sūtras to form *uṭra*. This ushers in the most fateful of the moments in the life of the couple. Kālidāsa confesses his total ignorance of the Śāstras and reveals the stunning truth that he had been persuaded by the vanquished Pandits to marry her by proclaiming him a scholar in silence. Vidyottamā first takes it a joke. How come, she asks him, he could answer her questions in the Śāstrārtha ? He then explains to her as to what he had meant by his signs. Vidyottamā, feeling convinced that he is a dud, refuses to accept him as her husband, who, thinking that he is so now, whether dud or otherwise, invites her to him to satisfy him. An argument ensues between the two : Vidyottamā refusing to accept him and he pleading with her to show due consideration to him, she having married him. He is not a fool, says he, in the sense that he follows his routine all right, which is to lumber wood in the forest. Vidyottamā orders him out of her room. Or else she would have to call the King. All the entreaties of Kālidāsa to change her mind fall flat on her. He tells her that she, being an Indian wife, should be knowing the duties of a Pativratā and should not, therefore, insult him. Vidyottamā tells him that if he wants respect from her, he should acquire learning, be a scholar and come back to her. Then only would she accept him as her husband. Her vow was that only the one defeating her with his superior knowledge could be her husband. He has, therefore, to be learned to be accepted by her. She would wait for him till then. Kālidāsa agrees to this and gets ready to leave for the Gurukula from where he had come to marry her. He requests her not to keep him away from her mind. She on her part prays to gods for his wisdom and wellbeing. With this the poor fellow repairs to the Gurukula and the hopeless Princess falls listless (Canto IX).

In the Gurukula Kālidāsa tells his classfellows all that happened to him. They suggest that he should approach the Guru, engage in study and become learned to have the princess for him. Accordingly Kālidāsa approaches Śivanātha and tells him that the Princess has turned him out. He is a fool. She is learned. Only a learned person can be her husband. The whole problem according to Śivanātha arose because Kālidāsa had given up silence. Vidyottamā could make out thereby that she had been deceived by the defeated Pandits. Kālidāsa tells Śivanātha that he being her husband now she should have better taught him and educated him, if she felt that he was not so. She however, did not listen to all this and instead turned him out. He requests Śivanātha to teach him so that he could be wise. The latter advises him to devote himself to studies and bring Vidyottamā home by winning her by his speech. His line on the palm indicates that he is going to be a poet. He asks him to take up the study of metres. Kālidāsa requests him to teach him all that so that he could get his wife. Śivanātha is surprised at his attachment to her though forsaken by her. Following the principle of wickedness for the wicked, he asks him to forsake her too. He advises him not to study in the Gurukula for he feels that the King having come to know that his son-in-law is a fool may come there to enquire of him as to why he had arranged a fake marriage by declaring a silent fool a great scholar. It would be better from him, therefore, to go somewhere else so that the King is not able to find him over there. If he finds him, he would have him put in chains there and then. He tells him to go about places and study wherever he likes. Kālidāsa says that when he becomes learned, the Princess would accept him. And that would be the time for him to forsake her. If she begs of him he would accept her as his wife. That should be enough punishment for her. With these words which he asks the Ācārya to keep in mind and in quick steps he goes out. It is a quirk of destiny that the husband of a Princess the previous night was going out to move from place to place the following day. The husband and wife were separated from each other now. Since he left the Gurukula for fear of the King nobody could see him (Canto X). Now back in the capital the King was happy that his daughter had got a husband. That he is a fool he did not know. Kuśalikā, the maid sent by him to enquire of Vidyottamā's welfare, told him that she was sitting sad in her room with her silent philosopher husband missing. It appears that her husband has gone out somewhere. It was about him that she was having a talk with her mother with sorrowful heart. The Queen had asked her to tell the King to come immediately. On hearing this the King leaves for the room of his daughter. There the Queen tells him as to how the daughter had been cheated by the defeated Pandīts by arranging the game of signs. Her husband is the fool of the first water. Silence for him was the cover for his ignorance which came to the fore the moment words escaped his lips. Vidyottamā had turned him out. She does not agree with her father that since she is married now to Kālidāsa, she should accept him, fool or no fool. Her vow had been that she would accept only that man as her husband who would score a victory over her in Śāstrārtha which in the present case was with one who was observing silence which was just a ruse. She has nothing against the man but certainly against the Ācārya who cheated her by obtaining from her consent forcibly for silent Śāstrārtha. Had it been a verbal one, the fool would not have been able to vanquish her. The King does not approve of her expulsion of the fool. She could have taught him if she could cooperate with him which she did not do. Even as it is, the fool can turn, through her reprimand, into a scholar. Her abandoning him may usher in a happy moment in his life. She tells the King that in her presence he had made the promise before leaving that he would become a scholar. The King blesses her to have a learned husband. She would have to wait till then. He then leaves along with the Queen to the Gurukula to enquire of Śivanātha as to why he should have his daughter married to a fool. Śivanātha denies his having done so and does not accept Vidyottamā's version. He couldn't have broken his silence before the stipulated period of one year. He sticks to his version that he is a great scholar and philosopher and lays all the blame at the door of the Princess. In her conceit she had been insulting scholars, says he. She has now branded her husband a fool for his not speaking anything because of his vow of silence. The royal couple then leaves back for the Palace in the hope that the Princess could one day be united with her learned husband (Canto XI).

As for Kālidāsa, he on coming out of the Gurukula meets a holy man, a Sādhu, with whom he moves about to different places like Ayodhyā, Prayāga, Kānyakubja, Hastināpura, the river Carmaṇvatī, the Vindhya mountain and the cities in between like Daśapura, Devagiri, Ujjayinī as also several rivers. Through intimate association with him for three years he acquires good knowledge of the Śāstras. He then thinks himself fit enough to go to Kāśī. He reaches first the Gurukula, meets ths Ācārya who sends the information to the King about the Śāstrārtha. The King conveys the same through a letter to Vidyottamā who sends her reply, also through a letter, wherein she says that the Śāstrārtha that she had last was her final one. It was after that that she was made to wed Kālidāsa. He is her husband. If there is to be a Śāstrārtha it could be with him only. Let him come alone to her Palace and prove his learning in words (and not by signs as he had done earlier). Nobody in the talk is to act as judge. The King drafts a letter on these lines and has it despatched to the Ācārya who gets the King's idea and sends Kālidāsa to Vidyottamā. Before leaving, Kālidāsa has a talk with his classfellows who tell him all sorts of things. He then comes to Vidyottamā and tells her what he has studied. It is something of Grammar and something of literature. Vidyottamā puts it to him that if he is able to answer her question *asti kaścid vāgviśeṣaḥ* in verse she would accept him a learned man. This renders Kālidāsa speechless. He wants time which the Princess allows. He decides then to go to the Gurukula from where, he says, he would be back only when he is able to compose poetry. The Princess assures him that she would wait for him till then and offers him all her good wishes for the success of his mission (Canto XII). After his departure Sāradānanda, the King of Kāśī, comes to Vidyottamā to know as to how things stand with her. He comes to know from the female attendant that Kālidāsa had come to the Princess and that he could answer her questions. She, however, wanted him to answer a particular question in verse which he could not do. The King is surprised at the condition of verse and enquires of the Princess whether she has no liking for Kālidāsa. From an uneducated person he has turned an educated person now. Does she want to turn him into a learned person ? The Princess tells the King that she wants him to be a poet, a wise man and not half wise and half ignorant. He is expected to spend some time in practising poetry and would turn into a poet through separation from her, his beloved. The poet knows the worldly ways. He knows how to love his wife. He has to be intelligent, with deep insight into the feelings of the people. He thus wins love of the people and honour from the King. She, therefore, would like him to be a poet. She is sure that he would give the answer to her questions in poetry and would come back to her one day. It is only then that she will decide whether he can be her husband or not. She assures her father that she has no feeling of indifference for him. All that she is doing is for his betterment only. The King leaves at this and enters then Suśīlā, the friend of the Princess. An interesting talk ensues between the two. Vidyottamā tells Suśīlā that Kālidāsa is striving to be what she wants him to be. Suśīlā on the other hand wants that Vidyottamā should invite Kālidāsa. There is no life for a woman without husband. It is just wastage of time. It is from him that she gets all the joys and all the pleaures of life. She further cautions that the Palace and all that it contains belongs to her father. What belongs to her is her husband who in reality is hers. Vidyottamā counters this by saying that like a son a daughter too has a share in her father's property. Being the only child all that which belongs to her father is hers. Suśīlā disagrees with her. According to her, if a woman does not have the joy of having a husband, then all other kinds of happiness have no meaning for her. All this a woman feels only, says Vidyottamā, if she has a husband of her liking. She has all regard for Suśīlā's views. She is, however, firm in her resolve to accept Kālidāsa as her husband only if he were to pass the test as and when he comes to her as per his own words. She does not listen to anybody, her father, mother, friends and attendants and remains unbending. On the other hand, Kālidāsa begins practising poetry and comes to be known as poet Kālidāsa. Every day passing brings him more and more of fame in Kāśī. Once as he was practising poetry, some friends, Tapanadāsa, Pavanadāsa, Somadāsa and Vipinadāsa approach him and have a light talk with him. The main subject is the Princess. Some have doubts about her accepting him. Others are sure that she would, now that he is writing beautiful poetry. Some think that he may not be lucky enough to get her. Others are of the view that luck would favour him and that he would be able to have her. One of the friends has a dig at Kālidāsa whom the Princess did not accept when he went to her the first two times. Now the third time he would bring her round with his poetry. Kālidāsa checks him and says that he would simply fulfil his word and do nothing in bringing her round. On being asked to recite the verses composed by him, he recites those from the *Ṛtusaṁāhra.* He goes on practising poetry daily. One day Vidyottamā has a talk with her friends who tell her about Kālidāsa and his beautiful Kāvyas as also fame he attained in the poetic symposia. One of them, Suśīlā had heard his description of six seasons in verse last spring. Vimalā and Suśīlā tell the Princess that she had wanted a poet to be her husband. That desire of hers is now going to be fulfilled. Vidyottamā is exceedingly happy at Suśīlā's remark that Kālidāsa will now be able to answer her questions in verse and that of Kamalā that he would compose a poem on her under the inspiration of separation. As the talk among the ladies is on, a knock is heard at the door. The attendant enters and informs that it is poet Kālidāsa. The friends of Vidyottamā leave at this while she invites him to the bed which be declines. He tells her that in answer to her question he has composed three Kāvyas each beginning with each of her words, the *Kumārasambhava* in which she is depicted as Pārvatī who could not but obtain Śiva with her hard penance, the *Meghadūta* wherein she is depicted as Yakṣī in whose separation a Yakṣa sends her message through cloud and the *Raghuvaṁśa* were husband-wife relationship is depicted in such union as can be visualized in words and meanings. It is she who peeps through her female characters like Sudakṣiṇā, Indumatī and Sītā. He hands her over all the three works which gratifies her. She now has the kind of husband she had been wanting to have. He is a poet, a scholar and expert in Prosody. His speech is refined. She invites him to bed to satisfy her. Kālidāsa refuses it on the ground that what she has done to him is what a *guru,* a teacher, would do to a *śiṣya,* a pupil. Since he now looks upon her as *guru,* it will not be possible for him to take her as his wife. This introduces altogether a new situation for Vidyottamā who strives to explain to Kālidāsa that what she had done to him is what a good wife would do to a husband. She had been duly married to him.

She has a right to his love. Why should the poet feel otherwise ? Kālidāsa sticks to his view, refers to the honeymoon night and his expulsion which Vidyottamā wants him to forget. All her explanations that she was out to improve him and seductions and force to make love to her fail to move him. He runs away from her leaving her weeping and cursing herself for her scholarship which made her insult her husband. Her vow had ruined her. Though married, she is without a husband as if she were a widow. She thinks of a number of possibilities to bring him under her control, one of which is to put him under arrest which on second thought she does not find going well with love which, being a matter of the heart, cannot be forced on anybody. She tells the attendant that Kālidāsa having become a poet is angry with her. By undertaking the vow she has set everything at naught. The attendant advises her not to give up but try to bring the husband round. She feels certain that like Śakuntalā she would meet with success ultimately. She should first try all means to trace him. Enquiry may first have to be made with the Gurukula. She should use all her ingenuity in retrieving the situation, the ingenuity by which she had vanquished all the Pandits. Mere crying won't do. Vidyottamā then asks her to bring her parents to her who come to her and find out from her all that had transpired between her and Kālidāsa which prompts her father to remark that the wise follow the policy of doing to others what they do to them which exactly is what Kālidāsa has done. He disapproves of Vidyottamā's suggestion to go to the Gurukula with an army. Force won't work in the present circumstances, says he. A husband has to be won over by begging of him, by being humble. His suggestion to her, therefore, is that she should go to the Gurukula alone and bring Kālidāsa round. In accordance with this she goes to the Gurukula and meets Śivanātha who tells her that Kālidāsa had come to her from Ujjayinī and possibly had gone back to it. He advises her to go there, report the matter to its justice-loving ruler Vikramāditya and get her husband back through his good offices. As an encouragement to her he tells her that it is her insult that has turned him wise. Making up her mind to go to Ujjayinī and to file a suit with Vikramāditya she returns to Kāśī, takes leave of her parents and proceeds to Ujjayinī (Canto XIV). Reaching Ujjaynī she first prays at Mahākāla temple for the success of her mission. She then goes to the Royal Office and files an application for her husband which the Minister-in-charge places before the King. Vidyottamā is called to the Court. She introduces herself as the daughter of the ruler of Kāśī. She declines the chair ordered for her by the King and wants justice like any other of his subjects. If the position is that the wife has to be with the husband, she has to be with Kālidāsa who, even when having married her through sacred rites, refuses to accept her. Justice it is that a wedded wife should go to the man who wedded her. The Courtiers echo her sentiments and request the King to provide her the opportunity to serve the poet so that she may not have to court unhappiness in separation from him. The King now wants to hear

Kālidāsa according to whom what Vidyottamā has said is all untrue. When he took her as his wife she refused to take him as her husband giving the go-by to the husband-wife relationship. Vidyottamā then tells the King all that had happened with her : the plan of the defeated Pandits to arrange a disquisition in signs with a fool which Kālidāsa was at that time declaring him to be a scholar observing silence, her defeat, her marriage with him, her joy at that and his (Kālidāsa's) being a dud in reality. She had accepted him as husband and accepts him even now. Kālidāsa disputes this by saying that on the honeymoon night she had charged him with being a fool and not accepting him as her husband, had abandoned him. Vidyottamā's reply is that never had she said that he was not her husband. For Kālidāsa the situation is different. He harps on the fact of his having not been accepted as husband on the first night. Had it been otherwise, the present situation would not have arisen. He refuses to accept one who has not accorded him the position of a husband. To him she is an opportunist. Hence his request that his application for divorce be accepted. He charges Vidyottamā with placing obstacles every time in his life, not giving herself over to him, having never had any physical contact with him, expelling him from the house and chiding him. He also accuses her of being conceited, coming to him only when he is well off, not having accepted him as husband when he was not so. Vidyottamā on being questioned accepts everything, but adds that she accepts the poet Kālidāsa as her husband and not the dud one. She joins issue with Vikramāditya in pointing out that she was actuated by the desire to be good to her husband—from a fool he has turned a wise man now—which is the duty of a wife when he finds fault with her in not adhering to the tradition of Indian wifehood in serving even a fool and abandoning him. Kālidāsa does not dispute Vidyottamā's statement and accepts it. Since Vikramādiya finds the statements of both not untrue, he feels that they are man and wife and rejects Kālidāsa's application for divorce. The position with Kālidāsa is that on his own admission he has taken Vidyottamā as his wife. Further, he did not remarry on separation. As for Vidyottamā, she accepts him as her husband. Both are intelligent. The King decides that both should engage in a poetic bout. If Kālidāsa scores victory in it, it will be upto him to accept or not to accept Vidyottamā. If it were otherwise, he shall have to accept her. This decision of the King elicits all praise from his Courtiers. Next day Vidyottamā and Kālidāsa present themselves in the Court, the former pleading with the latter in most poignant terms to accept her and the latter asking her to go to Kāśī trading all the oft-repeated charges. Ultimately it is Kālidāsa who bends and accepts Vidyottamā. She then comes together with Kālidāsa to his house. The priest makes for its ceremonial entry into it to the accompaniment of ladies songs (Canto XVI). In their house Kālidāsa and Vidyottamā have a nice time. Vidyottamā gives birth to a son. The event is celebrated with great fanfare. From the King and the Queen downward all senior officials of the State as also prominent citizens bless the new-born (Canto XVII). The poet and his wife mention a number of possibilities on names for the child who is fondled affectionately by them and when grown up is asked by the mother to play with the father. The child asks the mother to tell a story which she does. The story is that of a crow on a post dropping a gram into a pit, approaching the village carpenter to make an axe to cut the post, the carpenter not agreeing to do so, the crow approaching the King to kill the carpenter, the King not obliging him, the crow approaching the Queen to show her anger to the King, she refusing to do so, the crow approaching a rat to nibble off the dress of the Queen, it not doing so, the crow approaching a cat to kill the rat, the cat not doing so, the crow approaching a dog to kill the cat, the dog going out to kill the cat and the things starting happening in the reverse order from that onwards till the carpenter lumbers the post and the crow is able to retrieve the gram and eat it. Vidyottamā awakens the child by referring to all that which is associated with the morning (Canto XVIII). A daughter is born to Vidyottamā after some time. She contracts fever. No treatment works with her and she succumbs to it leaving the grieving parents (Canto XIX). After some time another son is born to Vidyottamā who tells him in the form of lullabys a number of stories. The poet asks him to learn Sanskrit (Canto XX). He teaches him nominal and verbal forms. He tells him the story of Vālmiki : How he was first a dacoit and later turned into a Ṛṣi due to contact with Nārada. He teaches him compounds. He asks him to try to learn composing poetry. The child recites his poem, his own composition. Vidyottamā praises the poet for his poems and the fame that they have won him. She asks him to work on a new composition. Both Kālidāsa and Vidyottamā lead a life of householders. Kalidāsa writes the lyrics, the *Ṛtusaṁhāra* and the *Meghadūta* ; the two Mahākāvyas, the *Raghuvaṁśa* and the *Kumārasambhava* and the three dramas, the *Malavikāgnimitra*, the *Vikramorvaśīya* and the *Abhijñānaśākuntala*. With these seven works, he wins acclaim and with his family life as also charming feelings becomes a poet of Śṛṅgāra Rasa, the sentiment of Love. With this ends the vo uminous Mahākāvya on Vidyottamā and Kālidāsa.

Critical Appreciation

The latest of the works on the traditional Vidyottamā-Kālidāsa narrative, it follows it to a point only, after which it takes an altogether independent line. The basic kernal of it maintains which is that a King had a daughter named Vidyottamā who was very learned and had taken the vow that she would marry that man only who would defeat her in Śāstrārtha. A number of scholars tried their luck at it but failed. They then conspired to wreak vergeance on her by arranging her marriage with a fool. They set out to look for one and came across him in one who was seen cutting the very branch of the tree on which he was sitting.

They presented him as a great scholar observing silence, arranged for his disquisition with the Princess in gestures which they explained ingeniously, thus bringing about the defeat of the Princess leading to her marriage with him. Later hearing the word *uṭra* from him, the Princess discovered him to be a fool and expelled him from the Palace. The next part of the narrative of Kālidāsa finding himself in the temple of Kālī crying before the idol, the appearance of the Goddess before him in person, her enquiring of Kālidāsa as to why he was crying, his uttering the word Vidyā meaning thereby that Vidyottamā had misbehaved with him and the Goddess taking it to mean that he wants *vidyā*, knowledge and her granting him that, his acquiring the name Kālidāsa thereby, the poet has just abandoned. He has retained only the last part of it; Kālidāsa coming back to the Princess, she enquiring of him, *asti kaścid vāgviśeṣaḥ*, is there any improvement in speech and Kālidāsa composing three of his works beginning with each of the words as above. Even upto the point the poet has followed the old narrative, he has introduced a number of innovations. He makes Vidyottamā the daughter of the ruler of Kāśī whose name he gives as Śāradānanda. To her mother he assigns the name Śāradā. Interestingly, he is in the habit of going in for connected names for husband and wife. This is noticeable in the names of Kālidāsa's father and mother too. She is Kālī and he is Kālīnātha, the lord of Kālī, the same position as in the case of Śāradā and Śāradānanda. The fool does not acquire the name Kālidāsa due to his being the recipient of the grace of Kālī. He is said to be already having it, the family tradition probably having something to do with it with the mother's name being Kālī and that of the father Kālīnātha, as noticed above. Among the other innovations are the introduction of the episodes of Bhairavanātha and Śivanātha and the ill-treatment by the Princess of the defeated scholars which is presented as the *raison d' etre* of teaching her a lesson by marrying her to a fool. The introduction of the Gurukula in the story is also original. It figures in quite a few places. Śivanātha is presented as the Ācārya of the Gurukula. The fool is brought to the Gurukula by Bhairavanātha from the forest where he was discovered by him, to be presented to Śivanātha for tutoring. Kālidāsa comes to the Gurukula after his expulsion by Vidyottamā. The King of Kāśī comes to it in search of him. Kālidāsa comes to it after having been turned away for the second time by the Princess to practise poetry. The other notable innovations are Vidyottamā's father approaching her to express concern at the possibility of her falling in the hands of an old man in terms of her vow and her mother urging her to withdraw it precisely for the same consideration and Vidyottama's assurance to her mother to marry one among those defeated. The entire incident of Kālidāsa going to the Gurukula after expulsion, his talk with its Brahmacārins, introduced as his classfellows, though he is nowhere said to be receiving his education there, with regard to what had transpired between him and the Princess, his meeting Śivanātha, his advice to him to go elsewhere to escape possible arrest, Kālidāsa's meeting a Sādhu and spending three years with him in visiting different places as also in learning, the King's coming to the Gurukula in search of Kālidāsa and his being put off by Śivanātha, Kālidāsa's going to the Princess after three years and her asking him to answer her query *asti kaścid vāgviśeṣaḥ* in verse, his not being able to do so, his coming to the Gurukula to practise poetry are all the creation of the author. So are the characters Suśīlā and Kamalā who, particularly the former, tell the Princess as friends as to what it means to have a husband and that she shouldn't have repudiated hers. By far the greatest innovation is the total abandoning of the incident of the grace of Kālī. Even the devotee in him could not persuade the author to believe that knowledge could descend on a person so suddenly that it could turn a blockhead into a great poet. Hence his mention of Kālidāsa's visiting different places to imbibe better awareness of the world, a necessary equipment of a successful poet and his acquistion of knowledge by learning the Śāstras and becoming a poet by practising poetry. In his attempt to introduce an element of rationality in Kālidāsa's acquistion of learning he has not been particularly successful in furnishing an explanation for the name Kālidāsa which the traditional narrative does far more rationally. In the poem Kālidāsa is shown already possessing it. There is no justification in the appearance of the word Kālī in it except for that it was continuation of the nomenclature of parents who too had it just as a matter of chance. The traditional narrative, the whole of it, flows out of this part of the name. The poem has nothing of the kind.

To make a poet out of Kālidāsa, the author has invented the story of Kālidāsa coming to the Princess three years after his expulsion, her asking him to answer hes question *asti kaścid vāgviśeṣaḥ* in verse, his practising poetry and coming back to her with his three poems each beginning with each word of the above and his handing over of them to her. The traditional narrative with all the innovations and novelties closes here. What follows is the author's own imagination and innovation. The author had almost come to the end of the Kāvya at one point. He thought later—on his own admission he composed his work in two instalments, the second instalment in 2041 V.S. following the first in 2035 V.S. after a gap of six years—to extend it to carry it forward by inventing many new situations and incidents mainly to show his skill in writing Sanskrit songs in which he simply excels. It is in this part that such modern ideas as divorce appear.

Since it is a Mahākāvya, it is natural for it to have some events incidental to the main narrative. These are the announcement of the marriage of Vidyottamā on the very night of her defeat, the festivities going with it, the marriage procession of Kālidāsa, the details about the wedding, the ladies' songs and the like. The author seems a trifle too much wedded to the marriage tradition of his area to have introduced everything of it in the description of Kālidāsa's wedding including the taunts of the ladies and their catcalls. The wedding feast has all the wide variety of delicacies which find copious mention in the work. The common enough scene in Indian weddings with shouts and noise that go with reception is vividly captured by the author as can be seen from the following :

कोऽपि—मोदकान् देहि मह्यं तु
अन्य:—मोहनभोगमिच्छसि ?
कोऽपि—कथं नेच्छामि तं देहि
अन्य:—गृहाण पण्डितवर !
....
अन्य:—स्वदते रसगोलान्नं
इतर:—पिण्डान् देहि महाशय[1]

Though the author has tried to be consistent in his approach all through, there are inconsistencies in his work here and there. When an attendant comes to Vidyottamā with the message of the King that she may start necessary preparations for the Śāstrārtha scheduled for eight days thence and that there could be questions on Philosophy, she tells her mother that Śivanātha or one of his pupils would be coming to have Śāstrārtha with her. The only possible explanation could be that she could have inferred this from the fact of the possibility of the questions on Philosophy. Śivanātha was known as an authority in that discipline. She could have thought that it could be he or one of his pupils trained by him in that discipline who could alone have the competence to challenge her in that. The only difficulty in this interpretation on Vidyottamā's words is that nowhere does she give the impression that what she was saying was her guess. She seems to be sure that it is Śivanātha. That is the import of her statement to her mother that an old man is coming to marry her, young lady of 18. It seems the coming event was very much present in the mind of the author when he put the above words in the mouth of Vidyottamā.

The other inconsistency is when Vidyottamā engages Kālidāsa in conversation in the first night of marriage. The conversation continues for some length. Except for some naive remarks of Kālidāsa which could well be interpreted as due to his not being initiated to the art of love, there is nothing of foolishness in him. It suddenly sprouts forth in his use of the word *uṭra*. That is the traditional narrative. There too the discovery is with *uṭra*. The same had to be in the present work too. Whether this goes well with its setting of grammatically correct and well-pronounced sentences by Kālidāsa earlier or not is a different matter.

There is obvious inconsistency in the behaviour of the fool which the

1. VIII. 42-44, p. 61.

poet seems to have ignored. He also does not seem to have succeeded well in presenting Kālidāsa as a fool. Except for the two traditional incidents of cutting the branch of the tree on which he was perching and his mispronouncing the word *uṣṭra* as *uṭra* as also the talk of his with Bhairavanātha where he indulges in pranks like jumping down the tree and his unidiomatic expressions like *kena vivāhṁ mama kariṣyasi,*[1] with whom would you marry me, prompting Bhairavanātha to remark that he is a fool of the first water, *mūrkharājas tvam,*[2] in using the masculine *kena* for the feminine *kayā*, there is not much evidence of foolishness in Kālidāsa. Further, as has been pointed out earlier, there is talk after the marriage in the honeymoon night between him and Vidyottamā which goes on to a considerable length. There is no use by him therein of any grammatically incorrect word. Even for the word *uṭra* Kālidāsa begs apology of the Princess for the slip of tongue. Even when the Princess rejects him and orders him out, he pleads with her to accept him in the name of his being her husband.[3] Even while going out he asks her to keep him in mind which certainly is no nonsense. His behaviour, except of course a few patches here and there, does not go well with his image of a fool which the author seems to project by mentioning him as such. He even denies that he is a fool : *mūrkho'smi nāham*[4] and advises the Princess to have due regard for him : *kānto'smi te'haṁ kuru tasya mānam.*[5] It seems the poet is torn between the conflicting considerations, after his abandoning the incident of the grace of Kālī for the intelligence to dawn on Kālidāsa, of presenting him a perfect fool with no intelligence and presenting him with a modicum of that, with a spark lying buried under ashes of ignorance which could fly out when stoked by better contact with the people of different persuasions and constant application to literary pursuits. It is this which is responsible for the apparent contradiction in the poet's depiction of the character of Kālidāsa.

A poet has to be careful about propriety which should in no case be violated. The present poet has not been particularly careful in this. Śivanātha's remarks about the Princess having an affair with a Palace attendant to satisfy her lust which is the talk of the people, openly in the court, in her very presence and that of her father violate all norms of decency.

Equally indecent and inelegant is the seduction of Kālidāsa after marriage by Vidyottamā in most lurid expression, his naivette in not

1. VI. 30, p. 43.
2. VI. 31, p. 43.
3. स्वामी तवाहं मम सासि पत्नी
   यस्या विवाहो हि मया सहाभूत् ।
   पत्युस्त्वया मानततिर्विधेया
   पत्न्याः पतिर्वै परमेश्वरो ऽस्ति ।।
   IX. 51, p. 75.
4-5. IX. 52, p. 75.

responding to her overtures notwithstanding. A certain suggestiveness, an artful initiative in having the innocent young man close enough to generate the warmth of love could have far more appeal to aesthetic sense than the straight invitation :

वक्षःस्थितौ पश्यसि मे न कुम्भौ ?
यौ जीवनीयेन रसेन पूर्णौ ।।
एतौ हि सर्वः पिबतीति लोकः
प्रेम्णा गृहीत्वा स्वकरद्वयेन ।
एत्या त्वमग्रे नय मां स्वपार्श्वे
पीत्वा रसं तं शमयेः पिपासाम् ।।[1]

The poet paints the Princess with urge for sex and Kālidāsa without it :

सा राजपुत्री रतिरक्तनेत्रा
मुग्धं पतिं सन्ततमीक्षते स्म ।
चाञ्चल्यमासीन्न तु तस्य काये
प्राप्तुं च पत्नीं न स कामभावः ।।[2]

If this lack of urge was to be attributed to his foolishness even the biggest of the fools do have this natural instinct when even the most overt attempts to turn them on don't succeed, how come that the same fool talks of making love when the Princess on discovering that he is so refuses to accept him her husband :

त्वं सुन्दरी मां प्रतिभासि जाये
आयाहि मां पूरय मे च कामम् ।।[3]

One of the most prominent features of the Kāvya is, as mentioned by the poet's wife in her introduction of him towards the end, its new metre which is his own invention, *svāviṣkṛta*, brushing aside older ones, *purātanaṁ taṁ chandomārgaṁ tyaktvā* which obviously is an overstatement, the poem having a good sprinkling of the older metres like Anuṣṭubh in Canto 1, verse 1, Canto III, verses 1-32, Canto IV, verse 1, Canto VII, verses 11-12, the whole of Canto VIII except verses, 30 and 35, Cnato IX, verse 68, Canto XII, verses 5-40, 42-46; Indravajrā in Canto II, verses 34, 38, 44, 46, 47, 49, Canto IX, verses 1-15 and 17-76; Upendravajrā in Canto II, verse 48; Upajāti in Canto II, verses 33, 36, 37, 41-43, 45, Canto IX, verse 16; Vaṁśastha in Canto VII, verse 1; Drutavilambita in Canto X,

1. IX. 18-19, p. 70.
2. IX. 27, p. 71.
3. IX. 47, p. 75.

verses 2, 32-34; Hariṇī in Canto II, verses 31-32, 39, 40; Śārdūlavikrīḍita in Canto I, verses 8-16. By and large, however, the poet has used the new metre and handled it successfully and with telling effect. His poem which has rightly been termed by his wife as lyric, has achieved thereby fluency which has few parallels in contemporary Sanskrit literature.

The other prominent feature of the poem is its conversational style, except for supplement-looking addition after Canto XVI making the work unique in every respect. Some of the Cantos the poet composes with final alliteration, the Antyānuprsāsa, which again is the special feature of the work. So also is the Rhyme. The classic example of both these is the Sixteenth Canto where they have been employed in the context of the poetic bout between Kālidāsa and Vidyottamā with a very happy effect. A stanza or two from the same would be worth reproduction by way of specimen :

विद्योत्तमा—-न देवयानिरहं शर्मिष्ठा प्रेमी त्वमसि ययातिः ।
या कामयते तवानुग्रहं सा देव्यहं नृजातिः ॥
करं गृहाण, गृहं नय, गमय न यौवने वनं माम् इतो मे राम विलोकय माम् ॥[1]

कलिदासः—-गुणाः क्व मयि ते सन्ति गुणास्त्वयि धनसम्पदः समस्ताः
मां प्राप्नुया न वा द्विधापि सा त्वं प्रियमोदकहस्ता ।
राजसुता त्वं मादृशा जनाः समेषितारस्त्वाम्
गच्छ काशीं त्वं विस्मर माम् ॥[2]

Rhyme is employed by the poet quite successfully in Cantos III and V in the context of the conversation between the King and the Princess and the Queen and the Princess respectively. In the conversation the last line of the verse uttered by the King is

सुते प्रतिज्ञा विहिता त्वया कथम् ?

that by the Princess is

पितस्त्वया चिन्ता नो विधेया

that by the Queen is

वत्से प्रतिज्ञामधुना त्यजेरिमाम्

that by the Princess is

भविता विवाहो मातस्त्यजेः शुचम्

In the songs from Canto XVII onwards Antyānuprāsa and Rhyme are almost the regular features. The songs are very happily worded and have a flow which is unique in many respects. A few stanzas from the same are reproduced below by way of specimen :

---

1. XVI. 10, p. 138.
2. XVI. 25, p. 141.

(1) काशिराजसुते ! अहं ते प्रेमवचने सदा रंस्ये ।
त्वमसि विद्योत्तमे ! विद्या, तद्वचस्तु कथं न मंस्ये ?
मां प्रिये ! भवती स्वकीये प्रेमकारागृहे क्षिपति ।
पुनः मातुः स्मृतिर्भवति ?[1]

(2) मातः श्रावय कामपि गाथां शृणु सुत चटकाकथां स्मरामि
यस्यां काकः कथयति सततम् 'अग्रे त्वं चल पुनरायामि' ।।
चटकाकाकावेकपादपे मित्रे भूत्वा प्रतिवसतः स्म
क्षेत्रे विकीर्णगोधूमकणान् तौ सह गत्वा भक्षयतः स्म ।।[2]

(3) त्रेतायां साकेतसमीपे वने दस्युरेको वसति स्म
इतस्ततो गच्छतो मार्गिणो लगुडप्रहारात्स लुण्ठति स्म ।
तत्र गतो नारदो वदति तं दस्युराज कथमिदं करोषि ?
हुङ्कुरु रे सुत ! कथां शृणोषि[3]

The Antyānuprāsa, it may be mentioned in passing, appears rather laboured at places. In his anxiety to create it the poet sometimes introduces words which are rather uncommon. The refrain in one of the songs is *priye viṣamaṁ kathaṁ calasi.* Since it ends in *lasi* the poet strives to end the previous line also in the song to end in it going for this sake rather uncommon and, more often than not, contrived forms : *lāvaṇyam alasi, Kāśījigamiṣāṁ khalasi, bhāvinīm* (*bhāvanām ?*) *alasi, Ujjayinyām eva palasi, māmakīnadāmpatye valasi.*[4] This labouredness is noticeable in the author's use of a particle to create an Antyānuprasa when it is not possible otherwise as can be seen in the following song :

(1) सुभगे तव रोदनेन नयने रक्ते भूते स्मरणं जहि हि
शान्तिं धारय प्रिये न रुदिहि

(2) क्षिप्राजले गृहीता शान्तिस्तया प्रिये ! तन्मोहं जहिहि
शान्तिं धारय प्रिये ! न रुदिहि

(3) गमनागमनं भवति भवेस्मिन् सांसारिकीं स्मृतिं नो तनु हि
शान्तिं धारय प्रिये ! न रुदिहि

(4) तस्य शिवस्य भगवतः स्तवनं तस्या आत्मशान्तये कुरु हि
शान्तिं धारय प्रिये ! न रुदिहि

(5) शयेऽधुनाहं त्वमपि च स्वपिहि
शान्तिं धारय प्रिये न रुदिहि[5]

Here the refrain ends in *rudihi.* Not every verb being possible of ending in *hi* the author puts the particle *hi* after such of them as do not have it

1. XVIII, 4.4, p. 175.
2. XX. 20.1, p. 205.
3. XXI. 5.1, p. 210.
4. XVII. 7, p. 165.
5. XIX.9.1-5.

to conform to the last word of the refrain creating thereby an impression of a forced Antyānuprāsa.

Occasionally the final *a* interferes with the Rhyme, e g.,

(1) तव कामं मंस्ये किं त्वं नो यास्यसि मे वशताम् ?
प्रिये त्वं गच्छेः काशीधाम ।।[1]

(2) यदा समर्पितवती स्वं न तत्कथं जिघृक्षसि माम्
प्रिये! त्वं गच्छेः काशीधाम[2]

This probably has something to do with pronunciation. It is not uncommon to see the final *a* not pronounced. With this the Rhyme would be fine.

Occasionally it is *visarga* which interferes with the Rhyme, e.g.,

कविरयमस्ति मदीयां कवितां शृणुत सभासत्सन्तः !
कविपत्नी कवयत्री का स्यान्मामन्तरेण हन्त ![3]

It could be *n* and *ṇ* in an odd case :

शृणुत हि कर्णधारमुख्यानां कर्णा ! वदत मुखानि !
अन्यायोऽयं नरस्य नारीं प्रति, किमहं करवाणि ?[4]

Since it is the new metre invented by the poet, he is not bound by the old convention of Sandhi between the last vowel of the First Pāda and the first vowel of the Second one as can be seen in some of the examples as given above.

There are dialogues generally in full stanzas or hemistichs or even a line. Occasionally even the line is split to form short question and answer sentences :

विद्योत्तमा किं चिन्त्यते ?
कालिदासः किञ्चिन्नहि ।
विद्योत्तमा किं वाञ्छसि ?
कालिदासः काल प्रिये !
विद्योत्तमा ददामि तम् ।
कालिदासः तद् गच्छामि ।
विद्योत्तमा कदैष्यसि ?
कालिदासः काव्यं कृत्वा ।।
विद्योत्तमा क्व यास्यसि ?
कालिदासः गुरुकुलम् ।
विद्योत्तमा प्रतीक्षिष्ये
कालिदासः आयास्यामि[5]

1. XVI. 9, p. 138.
2. XVI. 19, p. 140.
3. XVI. 49, p. 145.
4. XVI, 53, p. 146.
5. XII. 47-49, p. 102-3.

The poet has studded his work with traditional wedding songs, as stated while dealing with the theme, of ladies, one stanza out of which would do to give an idea :

मया गौरवर्णस्त्वाहूतः
कथमागतः पुनः कृष्णस्त्वम् ?
मया महाकवितस्त्वाहूतः,
समागतः कथमकिञ्चनस्त्वम् ?[1]

There was a practice widely prevalent in India till recently which is the case even now in the countryside and smaller towns of presenting utensils to the members of the marriage party. The poet refers to it in the context of Vidyottamā wedding :

राज्ञा दत्ता हि सादरम्
....
स्थालिकाश्चमसाः स्थाला वेलाकटोरकंसकाः ।
धिषणाश्चषका स्थाल्यो हसन्त्यः स्वेदनीयुताः ।।
ऋजीषाणि जलद्रोण्यः शरावा कलशीमुखाः ।
उदञ्चनानि सन्दंशाः कुम्भाश्च कटकैर्युताः ।।[2]

Occasionally the poet's expressions are influenced by those in Hindi :

1. इयं योजना चतुरः कर्णान् नोल्लङ्घ्य प्रसरेत्[3]
   Hindi : यह योजना चार कानों से बाहर नहीं जानी चाहिए
2. भ्रामराः पतितास्तस्याः[4]
   Hindi : उसकी भावरें पड़ीं
3. तस्य तौ चरणौ···विपिनं प्रत्यवर्धेताम्[5]
   Hindi : उसके पांव जंगल की ओर बढ़ते जा रहे थे
4. सा यदा सहयोगं करोति[6]
   Hindi : वह जब सहयोग करती है
5. मह्यं सहयोगं न ददाति[7]
   Hindi : मुझे सहयोग नहीं देती
6. ततः सोऽभवदवाक् श्रुत्वा[8]
   Hindi : तब वह सुनकर अवाक् रह गया
7. कालिदासस्य सा दृष्टिर्नीचैर्निपत्य नोन्नता[9]
   Hindi : कालिदास की नज़र नीचे गिर कर उठी नहीं

1. VIII. 30, p. 59.
2. VIII. 26-27, p. 58.
3. VI. 17, p. 40.
4. VIII. 79, p. 65.
5. X. 1, p. 79.
6. XI. 37. p, 93.
7. XVII. 4.3, p. 162.
8. XII. 46, p. 102.
9. Ibid.

8. तुकबन्धनं करोषि कवे त्वम्[1]
Hindi : कवि, तुम तुकबन्दी कर रहे हो

9. परं तया न गृहीतं कस्मादपि शिक्षणम्[2]
Hindi : पर उसने किसी से भी सीख नहीं ली

10. ध्यातेग वाक्य शृणु राजपुत्रि ![3]
Hindi : राजकुमारी, ध्यान से बात सुन

11. एवं भवेत्तत्सखि ते मुखे ऽस्मिन्,[4]
क्षेप्स्यामि शीले घृतशर्करे हि
Hindi : ···तेरे मुंह में घी शक्कर

12. तं···राजानं कुरु मनसः···[5]
Hindi : उसे मन का राजा बना लो

13. सत्यं समक्षमागच्छति[6]
Hindi : सच सामने आ रहा है

14. सभासदां जयजयकारशब्दैः[7]
Hindi : दरबारियों की जयजयकार से

15. निष्पक्षोऽयं भवतो न्यायो[8]
येन पयो दुग्धे पृथक्कृते
Hindi : यह आपका न्याय पक्षपातरहित है जिसने दूध का दूध और पानी का पानी अलग कर दिया

16. त्वं रुष्टस्त्यक्त्वा मामुपविष्टः[9]
Hindi : तुम रूठ कर मुझे छोड़कर बैठ गये हो

17. पतिरासीन् मूर्खो विज्ञो वा सो ऽमन्यत तु त्वाम्[10]
Hindi ; ···वह तुम्हें मानता था (इज़्ज़त देता था)

18. अहो दैव···स कः खेलस्त्वया प्रसूतः[11]
Hindi : अरी किस्मत यह क्या खेल तुमने खेला

19 ···नित्यमकरवं निजमात्मानं ह्यनुरक्तम्[12]
Hindi : ···अपने आपको···

20. त्वत्तः पराजितमनुभवामि स्वात्मानम्[13]
Hindi : अपने आपको···

1. XIII. 34, p. 109.
2. XIII. 28, p. 108.
3. XIV. 2. p. 113.
4. XIV. 6, p. 114.
5. XVI. 11, p. 115.
6. XV. 9, p. 128.
7. XV. 41, p. 132.
8. XV. 68, p. 136.
9. XVI. 12, 139.
10. XVI. 29, p. 142.
11. XVI. 50, p. 145.
12. XVIII. 1.11, p. 173.
13. XVIII. 4.8, p. 176.

21. गिरा नो मारय[1]
Hindi : बोली मत मार

22. ते लोका रसरहिता: सन्ति येषां सुतबाला न भवन्ति[2]
Hindi : जिनके बालबच्चे नहीं होते

23. रामो नाम सत्यमिति वदन्
Hindi : राम नाम सत्य है यह बोलते हुए[3]

24. यस्या भ्रमरे गतस्तव प्रियश्चक्रमश्नुते[4]
Hindi : जिसकी भंवर में पड़ा तुम्हारा प्रेमी चक्कर काट रहा है

25. येनेमामावां रक्षाव:
Hindi : जिस कारण हम इसे (गाय को) रखते हैं[5]
This is colloquial Hindi. Normal expression :
गाय पालते हैं

Writing in the present century it was not unusual for the poet to be influenced by modern concepts and go in for new words for the same. Thus the poet uses the word *patnītyāgapatra*[6] for application for wife's divorce, *patnītyāgapatrarakṣaka*[7] for person in charge of application (for wife's) divorce, *parivāraniyojana* (*parivāraṁ tu niyojaya*)[8] for family planning, *sahavāsanirodha*[9] for practice of continence. Even when the concepts are old, he permits himself new words which carry on them the unmistakable impact of vernaculars, e.g., *melasya rātriḥ*,[10] *melaniśāyām*,[11] *melarākāyām*,[12] for the first night, the honeymoon night (vide Hindi *milan ki rat*), *mela* for (Hindi *milan*), *yaunasambandha*[13] for sexual relationship, *śiśusāhitya*[14] for children's literature, *mṛtaghaṭṭa*[15] for cremation ground (Cp. Hindi *murdghat* whose Sanskritization it is). The word *kavisammelana*[16] for poetic symposium is also modern. The old Sanskrit word for it is *kavigoṣṭhī*. Equally modern is the word *auṣadhālaya*[17] for a dispensary or a clinic. Occasionally words which have a different meaning in Sanskrit are used in their vernacular meanings. *Sambhrānta* in Sanskrit should mean in a flurry. In Bengali as also in Hindi it means 'of high family'. It is in this sense that it is used in the present work : *sambhrāntamahilāgītaiḥ*.[18] *Darī* in Sanskrit means a cave. The author uses it in the sense of a carpet[19] (There is a word

1. XVIII. 3.5, p. 174.
2. XX. 1.2, p. 193.
3. XX. 2.5, p. 194.
4. XX. 6.5, p. 198.
5. XXI. 2.2, p. 208.
6. XV. 45, p. 133.
7. XV. 46, p. 133.
8. XIX. 2.6, p, 184.
9. Ibid.
10. IX. 4, p. 67.
11. XV. 36, p. 131.
12. XV. 43, p. 132.
13. XVI. 45, p. 144.
14. XXI. 8.10, p. 214.
15. XIX. 3.5, p. 185.
16. XIII. 51, p. 112; XXI. 7.3, p. 213.
17. XIX. 8.2, p. 191.
18. VIII. 62, p. 63.
19. VIII. 24, p. 58.

dari for it in Hindi. The author Sanskritizes it and uses the Sanskrit word *dari* for the same changing its sense altogether). The word *udgala* he uses in its Hindi sense of *ugalanā*, vomitting.[1]

Such expressions as *svāgataṁ karoti*, welcomes, are not genuine Sanskrit. It is *svāgataṁ vyāharati*. *Susvāgata*, also used by the author, *susvāgataṁ kurvan*,[2] which is fast catching up in modern Sanskrit is a further departure from the established practice.

Sometimes a word which cannot be termed as altogether a new coinage is used by the author. It is a Sanskrit word in its own right but suffers from the Aprasiddhatvadoṣa. Such, for instance, is the word *janapa*[3] for King. The author probably thought if it could be *nṛpa* or *nṛpāla* why can't it be *janapa* But he did not pay heed to the fact of its currency in Sanskrit. Similar is his use of the word *śaileśānasutā*[4] for Pārvatī in which *īśāna* is employed by him in the sense of *īśa*, lord, only unmindful of the fact that it has developed a convention in the sense of Śiva. The expression *śaileśa* would have been appropriate here.

In an odd case the author uses the Hindi word in Sanskrit, e.g., *naṭakhaṭaḥ*[5] for naughty.

While talking of the usage it may not be out of point to mention that it restricts the use of certain roots with certain prepositions only. Thus *lok* in the sense 'to see' has to be with *āṅ*, *loc* in the sense 'to think of', 'to discuss' has to be with *āṅ* again, *viś* in the sense 'to sit' has to be with *upa*, ḍī (ṅ) in the sense 'to fly' has to be with *ud*, the denominative form of *karṇa* in the sense 'to listen' has to be with *āṅ*. That is the usage, the all-powerful one. The author does not seem to observe it as can be seen from the following :

तन्न लोकसे यदहं कुर्वे[6]
लोके हं सुत रेवतीं निजां प्रिय ! बलरामं त्वाम्[7]
लोच्े तन्नयताम्[8]
चित्रित इव स्वस्थाने विष्ट: कवितां कुर्वन् भवान् विभाति[9]
घण्टाध्वनिं निशम्य डयन्ते राजसुते गगने विहङ्गमा:[10]
भवन्त: कर्णयन्तु मम निर्णयरीतिम्[11]
यो यो जन: कर्णयितुकामो गच्छेत्[12]

The beginning of the sentences with *cet* is a common enough occurrence in modern Sanskrit though against the Sanskrit usage. Our author is no exception to it. He resorts to it in

1. XVII. 5.1, p. 163.
2. XI. 44, p. 94.
3. XIV. 94, p. 125.
4. I. 9, p. 2.
5. XVIII. 6.5, p. 178.
6. VI. 20, p. 41.
7. XVI. 78, p. 150.
8. XVI. 57, p. 136.
9. XIX. 5.1, p. 187.
10. XVII. 3.5, p. 161.
11. XV. 34, p. 131.
12. XVI. 2, p. 137.

चेदनृतं स वदेन्निखिलं[1]

It is again the force of usage which does not permit verbal forms of certain roots that are possible grammatically in place of the more current nominal ones. Thus *unnayati* be better avoided in favour of *unnatiṁ karoti* as has not been done by the author in lines :

परिवर्तनं जीवने भवति
कोऽपि जनो नोन्नयति यद्विना ।[2]

In the same strain *ānandāmi*[3] for *ānandam anubhavāmi* is rare. The genuine coin is either just *nandāmi* or *ānandam anubhavāmi* as said above.

Usage restricts certain prepositions to certain roots in certain senses. They cannot be used indiscriminately, with any root any time. To illustrate the point, if one has to convey the idea of 'to forsake, to abandon', one can use the prepositions *sam* and *pari* with *tyaj* but not *anu* and *vi.* There is no convention for them in this regard. Proper care needs, therefore, to be exercised in their use which some of the modern writers including the present one have not. Our author permits himself their promiscuous use.

Sometimes the preposition is unnecessary and, if used, may create confusion. In *paśya priya te tatra gatvā kīdṛśo māno vibhavati*[4] *vi,* with *bhavati* is unnecessary. Similarly in *kathaṁ tvaṁ virodiṣi bāle,*[5] *rodiṣi* would do. *Pra* in *manye hi mattaḥ praparājitā ye,*[6] *patnyāh patiḥ prapūjyo bhavati*[7] is unnecessary padding. So is it in *prakakṣaṁ yātā*[8] and *lambavakrapraśuṇḍam.*[9] In the same strain is *sam* in...*probhūtasaṁjyotsnayā.*[10] Occasionally the preposition would make the word look very unfamiliar and obscure in sense. One such word used by the author is *pratibhāva* in... *jñātvā te pratibhāvaṁ nirmātum*[11] which seems to have the meaning 'capacity'.

Just as with the prepositions, so it is with particles sometimes. They could be an unnecessary padding. This is the case with *kila* in *prājñaṁ patiṁ prāpsyasi kila mamāśīh,*[12] the words uttered by Vidyottamā's father while blessing her.

Ka in some words is their integral part, though an addition, which gain in their identity with it. Sometimes the meaning may change if it is avoided. A prominent example of this could be *mūlaka* for radish. Avoid the *ka* and the word will mean a root. This may not be the case with

1. XV. 21, p. 129.
2. XIV. 32, p. 117.
3. VII. 59, p. 55.
S. XVIII. 4.5, p. 175.
5. XIX. 7.3, p. 190.
6. IX. 58, p. 76.
7. XIV. 56, p. 120.
8. XVII. 9.6, p. 167.
9. I. 15, p. 3.
10. I. 11, p. 3.
11. XVI. 40, p. 143.
12. XI. 40, p. 93.

other words but they are more frequent with *ka* than without it. The author, however, prefers them in their form of without *ka* as can be seen in his use of three of them : *ghoṭaka, mūṣaka* and *caṇaka* without *ka*.

While two of these are met with in literature, the third one is not.

1. निशि मूषान् खादितुमायाता[1]
2. चालय स्वमिमं काष्ठघोटम्[2]
3. येन लब्धश्चण एकः[3]

Conversely the addition of *ka* may make a word look incongruous sometimes. *Kavigoṣthiṣu* would look more natural than the author's *kavigoṣṭhikāsu*.[4]

Tvat and *mat*, the Ablative singular of *yuṣmad* and *asmad*, meaning 'from you' and 'from me' respectively are perfectly correct grammatically but do carry about them a certain ring of unfamiliarity. The author resorts to them a couple of times in his work :

1. त्वद्भविता कश्चन परिवारः[5]
2. वाञ्छाम्यधीतुं त्वदहं तु विद्याम्[6]
3. ये पराजिता बुधा मत्तु[7]

The addition of *tasil* to the Ablative-ending pronouns is optional. Though it may not be necessary to use it strictly grammatically, its use would add to the familarity of the words. If instead of saying *tvad vidyām adhītuṁ vāñchāmi*, if one were to say *tvattaḥ vidyām adhītuṁ vāñchāmi*, it would have more *svārasya*. *Aprasiddhatva* or unfamiliarity may better be avoided if it can conveniently be done so.

The *aprasiddhatva* is noticeable in the work in vocabulary too, though in extremely limited cases. The words like *jambo*,[8] and *lumī*[9] are very unfamiliar not listed even in the lexica. From the context *jambo* seems to mean lemon. The meaning of *lūmī* could be an animal with a tail. *Śatāṅga*[10] is another unfamiliar word which means a chariot and is to be met with only in the lexica. So is *jtviṣ-tveṣayati, tveṣa*[11] in the sense, as it appears from the context, 'to play'. The Pāṇinīya *Dhātupāṭha* lists it in the sense 'to gleam, to glitter', *tviṣa dīptau*. Monier Williams traces its use only in the Veda and notices among its meanings, apart from those noticed

---

1. XVII. 10.2, p. 168.
2. XVII. 6.4, p. 178.
3. XVIII. 8.1, p. 168.
Interestingly, the Hindi derivatives of such words like *mūlī*, *mūsā*, *canā*, etc. are all from their *ka*-less forms.
4. XIV. 2, p. 113.
5. II. 28, p. 13.
6. IX. 11, p. 69.
7. XV. 29, p. 131.
8. XVII. 5.2, p. 163.
9. XVIII. 4.11, p. 176.
10. XI. 60, p. 97.
11. XVIII. 6.4, p. 178.

above, 'to cause excitement' which can also fit in the context. The same unfamiliarity characterizes the use of *cit* in separation from *katham* as in :

मात्रादेशं विनान्त: कथमपि चिदथादत्त तातप्रवेशम्[1]

The work has here and there some words which are clearly superfluous. Thus in *sarvārcāmukhyadeśaṁ samahitakaradam*[2] *da* is unnecessary. *Samahitakaram* would just do.

The author is very liberal in the use of particles and pronouns. He just puts them here and there without any rhyme or reason. So is the case with *vai* which only can serve metrical padding.

Though the language of the author is fairly correct, one does come across in his work words and expressions which are hard to defend. In *mudā paryaṭatīt*[3] *sa dhīmān*, *paryaṭatīt* is very peculiar. If the root here is *aṭ*, the form should have been *paryāṭīt*, if it is *at* it should have been *paryātīt*. It looks both the roots got jumbled up in the mind of the author and caused confusion. The expression *akhādati sma*[4] should have either been *khādati sma* or *akhādat*. Periphrastic Future, *Luṭ*, is permissible only for an event which does not belong to the same day, vide Pāṇ *anadyatane luṭ* (3.3.15). This is not observed by the author in the use : *adya śāstrārtho bhavitā.*[5] The conditional *Lṛṅ* formation is always in Ātmanepada. Hence *abhindiṣyat* should have been *abhindiṣyata.*[6] The form *prasīditā*[7] should have been *prasannā*. Even in casual it could only be *prasāditā*. In *tacchandānām racananiyamān*[8] *chandas* being *s* ending *chandānām* should have been *chandasām*. In *tanmantriṁ brūhi māṁ mitra,*[9] *mantrim* should have been *mantriṇam*. *Man* being *aniṭ*, *manisye* used in *tadā maniṣye tvām*[10] should have been *maṅsye*. Twice the author uses the word *manvate* in singular : (1) *patnyāh sukhaṁ kṣaṇikaṁ manvate yaḥ,*[11] (2) *nārī...patiṁ svaparameśvaram eva manvate.*[12] This is not possible. The only forms possible are *manute* or *manyate*. In *dharmaṁ dhartā*[13] the use of Accusative is irregular. By *kartṛkarmaṇoh kṛti* (2.3.65) Pāṇini enjoins Genitive with Kṛdanta forms.

In a few places the author uses casual forms even without the casual sense. Such forms are : *anveṣayitum*[14] for *anveṣṭum*, *harṣitavān*[15] for *hṛṣṭavān*, *vitaritāḥ*[16] for *vitīrṇāḥ* (*modakāh*). In an isolated case Sandhi is avoided in the same line : *viduṣī ujjayininyāyālayam etya.*[17]

1. I. 14, p. 3.
2. Ibid.
3. I. 29, p. 6.
4. II. 43, p. 16.
5. IV. 7, p. 27.
6. IV. 17, p. 28.
7. V. 17, p. 35.
8. X. 19, p. 82.
9. XII. 37, p. 101.
10. XVI. 37, p. 143.
11. XI. 20, p. 90.
12. XI. 30, p. 92.
13. XI. 12, p. 89.
14. VI. 18, p. 41.
15. IX. 69, p. 78.
16. XVII. 10, p. 168.
17. XIX. 1.2, p. 83.

Among the more glaring of the grammatical anomalies is the poet's compounding of *nañ* with a verbal form as in *prāṇena yady amilati patir yuvā*[1] and *yaḥ pariṇītām asvīkurute*[2] and the use of *kadānīm* in *dugdhaṁ kadānīṁ salilaṁ kadācit*[3] and *dṛṣṭvā prasuptāṁ jananīṁ kadānīm*[4] which does not exist in Sanskrit, dānīm being limited by Pāṇ to *idam* only, vide his *sūtra : dānīṁ ca* (5.3 18). *Jñapa* being *mit* is subject to the rule *mitāṁ hrasvah* (6.4.92). The expressions *jñāpaya,*[5] *vijñāpaya,*[6] *jñāpayatu*[7] and *vyajñāpayat*[8] are all unpāṇinian but not if from *jñā* with *puk* in the causal. So is *prajvālaya.*[9] The optional *mittva* is restricted in this case and in the case of certain other roots to their being not preceded by a preposition though justification for this is offered by Bhaṭṭojidīkṣita : *kathaṁ tarhi prajvālayati, unnāmayatīti, ghañantāt tat karotīti ṇau.*

In an odd case is noticeable a lack of symmetry as in

भवती पृच्छतु सङ्केतैः स्व
यंद्यत् प्रष्टुमीहसे तत्तत् ।[10]

At a couple of places Parasmaipada is used in place of Ātmanepada and vice versa. The root *ay* is Ātmanepadin. It is used by the author in Parasmaipada : *ayeh,*[11] *aya,*[12] *ayāmi.*[13] Similarly the root *dah* which is Parasmaipadin is used in Ātmanepada : (*svāntam*) *dagdhāse.*[14]

There is confusion in gender too. *Prāsāda* and *svapna* which are masculine are used in neuter :

1. तत्सर्वं पितुरस्ति मदीयं प्रासादं नगरं राज्यं च[15]
2. दृष्टं त्वया कीदृशं स्वप्नम्[16]

Conversely *antara* which is neuter is used in masculine :

वियुक्तकाले कृतः केनापि विवाहान्तरो नैव[17]

Some of the compound forms suffer from the *vyadhikaraṇadoṣa* ;

1. भक्तानां विपदां पराभवकरः[18]
2. अस्याः परिणयकालो ऽयम्[19]
3. शष्कुल्या भक्षणानुरक्त[20]

---

1. V. 25, p. 36.
2. XV. 39, p. 132.
3. II. 35, p. 14.
4. II. 38, p. 15.
5. X. 8, p. 82.
6. VII. 40, p. 52.
7. VII. 41, Ibid.
8. XI. 3, p. 87.
9. XX. 5.6, p. 197.
10. VII. 30, p. 50.
11. IX. 7, p. 68.
12. IX. 12, p. 69.
13. X. 28, p. 84.
14. XIX. 2.3, p. 184.
15. XIII. 23, p. 108.
16. XVII. 8.2, p. 166.
17. XV. 65, p. 136.
18. I. 9, p. 2.
19. VII. 39, p. 52.
20. XVIII. 2.4, p. 173.

4. त्वमसि पतिः पत्न्या कृतसेवः[1]
5. यस्य डमरुनादादृषिपाणिनिविरचितचतुर्दशसूत्रविकासाम्[2]

In *putra saṁskṛtāṁ paṭha nijabhāṣām*,[3] *saṁskṛta* as an epithet to bhāṣa has been used in the feminine.[4] If what is meant here is the name of the language, it should have been used in the neuter only. That is its gender as should be clear from Daṇḍin : *saṁskṛtaṁ nāma daivī vāk*[5] where though it goes with feminine *vāk*, it maintains its neuter gender.

The author sometimes does not pay due regard to economy of words. He uses more than one word in the same sense, the synonyms, in quick succession making out a distinction in their sense as it were, as can be seen from the following :

1. भवनं गृहं मन्दिरमपि च कस्मै[6]
2. किङ्करसेवकादिभृत्यानां कोलाहलेन[7]
3. मनोहरं हृद्यं रमणीयं तज्जनचित्ताकर्षणजनकम्[8]
4. प्रणं स्वकीयं प्रतिज्ञया ऽऽ चार्यवरेण पूरय[9]
5. तेभ्यश्च प्राप्नुवन् बोधं लौकिकं व्यावहारिकम्[10]

He also seems to make a distinction between the apparent synonymous words *jña*, *vijña* and *sujña*.[11]

The above-noted grammatical and other anomolies, however, do not take away much from the merit of the work which has at places brilliant flashes in the use of typical grammatical forms showing the author's sound knowledge of the science of Grammar. The use of such expressions as *kim vuktam*[12] which is possible of formation by Pāṇ *maya uño vā* (7.1.51) and *kṣīrasyati*[13] which is possible of formation by Pāṇ. *aśvakṣīravṛṣalavaṇānām ātmaprītau kyaci* (7.1.51) as also the Vārtika *kṣīralavaṇayor lālasāyām* as

---

1. XIX. 2.1, p. 184.
2. XXI. 1.2, p. 207.
3. XXI. 1.5, p. 207.
4. Like the present author the editor of the Sanskrit magazine *Sarvagandhā* of Lucknow has started using the word Saṁskṛtā for Sanskrit language offering all sorts of justification for it oblivious of the fact that it militates against usage. Nowhere has the word been used in the feminine in the sense of language in older literature. The use of it in a *Rāmāyaṇa* line *yadi vācaṁ pradāsyāmi dvijātir iva saṁskṛtām* may not necessarily refer to the language of that name. It could just mean a refined language. The tendency of using Saṁskṛtā for Sanskrit is very recent and is restricted happily to only a few individuals. One should in no case take liberties with the genius of a language in the name of being original or unconventional.
5. *Kāvyādrśa*, I. 33.
6. I. 32, p. 7.
7. VIII. 21, p. 58.
8. XX. 6.1, p. 198.
9. VII. 10, p. 47.
10. XII. 19, p. 100.
11. XIII. 5, p. 105.
12. XI. 51, p. 95; XIII. 44, p. 111.
13. II. 46, p. 16.

well as the Frequentative forms like *pepīyate*,[1] *jaṅgamyate*[2] would corroborate the above.

Conclusion

A careful study of the work reveals that the author is influenced by the culture of Western U.P. which is known for its rich variety of food to leave no opportunity of referring to it. First it is the birth of Vidyottamā. Then it is her marriage. Next it is her pregnancy. Every time the names of different kinds of sweets and other dishes have been mentioned. He strives to go in for Sanskrit names like Kalākanda, Mohanabhoga, Saṁyāva (which could mean a kind of pudding) or restores them to their Sanskrit form from where they might have come like Piṇḍa for sweet balls (Pinnī in Hindi), Modaka (Hindi Laddoo), Sūtrakas (Pheniyāṅ in Hindi), Amṛtī (Hindi Imritī), Pakvavaṭa (Hindi Pakauṛā), Dadhivaṭa (Hindi Dahī Vaḍā), Madhumantha (Hindi Mīṭhā Maṭhā), Mallapūpa (Hindi Mālpuā), Rasagola (Hindi Rasgullā), Dvidala (Hindi Dāl) Polikā for Phulka (Roti) and so on or new coinages for them such as Śaṣkulī for Jalebī, Kauṣmāṇḍa for Peṭhā, Dādheya for Rāitā or, with some phonetic changes here and there gives them the Sanskrit look such as Parpaṭa for Hindi Pāpaḍ, Pūrikā for Hindi Pūrī or just adopts the common Hindi words such as Roṭī for Chapātī, or Ālu for Potato. Sometimes for no readily available word he has to give a description of the thing to indicate it like Māṣagarbhā Pūrikā to indicate Kachaurī. So carried away is the author by the sweets that he derives his metaphors sometimes from them. Vidyottamā refers to her darling Kālidāsa as her Kalākanda !

In his wanderings through the country to gain worldly knowledge Kālidāsa follows the route which is the same as is described in the *Meghadūta*. As a matter of fact, the poet seems to have clearly been inspired by the immortal work to invent the incident in his work just to introduce it. He mentions precisely the same places, rivers and mountains as find mention in that work. In our poet's mind there is a link in this. If Kālidāsa were to undertake a tour, he would undertake it in the manner he has indicated for some one else in one of his works.

Though living in the modern age the poet has a fairly strong hold of tradition on him. This finds expression in his view of the position of married women. Her place is, according to him, in the feet of her husband :

विद्योत्तमा—अहमेतत् प्रष्टुं काङ्क्षामि
ज्ञापय पत्नीस्थानं कुत्र
विक्रमादित्यः—तदस्ति तत्पत्युर्हि पादयोः ।[3]

---

1. II. 46, p. 16. 2. II. 47, p. 16.
3. XV. 14, p. 128.

For her husband is her lord :

1. पत्न्या: पतिर्वै परमेश्वरो ऽस्ति[1]
2. शृणु भारतीय नारी सदैव[2]
   पतिं स्वपरमेश्वरमेव मन्वते

It is being really traditional to speak of the women the way the author has done in these days of Women's Lib.

With its 1317 stanzas, excluding the colophons, the Mahākāvya *Vidyottamākālidāsīyam* has a lot of originality in it, a lot of good descriptions and a lot of good lyrics to interest a discerning reader. As a matter of fact, the whole of its latter part from Canto XV onwards describing the poetic bout between Vidyottamā and Kālidāsa with stanzas flying from each other, Vidyottamā's pregnancy, the birth of a son, the festivities for that, the lullabys for the child, the stories for him, the birth of a daughter, her death, the birth of another son, the festivities for it, the stories for the second son, his initiation into the Sanskrit language and its rules as also into poetry-the entire labyrinth the poet has created to show off his talent as a lyricist. The theme is a mere tool for him to create songs in easy and simple Sanskrit which goes straight home. The end result of all this is that he is able to create a work of absorbing interest in which old narrative blends with the new, songs vie with each other in captivating the hearts of the people and originality and innovation surge forward again and again.

---

1. IX. 51, p. 75.
2. XI. 30, p. 92.

12

KAVIKĀLIDĀSĪYAM

Included in the collection *Madhurāmlam,* it is a play in seven Scenes. Its theme is an adaptation of the various accounts as found in the *Bhojaprabandha* of Vallālasena. It projects Kālidāsa as a compassionate and a humane person, apart from his being an excellent poet.

Theme

"The illustrious and learned King Bhoja of Dhārā was well-known for his ceaseless charities to poets and creative artists. The artists, therefore, used to visit him from far and near in expectation of wealth and acclamation.

Once Kālidāsa came to his Court and impressed him with his excellent poetical skill. He became the most favoured jewel of his Court. This was resented by other poets like Karpūra, Kokila and Mayūra. They began hatching a plot to bring about Kālidāsa's downfall.

There was a royal announcement that a citizen able to compose poems would get rich reward and would be allowed a stay in the Kingdom. One not able to do so would be ordered out. On hearing it three Brahmins well-versed in the Vedas began to compose a poem in a lonely park. Kālidāsa having been turned out by the King on account of his association with a courtesan Vilāsavatī happened to pass that side incognito. Taking pity on the poor Brahmins he composed a part of the poem for them for which they were trying hard for long. The Brahmins took the poem to the King the next morning and got the promised reward.

A learned lady of Bhoja's court named Sītā was critical of Bhoja on his turning out Kālidāsa from his Court. She told him that a brilliant poet like Kālidāsa should be allowed to have some freedom to be associated with a person of his choice.

The King on the advice of the chief Purohita announced the completion of the two lines of a verse within twenty four hours. It was announced that one not being able to do so would have to leave the Kingdom.

Kālidāsa was living incognito with Vilāsavatī in Dhārā itself. One evening he heard some noise of the people on the main road. Vilāsavatī told him of the announcement of the King and the decision of a number of poets not able to supply the last two lines of the verse of the King to leave the Kingdom in the night to avoid discomfiture. Kālidāsa was very sorry to hear of the sad plight of the worshippers of Sarasvatī. He disguised himself as a Cāraṇa and supplied the two lines to the first two of the King uttered to him by Karpūra.

Next morning Karpūra went to the King and showed him the complete verse and got a reward from him which created resentment among his (Karpūra's) other companions Mayūra and Kokila who were with him when the Cāraṇa had met him. They revealed everything to the King who came to know thereby that it was not Karpūra who had supplied the lines but an unknown Cāraṇa.

This gave the King the idea about the whereabouts of Kālidāsa. With the help of his spies he found out the secret place where Kālidāsa was living with Vilāsavatī. One evening when Kālidāsa had just finished his evening prayers, he was told by anxious Vilāsavatī that their house had been surrounded by royal soldiers. Before he could make out anything, he found the King standing before him begging of his forgiveness. He requested him to come back to the Court and bestowed on him the title of Kavikulaśiromaṇi. He also consented to Vilāsavatī staying with him in his Kingdom of Dhārā as his (Kālidāsa's) life companion. The play closes with Kālidāsa expressing gratefulness."

Critical appreciation

An adaptation of a portion of the *Bhojaprabandha* dealing with Kālidāsa, the present work follows the narrative of the parent work by and large. It does introduce some changes, though in no case major. One of these pertains to the poor Vedic Brahmins who try desperately to compose a verse. In the present work they are shown to try their hand at it under the compulsion of the royal announcement that only that person who is able to compose a poem would be allowed to stay in the Kingdom and the others would be ordered out. In the parent work there is nothing of this royal announcement. In that in line with its style, the scholars are introduced trying their hand at composing a poem because the King likes it : *rājānaṁ kavitāpriyaṁ jñātvā.* Further, the appearance of Kālidāsa in the present work is shown as a chance occurrence, he is said in it to pass by that side incognito, while in the parent work it is shown as due to Kālidāsa's going to a temple to offer worship. In that Kālidāsa is not incognito. He is recognized as Kālidāsa by the Brahmins who approach him to bail them out of their difficulty by providing the second hemistich which does not occur to them with all their efforts. There is nothing there of his stay in the house of the courtesan Vilāsavatī either which the present work mentions in passing. It does occur there but much later and certainly not in this context.

Again, Sītā, a learned lady in Bhoja's Court is shown in the parent work to be defending Kālidāsa when she notices the King nursing a grievance against him on account of his infatuation for a courtesan. She says that a person in love with qualities should not feel bad about a person, otherwise meritorious, if he has some shortcoming. Nowhere does she say in the parent work, as is made out in the adaptation, that a brilliant poet like Kālidāsa should be allowed freedom of association with a person of his choice.

Further, the present adaptation makes the King announce the Samasyā, the completion of the two lines—the adaptation gives their Sanskrit version while the original records it in Prakrit—on the advice of the chief Purohita while there is nothing of the kind in the original. Moreover, the two lines in the adaptation are to be completed within twenty four hours while in the original it is eight days. Further, it is not Vilāsavatī who informs Kālidāsa of the King's Court poets quitting Dhārā but a maid-servant sent out by him to find out the goings on, on hearing the hullabaloo on the road. Still further, the two lines supplied by Kālidāsa in his guise of Cāraṇā are recited to the King by Bāṇa in the original and not Karpūra as is made out in the adaptation. It is Bāṇa again who gets the reward from the King there and not Karpūra. And finally, the original does not say anything about Kālidāsa being permitted to stay in Dhārā with Vilāsavatī as his life companion which forms the denouement in the adaptation.

Perhaps these changes the author of the *Kavikālidāsīyam* thought necessary for a dramatic creation. To convert the eight days to twenty four hours for leaving the Kingdom in the event of non-supply of the two lines to those of Bhoja would make, so thought the playwright perhaps, the impact of the shock more severe which should go better with a drama. Kālidāsa being permitted to stay in Dhārā with Vilāsavatī as the life companion is also in line with the tradition of happy ending in traditional Indian drama. This also would reinforce the regard that the King is shown to have for Kālidāsa in tracing him and asking for his forgiveness in being over-harsh to him. Penitence on the part of the King would acquire further edge if he is shown shedding off his inhibition for Kālidāsa's association with a courtesan. The King accepts him along with her.

Everything else is fine with the play except its expression which needs improvement at places. Some of the glaring of the anomalies in it are : *yādṛśo Kālidāsaḥ*,[1] *nagaravadhau*,[2] *vivadantaḥ*,[3] *vivadanti*,[4] *Bhojarājānam*,[5]

1. p. 53.
2. Ibid.
3. p. 59.
4. p. 60.
5. Ibid.

vasiṣyāmaḥ,[1] *rājamārgam*,[2] *svapnam*,[3] *pūrvavṛttāntam*[4] which should have been *yādṛśaḥ Kālidāsaḥ*, *nagaravadhvām*, *vivadamānāḥ*, *vivadante*, *Bhojarājam*, *vatsyāmaḥ*, *rājamārgaḥ*, *svapnaḥ* and *pūrvavṛttāntaḥ* respectively.

The author more than once puts in Sanskrit the Hindi idioms, e.g.,

1. भित्तीनामपि श्रोत्राणि भवन्ति[5]
   दीवारों के भी कान होते हैं ।
2. उदरे च मूषका यातायातं कुर्वन्ति ।[6]
   पेट में चूहे कूद रहे हैं ।
3. सर्वे कारावासस्य वातमनुभविष्यामः ।[7]
   सभी जेल की हवा खायेंगे ।

A fine creation and the only one of its kind in drama form—in prose there is one, *Kālidāsasya Antimam Aitihyam* which too is noticed in the present Volume—it retells some of the anecdotes of the *Bhojaprabandha*. All through an attempt is made in it to bring about some sort of connection among the seemingly disparate events which are woven together. It is this which makes the work a real piece of art.

---

1. p. 61.
2. p. 60.
3-4. p. 64.
5. p. 53.
6. Ibid.
7. p. 55.

13

ŚRĪKĀLIDĀSĪYAM ANTIMAM AITIHYAM

It is a prose piece published in two instalments in the *Saṁskṛta Bhāratī*, Vol. II, No. 3, 1919 and Vol. III, No. 1, 1920, Vardhaman. The name of the author, as can be seen from the verse at the end of the composition, is Nārāyaṇa :

इति नारायणनामकभूसुरलिखितं पुरातनं वृत्तम् ।
कविवरकुलगुरुकालिदासस्य शुभप्रदं भूयात् ॥

Nothing is known about him, not even the period to which he belongs. The prose write-up is a jumble of different anecdotes about Kālidāsa, as the author might have heard or understood them. The anecdotes cover three lives—one, when the poet lived as Kālidāsa, the other, when he was reborn as the son of a Brahmin near Varanasi and the third, when he was reborn again as a dumb fellow in Kāñcīpura.

Theme

Once all the people like Śaṅkara, Bāṇa and Krīḍācandra went to Bhoja and complained to him of his partiality towards Kālidāsa in spite of their having composed profound works in contrast to the latter's works which are so easy that even a child can follow them. Bhoja did not agree with them. 'A great poet is he who caters to the public at large while the works of the complainants can provide enjoyment to the learned only', said he.

The complainants told the King that they would place before him a four-syllabic samasyā : क ख ग घ.

If Kālidāsa completes it, they would give due consideration to his words and accept what the King says. That very moment Kālidāsa happens to enter the assembly. The King places the samasyā before him. For a moment Kālidāsa gets lost in his thoughts. The goddess of learning, realizing that he is in a fix, appears before him in the form of a girl with a palm leaf to help him out of his difficulty. Kālidāsa enquires of her as to who she is. 'Kāñcanamālā', says she. 'Whose daughter,' asks he. 'Of Kanakalatā', says she. 'What is she holding in her hand,' further asks he. 'A palm leaf,' answers she.

का त्वं बाले काञ्चनमाला कस्याः पुत्री कनकलतायाः ।
किं ते हस्ते तालीपत्रं का वा रेखा क ख ग घ ॥

The complainants see this and together with the King feel surprised and happy.

Two or three years pass after this. Kālidāsa falls ill and is confined to the house of Vilāsavatī only. Occasionally the King would go to him and meet him. Once he (the King) charmed by the beauty of his Queen Līlāvatī speaks out Anuṣṭubh hemistich : *kusume kusumotpattiḥ śrūyate nahi dṛśyate*, the appearance of a flower on a flower is heard but not seen. The next morning the King places the same as a samasyā before his learned poets. None is able to complete it. He then makes an announcement that anybody completing it would be rewarded with the half of his kingdom and has a bell installed in his palace. Thinking that to be her opportunity, Vilāsavatī writes it in Kālidāsa's room while he is asleep. He notices it after getting up and writes below it : *bāle tava mukhāmbhoje dṛṣṭam indīvaradvayam*, O girl, on your lotus-like face are seen two lotuses and goes to sleep again. Thinking that if Kālidāsa were to continue to live, the truth would be out, Vilāsavatī cuts him into pieces and throws him in a deep well in her house. She then goes to the palace, rings the bell, is received in audience by the King before whom she recites the second hemistich, written by Kālidāsa as above, as her own composition. The shrewd King realizes that it must be that of Kālidāsa and asks her pointedly whether Kālidāsa was alive or not. Knowing from her the whole thing, he rushes to the well, has all the pieces of the body of the great poet taken out and with the help of divine herbs like *Viśalyakaraṇi and Mṛtasañjīvanī* has him revived. Getting up as if from sleep, Kālidāsa asks the King as to why he has brought him back to life. He (Kālidāsa) is destined to die at the hands of a woman. He asks the King not to grieve for him because even when revived, he (Kālidāsa) would live only for a while. He enquires from the King as to what he wants. The King tells him that he wants that like him he too may enjoy eternal fame. Kālidāsa tells him to sing the life of Rāma in verse. In prose he would help him. The work would, however, go by the name of the King. As the two go upto the Sundarakāṇḍa, there comes Kālidāsa's end. Telling the King that the work would be known as *Bhojacampū* or the *Campūrāmāyaṇa* the great poet goes into eternal sleep. Satisfied even with what has been achieved, the King performs the last rites of Kālidāsa and finding no meaning for his life transfers the kingdom to his son and retires to the forest with his wife and finally gives up his life with Yogic rites.

Now, when Kālidāsa was thinking over the *samasyā* and Sarasvatī was taking long to appear, he addressed her *raṇḍe*, you whore. Even though she loved him, she could not withstand the insult and told him that in the next birth he would be dumb, *mūka*, though omniscient, the whole life.

In the next birth Kālidāsa was born as the son of an old Brahmin near Varanasi.

Once lord Śaṅkara appeared as Śaṅkarācārya and wanted his *Śārīrakabhaṣya* on the *Brahmasūtras* to be revised in the light of his comments agreeing with their author or not. He prayed to lord Śaṅkara to arrange for this. The lord appeared before him in dream and told him that he should place his Bhāṣya on the steps of the Gaṅgā in the morning. Bhairava would appear there and would revise it, as he would read it out to him. The next morning Śaṅkarācārya did as directed. Vedavyāsa, the author of the *Brahmasūtras* himself appeared there in the form of Bhairava. Śaṅkarācārya read out to him his *Bhāṣya*. Whatever he did not approve, he licked out. This he went on doing right up to the Ninth Āhnika, much to the surprise of Śaṅkarācārya. After this he just went away. One fourth of the Bhāṣya was still to be revised. Śaṅkarācārya prayed to Śiva again. The Lord appeared before him and told him that Bhairavas do not stay for long at one place. That is why the Bhairava revised the work upto a part only. The part subsequent to that he advised Śaṅkarācārya to read out to the son of an old householder in a Brahmin village near Kāśī and have it revised by him. Śaṅkara did accordingly and the entire work was thus revised. Śaṅkarācārya then set on his journey for propagating his philosophy of Advaita which took him to Kāñcī where the Vaiṣṇavas not falling in line with his views told him that they would agree with him only if he were to provide speech to a dumb fellow roaming about here and there with no consideration for what to eat and where and with no attachment. Śaṅkara told them that if he could go to the Kāmākṣī temple he would do so. The dumb fellow was the same one who had heard as the son of an old Brahmin in the previous birth his *Śārīrakabhāṣya* and in the present state of dumbness also remembered of it everything. Being in the state of *samabuddhi* he moved about everywhere and had come over to Kāñcī which had surprised him with its prosperity and had stayed on there for quite some time though ridiculed and humiliated by the people. As soon as Śaṅkarācārya saw him, he could know that he was the same person who had heard from him in the form of a Brahmin boy his *Śārīrakabhāṣya*. He asked him to sing a hymn in praise of Goddess Kāmākṣī. And there came out the dumb one with five hymns, the *Āryāsaptaśatī* and so on, much to the surprise and delight of everybody.

It was no other than Kālidāsa who was born in his third life as a dumb fellow and had attained the divine state through the favour of

Śaṅkarācārya. His work the *Mūkapañcaśatī* is read by people with respect and devotion.

Critical appreciation

Written in flawless Sanskrit, the prose piece is a fine blend of anecdote and mythology. Some admirer of Mūka in appreciation of his poetic talents, must have invented the story by connecting him with Kālidāsa and making him his incarnation through very spicy anecdotes. As for the real Kālidāsa, his story came to an end with the chopping off of his body by the harlot Vilāsavatī—there are various anecdotes connecting him with some woman or the other. The rest of the story leading to the composition of the *Bhojacampū* or the *Rāmāyaṇacampū* has also apparently been invented to lend respectability to that work by showing its prose portion at least to have been that from Kālidāsa. In the midst of tradition and anecdote, it is very difficult to know what the reality is. Kālidāsa, being the tallest of Indian poets so much of anecdote has got woven round him that he has himself begun sliding into a mythical personality.

The work under study is composed in an easy, fluent and narrative style and being one of very very few works on Kālidāsa in prose is particularly welcome.

14

ŚRĪKĀLIDĀSACARITASAṂGRAHAḤ

Published in the *Mañjūṣā*, Calcutta, Vol. IV, No. 9, May 1950, *Śrīkālidāsacaritasaṁgrahaḥ* by the celebrated Sanskrit author Sri Y. Mahalinga Sastri, is a queer composition. A summary initially of an account of Kālidāsa's life, based on tradition and his works in eighteen verses, it is followed by a dialogue between imaginary characters Gautama and Śāṇḍilya in which the third one Kauṇḍinya, also joins at a later stage, and all problems relating to the master poet are discussed.

The dialogue opens with the reproduction of the eulogies for Kālidāsa by an anonymous poet (*purā kavīnāṁ gaṇanāprasaṅge*, etc.) as well as Bāṇa and Daṇḍin. Next is pointed out the fact of his having a critic in Diṅnāga but an admirer in Nicula, a king of that name, as could be inferred from the supposed oblique references to them in a *Meghadūta* verse. After that is taken up the question of the propriety of making a non-sentient thing serve as a messenger. Attention is drawn in this connection to Kālidāsa's own answer to this, viz., the love-lorn are by their very being incapable of distinguishing between things sentient or otherwise—a view also upheld by the well-known rhetorician Bhāmaha. Next is raised the question (it is at this stage that Kauṇḍinya is shown to join) as to why Kālidāsa should have stopped at the description of the marriage of Śiva and Pārvatī and not gone upto the description of the birth of Kumāra as would suggest the title of the work, the *Kumārasambhava*. The traditional view that the poet invited the curse on him of Pārvatī for a little too graphic description of the love-sports of the divine couple which cut short his composition is discounted with the approval of Ānandavardhana. After that is raised the doubt, in view of Kālidāsa's acknowledged supremacy in the description of the sentiment of love, about his indifference to or inability in the description of other sentiments like Heroic, Pathetic, etc., which is dispelled by pointing out instances from the *Raghuvaṁśa* and the *Kumārasambhava* where he excels the delineation of the Heroic and the Pathetic.

The verse in Canto XIV of the *Raghuvaṁśa* in the episode of Sītā's exile : *tad eṣa sargah karuṇārdracittaih*, etc. is taken to represent cleverly the poet's own assessment of his heartrending description of Pathos.

The dialogue takes a different turn here. It must not be Kālidāsa who would engage himself in the childish Yamaka word-play in the 9th Canto of the *Raghuvaṁśa* and that from that Canto onward the work is of some other poet, a view held by some, is taken up for consideration. It is discounted on two counts : one, if it is mere Yamaka, a particular arrangement of syllables, it could well mean inferior poetry, *adhama kāvya,* as says Ānandavardhana, but if the same were to be employed occasionally as a diversion by a poetic genius, the case would be different. Second, Kālidāsa might have indulged in this to humble the pride of his alleged contemporary, Ghaṭakarpara whose view it was to carry water in a pot-sherd, *ghaṭakarpara,* for one who were to defeat him in the use of Yamaka. But that as it may, Yamaka, if it is sweet, clear, significant and delightful, would add to the beauty of a composition. It need not be underrated simply because it is Yamaka.

Next is repudiated the view that Kālidāsa was one of the nine jewels in the Court of Vikramāditya, on the authority of the verses recording their names occurring in the *Jyotirvidābharaṇa* ascribed to Kālidāsa but not actually his and consequently unreliable, more so, because those who find mention in the said verses are not all contemporaries. It is possible that a later poet carrying the pseudonym of Kalidāsa would have composed them. There seem to have been many who carried this pseudonym. That one Parimala or Padmagupta in the court of Muñja carried it is well-known, even if Rājaśekhara's mention of three Kālidāsas may lack naturalness. The *Bhojaprabandha* story making *Kālidāsa,* Bāṇa, Māgha, etc. contemporaries is simply not acceptable for they were not really so. Equally unacceptable is the theory that Kālidāsa had friends in the *Setubandha*-author Kuntala king Pravarasena and the *Jānakīharaṇa* author Simhalese King Kumāradāsa and that they wrote their works with his help. It could only be interpreted to underscore Kālidāsa's superiority over the two. Still equally unacceptable is the theory that Vikramāditya, i.e., Candragupta II, got the *Setubandha* written from Kālidāsa in the name of his daughter's son Pravarasena II, and grandson of Vākāṭaka Pṛthivīsena I on the basis of the tradition that he (Kālidāsa) uttered a verse at each opportune moment as recorded in the text (of the *Setubandha*) itself while he acted a messenger between Vikramāditya and the Kuntala king on the ground that he (Kālidāsa) is far removed from Vikramāditya and Pravarasena and that there is a marked difference in style in the *Setubandha* and the Prakrit verses in his works. The theory that Mātṛ-gupta described by Kalhaṇa is Kālidāsa is simply absurd. More probable it is that he was a contemporary of Agnimitra. His *Mālavikāgnimitra* describes characters of whom he seems to have had direct experience. The indication of the contemporaneity in the line आशास्यमीतिविगमप्रभृति प्रजानां

सम्पत्स्यते न खलु गोप्तरि नाग्निमित्रे is difficult to lose sight of. Further, his contemporaneity with Agnimitra would not conflict with his occupying an honoured place in Vikrama's court, the two kings not being far removed from each other. The title of the play *Vikramorvaśīya* indicates his association with *Vikramāditya.* So does the sentence अनुत्सेक: खलु विक्रमालङ्कार: where Vikrama could cleverly refer to Vikramāditya.

The view that the poet had an association with an harlot and spent his time in her company is the imagination of the perverted. How could he, with his heart set on Śiva, intent on salvation, be a Viṭa ? The fact of the matter is that when the Buddhists had attacked the Vedic path and the country was troubled by the Mlecchas, the poet and the king (Vikramāditya) once again established the supremacy of the Veda and the Vedic way of life and restored peace to the country by crushing the foreign invaders.

This brings to an end the lengthy dialogue, *the first of its kind in Sanskrit literature,* wherein all the different theories about Kālidāsa, old and new, are examined in brief and he is defended against criticism apiece with the approach of any of his devotees. There are few Sanskrit poets and writers who have become centres of so many theories and views as Kālidāsa has. It was partly due to his near total silence about himself. Any casual reference anywhere, just a name somewhere, was enough to make the scholars come out rushing with their theories. The situation now is that Kālidāsa has become a phenomenon rather than remain an individual. Much of the confusion about him is caused by the assumption of his name by a number of later poets and the uncritical approach of the ancients in accepting them all as the first Kālidāsa. Our author has a sharp dig at this. After repudiating the view that Kālidāsa wrote the *Setubandha* in the name of Pravarasena, he says through one of his characters, Śāṇḍilya :

शाण्डिल्य:—साहित्यसंसारे खल्वस्मत्पूर्वपुरुषाणां न केवलं य: कालिदास: स कालिदास:, न केवलं येऽर्वाचीना: तद्विरुदभाज: ते कालिदासा:, परन्तु ये सरसोदारपद्यनिर्मातार: अज्ञातविशेषा: तेऽपि कालिदासा: । येषामनाकलितनामस्वरूपाणाम् आदिरसोद्गारसौरभ्योद्रिक्ता वाचस्तेऽपि नाम कालिदासा, ये दुर्ग्रहचित्रकटुकाव्यकर्तृतया क्रमेलकप्रायरसना वैदग्ध्यवित्तकानाम् अभ्यर्हणास्पदं तेऽपि खलु कालिदासा:, ये च व्रीडाकरमुक्त्वा ग्रन्थप्रचारार्थिन: निजनामनिगूहनश्रद्धालव: तेऽपि बत कालिदासा: । (सर्वे हसन्ति)

Śāṇḍilya : In the world of literature for our ancestors not only that one was Kālidāsa who (really) was so nor were later ones so who carried that title, but also those writers of verses full of Rasa about whom nothing particular is known. Such ones whose name and form are not known and whose words are full of the perfume of over-flowing sentiment of Love are also

Kālidāsas. Those whose tongues are very similar to those of camels because of their creating harsh and pictorial poetry not easy to comprehend are also Kālidāsas. And they too are Kālidāsas who desirous of propagating their works believe in withholding their names on the plea that it may be embarrassing to them. (All laugh).

Though our author gives enough evidence of critical spirit in examining various theories about the master poet, rejecting or accepting them, he seems to fail it in asserting that he (the master poet) would have lived in the reigns of both, Agnimitra and Vikramāditya since both of them were not far removed from each other in point of time. As for Agnimitra, there is near certainty about his identity. He was the son of Puṣyamitra, the founder of the Śuṅga dynasty. As for Vikramāditya, there is considerable doubt. If he is identified with Candragupta II, as is the consensus, there should be a big time gap between him and Agnimitra. The dynasty of the Śuṅgas was succeeded by that of the Guptas. The reign of Candragupta II was preceded by a short reign of his brother Rāmagupta and a long one of that of his father Samudragupta. There was easily a time gap of some 200 years between the two celebrities and to place Kālidāsa in the reign of both would, on the face of it, be ridiculous. Here our author seems more to have been carried away by tradition than reason. Tradition makes Kālidāsa one of the nine jewels in Vikrama's court. The name Agnimitra in the *Mālavikāgnimitra* indicates his association with the King of that name. In his effort to reconcile the two, our author has landed himself in a difficult position. He seems to possess a poor sense of history.

The word *saṁgraha* seems to have been employed by our author in the twin senses of synopsis and compendium. The former would go well with the verse portion and the latter with the subsequent prose portion. The first eighteen verses give, as pointed out earlier, in summary form an account of the life and works of Kālidāsa, his grazing the goats in childhood, his cutting the root of the branch of the tree on which he was perching, the royal Pandits' notice of him in that state, their arranging his marriage with a princess who had vowed to marry only a learned man by pointing towards him as their guru, her expulsion of him from the house after realizing her mistake, his going to the Kālī temple, her laugh at his words, the slipping of betelnut juice out of laughter from her mouth into that of his, his becoming a unique poet, the acceptance of him by the princess, her asking him *asti kaścid vāgviśeṣaḥ*, is there any difference or improvement in his speech, his composing the three Kāvyas with each one of the three words as the first ones, his description of the royal duties in the *Raghuvaṁśa*, his delineation of the different types of Śṛṅgāra in his three plays, his honour by King Vikramāditya Śakāri, and his re-establishment of the authority of the King's routing the Mlecchas. The prose portion, as said earlier, gives a compendium of the different theories about Kālidāsa. Both portions, therefore, could appropriately be styled *Kālidāsacaritasaṁgraha*.

Since a multiplicity of the theories about Kālidāsa, both old and new, had to be examined, it was but natural that there should be a fair sprinkling of quotations in the composition. Apart from them, the entire work is the composition of the author himself. One of the most powerful writers of the modern age, he wields a facile pen. Though following for the most part an easy style, he does permit himself a high flown one occasionally, e.g.,

यमकोऽपि सरलः, सुकुमारः प्रसन्नो मधुरः, पुष्टार्थः, मनोहरः, प्रयुक्तः, अत्यनर्थकतामावहतीति अहो, प्रसन्नवाग्देवतानुवृत्तीनां कवितल्लजानां पारेगिरंमहिमातिशयः । प्रतिपक्षोक्तीनाम् अनुमानप्रायत्वं स्वच्छन्दभङ्गुरमूलावलम्बनदौर्बल्यं च त्वरयानुपतताम् अविश्रान्तिदौःस्थ्यमेव भूयः पर्युपस्थापयतः ।

Our author has a fine sense of humour. He is at his best in satire. An instance of it is the dig, referred to earlier, at the tendency of the ancient Indians accepting all kinds of poets, good, bad or indifferent, as Kālidāsa, if only they styled themselves so. The second is the ridicule poured on those who ascribe the authorship of certain works to Kālidāsa whether the first or the second, or the third and so on.

शण्डिल्यः— रघुबंशनबमसर्गे यमकक्रीडायां बालिश इव समासक्तः कविः कालिदासो न भवितुमर्हतीति केचित्तदुपक्रमाणां सर्गाणां कालिदासकृतित्वे प्रत्यवतिष्ठन्ते, तत्र का भवतः प्रतिपत्तिः ?

कौण्डिन्यः—या प्रतिपत्तिः काव्यत्रयं प्रथमेन, नाटकत्रयं द्वितीयेन, ऋतुसंहारं तृतीयेन, पुष्पबाणविलासशृङ्गारतिलकनवरत्नमालिकादिकं चतुर्थेन, ज्योतिर्विदाभरणं पञ्चमेन, लम्बोदरप्रहरणं षष्ठेन, श्रुतबोधं सप्तमेन, नलोदयमष्टमेन, अन्यदन्यच्च नवमेन दशमेन वा कालिदासेन रचितमाचक्षाणेषु । (उभौ हसतः)

Śāṇḍilya : What have you to say with regard to those who do not accept the Cantos of the *Raghuvaṁśa* from Canto IX onwards to be those of Kālidāsa on the plea that the poet who engages himself in the Yamaka-work like a child cannot be Kālidāsa.

Kauṇḍinya : That what I have to say with regard to those who pronounce that the three Kāvyas have been written by Kalidāsa I, the three plays by Kālidāsa II, *Ṛtusaṁhāra* by Kālidāsa, III, *Puṣpabāṇavilāsa*, *Śṛṅgāratilaka*, *Navaratnamālikā*, etc. by Kālidāsa IV, *Jyotirvidābharaṇa* by Kālidāsa V, *Lambodaraprahasana* by Kālidāsa VI, *Śrutabodha* by Kālidāsa VII, *Nalodaya* by Kālidāsa VIII and still others by Kālidāsa IX and X.

1. Since our author appreciates Yamaka if used properly, it is no wonder that he should resort to it in his composition :

कविमध्ये सार्वभौमः सार्वभौमसभाजितः ।
अजितः कालिदासोऽयं दासोऽयं प्रत्यसौ जनः ॥

Our author brings to bear on his work profundity of his knowledge of and about Kālidāsa and the science of poetics, quoting as he does such authorities as Bhāmaha, Daṇḍin and Ānandavardhana. Coming from the pen of one of modern India's foremost creative writers of Sanskrit, the summary verses and dialogue in the *Kālidāsacaritasaṁgraha* make a delightful reading and are a valuable addition to the growing modern literature on Kālidāsa.

INDEX OF WORKS STUDIED

Titlewise

Asti Kaścid Vāgarthīyam—Krishna Kumar, Mayank Prakashan, Moradabad, 1984.

Asti Kaścid Vāgviśeṣaḥ—Maheshwar Shastri N. Joshi, Samskrita Pratibha, New Delhi, Vol. XIV, No. 1, 1984.

Kālidāsacaritam—S.B. Velankar, Girvanasudha Prakashan, Bombay, 1961.

Kālidāsagauravam—Jivanath Jha Sharma, *Kālidāsīyoparūpakāṇāṁ Samuccayaḥ*, Kameshwar Singh Sanskrit Vishvavidyalaya, Darbhanga, 1963.

Kālidāsaḥ—Vaneshwar Pathak, *Kālidāsīyoparūpakānāṁ Samuccayaḥ*, Kameshwar Singh Sanskrit Vishvavidyalaya, Darbhanga, 1963.

Kālidāsiyakāvyasambhavam—Mathura Datt Pandey, *Viśvasaṁskṛtam*, Hoshiarpur, Vol. XVI, Nos. 3-4, May-August, 1979.

Kālidāsapāṇikaraṇam—Sabhanath Pathak, *Kālidāsīyoparūpakāṇāṁ Samuccayaḥ*, Kameshwar Singh Sanskrit Vishvavidyalaya, Darbhanga, 1963.

Kavikālidāsam—B.K. Bhattacharya, Sanskrit Pustak Bhandar, Calcutta, Saka Year 1890 or A.D. 1968.

Kavikālidāsīyam—Vinapani Patni, *Madhurāmlam*, Nag Publishers, Delhi, 1986.

Kavikulakokilam—Roma Chaudhuri, Pracyavani, Calcutta, 1970.

Mahākavikālidāsam—Srijiva Nyayatirtha, First published in *Praṇava-Pārijātaḥ*, Calcutta, Vol. VI, Nos. 2-4, 6 & 8, Saka Year 1885 or A.D. 1964. Subsequently published in the *Rūpakacakram*, Published by the author, Calcutta, 1968.

Śrikālidāsacaritasaṅgrahaḥ—Y. Mahalinga Sastri, *Mañjūṣā*, Calcutta, Vol. IV, No. 9, May, 1950.

Śrī Kālidāsīyam Antimam Aitihyam—Nārāyaṇa, *Saṁskṛta-Bhāratī*, Vol. II, No. 3, July-September, 1919, Vol. III, No. I, Jan.-March, 1920.

Vidyottamākālidāsīyam—Ram Kishore Mishra, Published by the author, M.M. College, Khekra (Meerut), 1984.

INDEX OF WORKS STUDIED

Authorwise

Bhattacharya, B.K., *Kavikālidāsam*, Sanskrit Putak Bhandar, Calcutta, Saka Year, 1890 or A.D. 1968.

Chaudhuri, Roma, *Kavikulakokilam*, Pracyavani, Calcutta, 1970.

Joshi, N., Maheshwar Shastri, *Asti Kaścid Vāgviśeṣaḥ*, Samskrita Pratibha, New Delhi, Vol. XIV, No. 1, 1984.

Krishna Kumar, *Asti Kaścid Vāgarthīyam*, Mayank Prakashan, Moradabad, 1984.

Mishra, Ram Kishore, *Vidyottamākālidāsīyam*, Published by the author, M.M. College, Khekra (Meerut), 1984.

Narayana, *Śrīkālidāsīyam Antimam Aitihyam*, Samskrta-Bharati, Vol. II, No. 3, July-September, 1919, Vol. III, No. 1. Jan.-March, 1920.

Nyayatirtha, Srijiva—*Mahākavikālidāsam*, First Published in *Praṇava-Pārijātaḥ*, Calcutta, Vol. VI, Nos. 2-4, 6 & 8, Saka Year 1885 or A.D. 1964. Subsequently published in the *Rūpakacakram*, Published by the author, Calcutta, 1968.

Pandey, Mathura Datt, *Kālidāsakāvyasambhavam*, *Viśvasaṁskṛtam*, Hoshiarpur, Vol. XVI, Nos. 3-4, May-August, 1979.

Pathak, Sabhanath, *Kālidāsapāṇikaraṇam*, *Kālidāsīyoparūpakāṇāṁ Samuccayaḥ*, Kameshwar Singh Sanskrit Vishvavidyalaya, Darbhanga 1963.

Pathak, Vaneshwar, *Kālidāsḥ*, *Kālidāsīyoparūpakāṇāṁ Samuccayaḥ*, Kameshwar Singh Sanskrit Vishvavidyalaya, Darbhanga, 1963.

Patni, Vinapani, *Kavikālidāsīyam*, *Madhurāmlam*, Nag Publishers, Delhi, 1986.

Sastri, Mahalinga, Y., *Śrīkālidāsacaritasaṅgrahaḥ*, *Mañjūṣā*, Calcutta, Vol. IV, No. 9, May, 1950.

Sharma, Jha, Jivanath, *Kālidāsagauravam*, *Kālidāsīyoparūpakāṇāṁ Samuccayaḥ*, Kameshwar Singh Sanskrit Vishvavidyalaya, Darbhanga, 1963.

Velankar, S.B., *Kālidāsacaritam*, Girvanasudha Prakashan, Bombay, 1961.

ERRATA

Page	*Line*	*Incorrect*	*Correct*
10	9	न जवेन	नु जवेन
28	2	lowing of a camel	grunting of a camel
28	12	oddess	Goddess
33	27	grāmjanabandhubhya	grāmajanabandhbhyas
34	4	डत्कृष्टता में	उत्कृष्टता में
39	44	Kāntāvirahguruṇa	Kāntāvirahaguruṇā
48	33	The Mālinī	Mālinī
51	18	श्रेणीभारा	श्रोणीभारा
53	12	शनैश्चक्राम्यर्णा	शनैश्चक्राभ्यर्णा
53	13	स्फुटितकमलेणु	स्फुटितकमलेषु
54	4	Kim	Kiṁ
54	17	ratnamaeva	ratnam eva
55	fn. 7	Prastāvana	Prastāvanā
55	fn. 8	Malavikāgnimitrā	Mālavikāganịmitra
58	6	Vālmikī	Vālmīki
60	15	Gaṇeṣa	Gaṇeśa
60	28	Meghaduta	Meghadūta
61	19	lavaṇyam ākarsayati	lāvaṇyam akarṣayati
64	4	arvācinena	arvācīnena
64	18	kāhinī	kahānī
65	8	शार्ग्ङनाद	शार्ङ्गनाद
66	27	छिद्रान्वेबी	छिद्रान्वेषी
78	28	Vidyavati	Vidyāvatī
85	4	आनन्दविह्व्लः	आनन्दविह्वलः
88	38	mandain	mandam
95	10	पाण्डित्मपि···भवेत	पाण्डित्यमपि···भवेत्
98	16	इत्युक्त्वा	इत्युक्त्वा
98	20	भोक्तं	भोक्तुं
98	36	suspician	suspicion
105	37	be a ringing	be ringing
109	22	मछिजगाक	मछिजगाम
109	26	ākrośamanā	ākrośamānā

110	1	jñāśrusmṛāṁ	jñāśrusmṛdṛśāṁ
111	9	na jūne	na jāne
116	44	disquistion	disquisition
117	12	statisfies	satisfierr
120	32	better from him	better for him
126	28	Vidyuttama	Vidyottamā
126	34	vouminous	voluminous
126	38	of it maintains	of it it maintains
126	42	vergeance	vengeance
128	15	acquistion	acquisition
131	9	एत्या	एत्य
131	13	रतिरक्तमेत्रा	रतिरक्तनेत्रा
136	5	ध्यातेग	ध्यानेन
136	20	रुष्टस्त्यक्ता	रुष्टस्त्यक्त्वा
140	29	J tviṣ	√ tviṣ
141	21, 31	casual	causal
142	14	सङ्कैतैः स्व-	सङ्केतैः स्वै-
148	21	cāraṇā	cāraṇa
154	29	he excels in	he excels in the
155	15	But that as it may	Be that as it may
156	4	Vikramorvaśtya	Vikramorvaśīya
156	36	श्रद्वालब:	श्रद्धालव:
157	44	of the king' routing the Mlecchas	of the Veda and Īśvara (God)
158	13	अनुमानप्रायत्बं	अनुमानप्रायत्वं